**1900** • Steering wheel
appears on some cars

**1901** • The buggy grows
a hood on its front . . .

**1905** • Rear side doors . . .
runningboards . . . top folds

**1909** • The Model T Fords
popularize automobiling

**1911** • Runningboard aprons
. . . four doors . . . windshield

**1923** • Radiators nickeled . . .
cylindrical lamps . . . bumpers

**1926** • Closed cars . . . integral
sun visor . . . balloon tires

**1928** • Radiator ornaments
. . . lacquer . . . chrome plate

**1935** • Vee windshield . . . long hood
large hubcaps . . . sloping rear . . .

**1937** • Grille and louvers blend . . .
hood hinged at rear . . . disc wheels

**1940** • Headlights are in fenders . . .
no runningboards . . . spare in trunk

**1950** • Both front and rear
take on squared shapes

**1953** • Low over-all height . . .
wraparound windows general

# A PICTORIAL HISTORY
# OF THE AUTOMOBILE

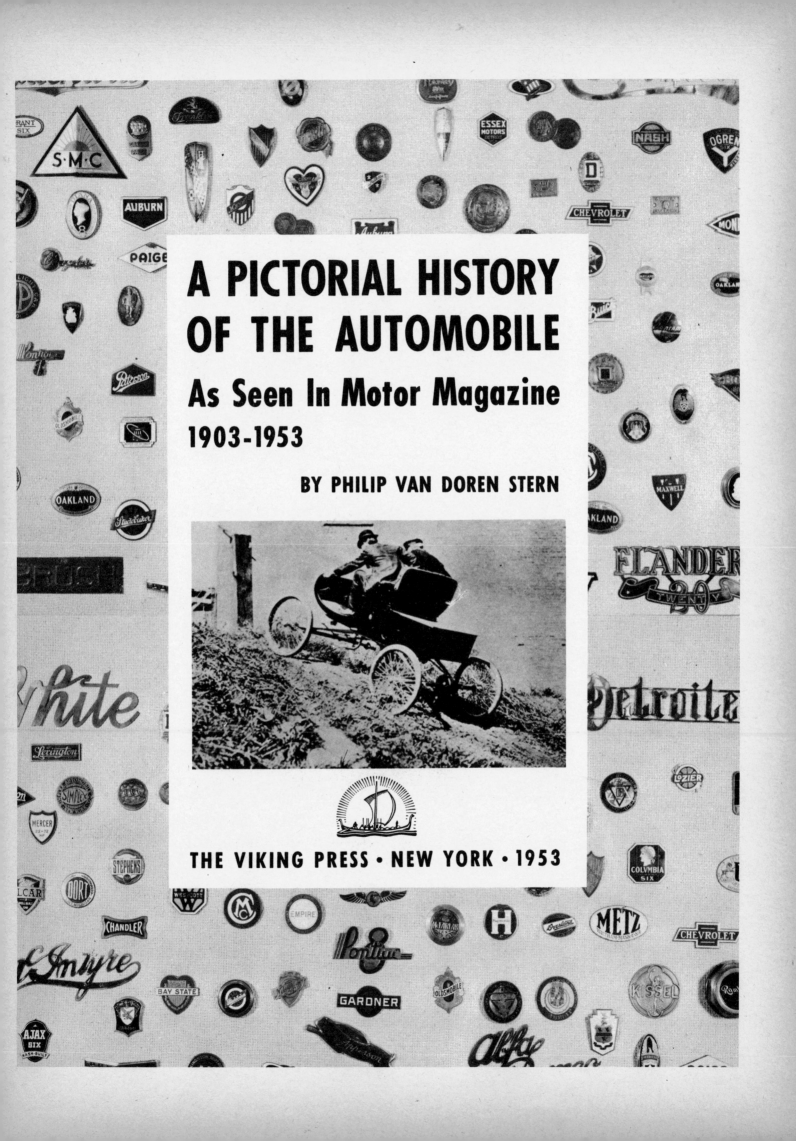

# A PICTORIAL HISTORY OF THE AUTOMOBILE

## As Seen In Motor Magazine

### 1903-1953

BY PHILIP VAN DOREN STERN

THE VIKING PRESS · NEW YORK · 1953

COPYRIGHT 1953 BY THE HEARST CORPORATION

PUBLISHED BY THE VIKING PRESS IN OCTOBER 1953

PUBLISHED ON THE SAME DAY IN THE DOMINION OF CANADA
BY THE MACMILLAN COMPANY OF CANADA LIMITED

Library of Congress catalog card number: 53-8619

LITHOGRAPHED IN U.S.A. BY W. S. KONECKY ASSOCIATES

# TABLE OF CONTENTS

# FOREWORD

I was born at the turn of the century and so grew up with the automobile. My earliest memories, of course, are of a horse-and-carriage world—a world of dirt roads, thank-you-ma'ams, hitching posts, watering troughs, back alleys, rich-smelling stables, and the clomp, clomp, clomp of horses' hoofs on the streets outside the front windows. Those streets were never clean; it is impossible for a young, city-bred American to appreciate the difference between our smooth and reasonably well-swept pavements of today and the mud-and-manure-littered streets that were almost universal before the coming of the automobile.

Its coming changed America from a slow-paced, predominantly rural country to a swift-moving, highly industrialized and highly urbanized nation. Whether or not that dynamic change was worthwhile is a fruitless question. The change had to come; it came; the results of it are upon us, and we have to live with them and adjust our lives and our thinking to the routines of a mechanical world.

We lost a great deal with the passing of the horse. People who live in those sections of our country, such as certain areas in the West, where the horse still plays some part in everyday life will attest to that. Horsemanship was and is a great art; anyone who learns to manage a horse learns a good deal about managing things in general. And the mutual attachment of man and horse has an emotional value that can never be replaced by any machine, no matter how fine.

The importance of the horse in shaping the character of a human being was brought home to me at an early age. I was fortunate in being in a position to observe horses and early automobiles at their best, for my favorite Aunt owned a farm in Hempstead, Long Island, which was then a center for fashionable society's interest in fine horses, and it was there, of course, that the famous Vanderbilt Cup Races were first held. My Aunt had a beautifully built closed carriage and a two-wheeled wicker dogcart (which we children much preferred), and, as was then the custom, she employed a professional coachman. But I remember that when her handsome black mare became skittish, my Aunt would order her coachman to step down; she herself would descend from the carriage, get up on the box, put on a pair of driving gloves, and with firm and decisive hands calm down the mare and drive her around until the high-spirited creature could be turned back to the coachman. Then my Aunt would take off her driving gloves, thrust them behind the seat cushion, get into the carriage, and be driven grandly into town.

I developed a great admiration for my Aunt on those occasions, and I have never lost it, for she was a remarkable woman. Photographs show that she was very beautiful; she was married for the first time at sixteen; after her second marriage ended she lived for the rest of her life on the two divorce settlements which the celebrated law firm of Howe and Hummel arranged for her.

It is to her that I owe my first clear recollections not only of horses but also of automobiles. The very first car I remember was the electric hansom cab she used in the city. The chauffeur sat up above and behind, while the passenger was splendidly isolated down below and sheltered from wind and rain by two beautifully curved waist-high doors. I remember that softly purring electric car calling at my Aunt's apartment to take her to Louis Martin's or Shanley's celebrated restaurants and then to the theaters near Herald Square.

At her country place in Hempstead she had a long succession of big open touring cars. Among them I recall a Metallurgique, a Lancia, a Mercedes, and later a Crane-Simplex. They were all very large, very impressive, gleaming with brass and smelling of well-dressed leather, and they shook and throbbed like living beings while they stood still with their motors idling. Since I was still only a child, the best I could hope for was to be allowed to sit in the front seat alongside the chauffeur and as a special favor be allowed to reach over and honk the rubber bulb horn. (Cars were all right-hand drive then; it was not until the introduction of the brass-fronted Model T Ford in 1908 that the American driver moved over for good to the left side.)

It was one of these early Model T's that gave me my first real association with automobiling. My Aunt's chauffeur bought a second-hand one, which he repainted and polished until it glistened like my Aunt's big foreign car. There was no room for it in the barn or the carriage house, so it was banished to the wagon shed, where he and I used to work on it in his spare time. I learned to drive on that car, guiding it under its owner's watchful eye along the gravel and macadam roads around Hempstead and Westbury.

It was about this time that my family decided to buy a car of its own. (We stayed at my Aunt's place only during the summer and spent the rest of the year in New Jersey.) Accordingly, we became the proud owners of a 1916 Overland, a round-hooded, tan-colored, four-cylinder touring car, with an electric self-starter that worked very satisfactorily until it chewed the gear teeth off the flywheel. The estimated repair bill for installing a new flywheel was so staggering that my father refused to have the work done. Since I had had plenty of experience cranking Fords, I had to crank that heavy Overland engine. It was a wicked brute to start, especially in cold weather. For the benefit of the younger generation who has never had to start a car by crank in wintertime, I give a detailed account of what such a truly onerous and muscle-straining task habitually entailed.

1. We did not use alcohol or any kind of antifreeze fluid. We purposely refrained from using such things so we could fill the radiator with boiling water in the morning to warm up the engine which had been exposed to bitter winter weather all night in an unheated garage. The metal had become so cold by then that drops of steaming hot water which splashed on the radiator immediately froze fast.

2. You opened the brass petcock on each cylinder and poured a few drops of gasoline into the engine. The petcocks were then closed, the spark retarded (so the engine wouldn't kick back and break your arm), and the hand throttle was set according to each owner's pet theory.

3. You then vigorously cranked the engine and hoped. If it coughed and caught and seemed about to start, you ran like mad to the steering wheel to advance the spark lever and reset the gas throttle. At this point the engine invariably sighed and stopped, so you had to start all over again.

4. Finally, when you got the thing going (and perhaps had to put on chains if there was snow on the streets), you rolled along at twenty or twenty-five miles an hour, hoping to arrive at your destination without a breakdown.

It was painfully cold in that open touring car. The wind howled around the sides of the windshield and came up through the cracks between the floor boards. And then, when you finally got to where you were going, you had to cover up the engine with old quilts to keep it warm. If you were staying for more than an hour or so, you had to go outdoors to start the engine again and let it run for a while to make sure it didn't freeze.

Such was motoring in those days. And this, of course, was nothing compared to what the very first motorists went through. But we learned one thing then that most drivers today never learn. We knew our cars; we knew how to take care of them, repair them on the road, and we always traveled with a full kit of tools. (I still do.) Nothing fazed us because we dealt with emergencies every day. We expected almost anything to happen—and it usually did. I have had the driveshaft drop right out of the car. I have had one of my rear wheels come off the axle and go spinning merrily down the road ahead of me while my car came to a quick jolting stop. I have been pulled out of mud, sand, and quagmires by horses, other cars, or trucks, and once by the good strong arms of a French-Canadian farmer who simply picked up one end of my Model T landaulet and lifted it back on the road.

Model T Fords (of which more than fifteen million were built) were the common denominator of automobiling from 1908 to 1927. During my college days we used to buy them second-hand for $25 and fix them up so as to get thousands of miles more use out of them. No one who was brought up on the Model T can ever forget it. It was a miracle of simplicity, with only two speeds forward and a reverse, but it was utterly different from the present-day automobile.

This is how it worked: first you made sure that the emergency brake was pulled all the way back. This threw out the clutch and firmly gripped the rear wheels so the car couldn't creep forward and run you down when the engine started. After that you set the spark lever and gas throttle on the brass quadrants under the steering wheel at what you considered the correct starting positions. Then you turned on the magneto switch.

You were now ready to go to work on the engine. You went forward and from underneath the radiator pulled out a long piece of wire by putting one finger into a loop at the end of it. This was the choke. You held this out with one hand while you thrust the crank into the starting notch and determinedly spun the engine with the other hand. When—and if—the engine started, you quickly let go of the choke and made the usual frantic dash to reset the gas and spark levers. Then you got into the car from the right (there was no door to the left of the driver's seat) and sat down behind the wheel, looking rather proud of yourself.

You glanced around carefully to make certain the road was clear; when assured that it was, you pushed the left one of three pedals in slightly and shoved the hand lever all the way forward; then you pushed harder on the same pedal, and the car moved forward with a harsh grinding of low-speed gears. When it had picked up enough speed you released the pedal, and the car thereupon leaped ahead like a jack rabbit. It was then in high gear (and direct drive) and could go somewhat better than forty mph on a good level road.

When you wanted to stop, you declutched, pressed in the right-hand pedal, and hauled back mightily on the hand brake. The center pedal was for reversing. To use it you had to throw out the clutch at the same time, so both feet were kept busy. The reverse gearing made the whole car shudder, but it applied so much power to the rear wheels that when you came to a hill too steep to climb in low gear, you simply turned the car around and backed up.

Model T's ran through my college days, but as soon as I got a job and had an income of my own I bought a second-hand 1921 Mercer Raceabout with two bucket seats on the floor and a folding canvas mother-in-law seat slung over the left runningboard. The car was completely open to the sky except for a temporary canvas roof, which could be put up on iron rods to keep off the rain. Water then collected in the sagging canvas, and you always got some of it down your neck when you tried to shake it off by slapping at the underside of the canvas.

But that Mercer was a great car. It sounded like a stampeding herd of buffalo when you stepped on the muffler cutout; it held the road like a housefly clinging to the ceiling; and it would go faster than any road in New Jersey would then permit. I bought it for three hundred dollars, drove it for a year and a half, and then sold it for three hundred and twenty-five dollars. It was a sorry profit to take, for of all the cars I have ever owned I loved that one most. I can still hear it roaring over the hills while I lay back in the driver's seat with the wind blowing in my face.

Perhaps my old Mercer still exists in some collection of old automobiles. I hope it does. It would have been a crime

## THE 1921 MERCER RACEABOUT

Four-cylinder 70-hp motor with 3¾″ bore and a 6¾″ stroke. Piston displacement 298.2 cubic inches. Wheelbase: 115 inches. Weight: 3800 pounds. Gas tank: 25 gallons. Extra oil tank for high-speed driving: 5 gallons. Tires: 32 x 4½ inches, high pressure. Gear ratios: fourth, 3.22 to 1; third, 4.72 to 1; second, 6.88 to 1; first, 11.91 to 1. Paint: Robin's Egg Blue No. 4798. Upholstery: genuine black leather. Price: $3950 F.O.B. Trenton, N.J.

to junk a car like that. The serial number, incidentally, was only 4861. The Mercer people didn't build many cars, but they built them well.

I sold my Mercer in 1928. After it I owned a succession of automobiles: a tenth-hand Chevrolet, vintage 1923; a 1929 Graham-Paige, which I finally gave to a country carpenter to settle a bill for $25; a lordly 1930 Cadillac; and several Chryslers and Dodges, one after another. They were all good cars, and they carried me and my family for many thousands of miles. But by then something had gone out of motoring—not only for me but for most American automobile owners. Manufacturers were building such mechanically perfect cars that they seldom got out of order, so we began to take them for granted like any other highly efficient, useful, but unobtrusive piece of machinery, such as an electric refrigerator or an automatic gas furnace. Talk about the automobile died down. It was just a means of transportation and no more worthy of conversation than a street car or a bus. And meanwhile so many cars were making their appearance on the road that they made summer week-end travel a nightmare.

Our present-day traffic jams are bad, but they do not compare with the dreadful overcrowding in the mid-1920's before our modern highways, bridges, and tunnels were built. I remember what used to take place in New Jersey on Sunday nights in summer before the Holland Tunnel was opened. The only way you could get to New York was by ferry, so thousands of cars all headed for the ferries at the same time. As a result, they backed up for miles while the ferry boats slowly nibbled away at the line. Each time a boatload of cars was taken away, the long column would move forward a few hundred feet; then you would shut off the motor and wait until signs of movement ahead indicated that another boatload of cars had been removed. This went on for hours—and I mean hours.

The transformation the automobile wrought upon American life had three major phases. The first extends from the earliest days of the motor car to about 1927. This was the period when dirt roads began to be covered over with some kind of pavement. A few new highways, bridges, and tunnels were built, and signposts were erected to guide the stranger on his way. But little attempt was made to cope with the ever-increasing numbers of automobiles that were being manufactured each year. This was the era of the Model T Ford, when people were so delighted with the novel idea of inexpensive individual transportation that they were perfectly satisfied with their simple, slow-moving cars which took them—often for the first time—out of their own immediate neighborhoods. The Model T and the cars contemporary with it opened up America; they ended forever the terrible isolation of lonely farms, where people were cut off from the mainstream of modern life as completely as though they were living on a feudal manor. One of the Model T's great virtues was that it could go almost anywhere. It was built with big wheels and high clearances so it could traverse the primitive roads of its time. Having fulfilled its function, it became obsolete when better roads were built and people demanded comfort, luxury, and speed in their cars.

The second period, which extended from 1927 to December 1941 (when Pearl Harbor abruptly put an end to all manufacturing of civilian automobiles and to road-building), was a time of tremendous growth. During it America established her great highway system, and began to study seriously the problems of traffic, parking, and modern road-building.

The third period began when the war ended. Automobile registrations soared during the postwar years, and city, country, state, and federal governments realized that they were faced with an enormous task. New roads that became inadequate even before they were finished were no longer an answer. Thruways had to be built, and the parking problem could no longer be left to individuals who rented vacant downtown lots and charged all they could get. Only by making use of the best brains in the country and by spending not merely millions but billions of dollars can the problem the automobile has thrust upon us be solved. But there is one thing certain: the American people want automobiles more than they want any other material thing, more even than good housing, for there are plenty of Americans who are perfectly content to live in a substandard dwelling so long as they can drive around in an automobile that is the last word in comfort, style, beauty, and speed.

During the Second World War, from 1942 to 1945, while production was suspended and gas rationed, the automobile began to take on new meaning to the American public. Driving was restricted, so for the first time we missed our cars and realized how much they had meant to us. And many of the young men in service were making an intensive study of the internal-combustion engine. They studied it in command cars, jeeps, trucks, tanks, airplanes, and PT boats. A whole new generation became gas-engine experts during those four years.

Then, when cars could be manufactured again, there was such a shortage of them that British, Italian, French, and German makers began sending their cars — especially the sports models—into this country. Interest in the sports car, which had nearly died out in America after the early days of automobiling, was revived. Existing cars were hopped up, customized, radically redesigned, and rebuilt at the expense of hundreds of hours of labor done by devoted amateur mechanics. Men who could afford to do so began collecting old cars and have them carefully restored. Something exciting was happening to the automobile. People were beginning to look at it as something more than a means of convenient transportation. It became a subject of popular conversation again. Men—especially young men— discussed it seriously in technical terms. Crowds began flocking to racing meets and sports-car shows. Artists made color prints of early automobiles, and people bought them eagerly for their homes. Fan magazines, which had literally become extinct during the 1930's, were issued again, and their circulation quickly soared into the hundreds of thousands. During this third phase of the automobile's evolution, people became very style-conscious, so American automobile manufacturers redesigned their regular models along new and more graceful lines. They also began to experiment with radically different-looking sports cars. They made power steering, power brakes, and air conditioning available as extras and pushed horsepower and speed steadily upward. As a result, enormous progress was made in American automobile building during the postwar years. Now cars are no longer being taken for granted. They have again become worth talking about, because they are beautiful to look at, mechanically more interesting, and a pleasure to drive.

Behind their sleek beauty and marvelous efficiency is a long period of evolution. Ever since the Duryea Brothers drove their first auto-buggy through the streets of Springfield, Massachusetts, in 1893, the American automobile has been going through a never-ending series of improvements. The pioneers who learned the hard way are now either dead or very old. But to them should go the credit of making the greatest civilizing force of the twentieth century a reality. Their brass-bound, snorting, and temperamental iron monsters opened the way, and everyone who drives smoothly along one of our superhighways owes something to the men and the cars that are pictured here.

\* \* \*

Nearly all the photographs used in this book have been reproduced directly from bound copies of *Motor*. Over a fifty-year period the quality of both photography and printing will naturally vary a great deal, so some pictures are decidedly less than perfect. But the originals had long since been destroyed, so there was no choice but to use what was available. Historical importance and documentary value will have to make up for ideal printing quality.

There is much more to a picture book than pictures. In preparing this one I particularly want to thank the entire staff of *Motor* for their help. A number of people, beginning with *Motor's* publisher, Clifford S. Bailey, Edward Ford, the editor; Harold F. Blanchard, special consultant to *Motor* on engineering; Emmet M. Greene, service editor, and Henry J. Lee, art editor, all deserve my gratitude for supplying information and being properly critical when criticism was needed.

I also want to thank those who in one way or another helped make the book possible. They are: Estelle Seif, Janet Frank, Virginia Crim, Betty Barclay, Miriam Rose Stern, Lillian Stern, Paul Jensen, and also W. L. Powlison, librarian of the Automobile Manufacturers Association.

And last of all I want to thank the automobile companies that kindly supplied photographs and information and extended every possible courtesy to me. They are: The Chrysler Corporation, The Ford Motor Company, General Motors Corporation, Hudson Motor Car Company, Kaiser-Frazer Corporation, Nash-Kelvinator Corporation, Packard Motor Car Company, The Studebaker Corporation, and Willys-Overland Company. Thanks also are due to the Key Wester for the photograph on page 155, to Henry W. Uhle for the Duesenberg photographs on pages 226 and 227, and to the Eaton Manufacturing Company for background and historical data.

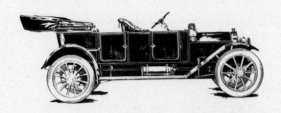

# A PICTORIAL HISTORY
# OF THE AUTOMOBILE

# THE EARLY ANCESTRY OF THE AUTOMOBILE

Land yacht built by Simon Stevin of Bruges in the 1700's

This steam carriage was built in England about 1803 by Richard Trevithick. Its driving wheels were 10 feet in diameter, and its body was 6 feet above the ground. Note the stoker at the rear

Oliver Evans' amphibian which he called "Orukter Amphibolis"

In 1824, David Gordon devised a steam-driven road vehicle pushed along by mechanical hoofs. It was noisy, and it ruined the roads

The James and Anderson British steam coach of 1829. It had two engines to avoid the use of a differential

One of the three buses built in England by Gurney in the 1830's. This one is said to have traveled 3644 miles

The steam bus of 1832 invented by Dr. Church for carrying large numbers of passengers. Note that it was a three-wheeler

The steam wagon built by Cugnot in France in 1769. (From a model.)

# THE AUTOMOBILE BEFORE 1903

*The first issue of* Motor *was published in October, 1903; it therefore could not cover the early history of the automobile except in retrospect in some of its later issues. Fortunately, it did this very thoroughly.*

The automobile was not invented by any one person; it evolved over a period of many years. When it finally appeared at the end of the nineteenth century, it was the result of the cross-breeding of ideas derived from the railroad locomotive, the bicycle, and the then recently invented internal-combustion engine. Long before this time, however, men had thought of driving road vehicles by mechanical force rather than by animal power. There were all kinds of strange early efforts—the land yacht driven by wind power acting on sails, wagons drawn by kites, and vehicles propelled by powerful wound-up springs.

But the most likely source of power was steam. It was being used in the eighteenth century for stationary engines and in the early nineteenth century was applied to boats and railroad locomotives.

Nicolas Joseph Cugnot (1725-1804), a French engineer, seems to have been the first person to have built a steam-driven vehicle that would actually go. Built in 1769, it was a three-wheeler carrying a boiler and a two-cylinder engine mounted over a single front wheel. It was a clumsy, heavily built, lumbering contraption that could travel only about as fast as a man could walk—about three miles an hour. It was very difficult to turn, so difficult, in fact, that Cugnot ran it into a wall and brought disaster and the police down upon him. He was jailed and his vehicle was impounded.

The steam-driven road vehicle had an early start in the United States, but it never got very far. In 1790, Nathan Reed of Warren, Mass. built one that had a smokestack. It

could move along the road, but it never got anywhere financially so it soon vanished from the scene. Oliver Evans, who was one of America's most brilliant early mechanics, in 1804 was faced with the problem of moving a flat-bottom steam dredge he had built in a Philadelphia yard to the river where it was to be launched. He solved the problem very neatly by mounting the boat on heavy iron wheels and axles to which he attached the steam engine and then triumphantly drove the boat to the river bank and launched it.

In England, during the first half of the nineteenth century, the steam-driven road vehicle reached a high stage of development. Quite a few of them were built and were used successfully as buses to carry passengers on fairly long trips. But the owners of horse-drawn stagecoaches were resentful, and the backers of the early railroads feared the competition of vehicles that could travel freely on the public roads without having to buy expensive right-of-ways and equip them with iron rails. They ganged up on the fledgling steam-buses and forced through Parliament the notorious Red Flag Law of 1865 limiting such vehicles to 3 mph. And then, as if this wasn't bad enough, each vehicle had to be preceded by a man carrying a red flag. This served to drive all power-driven vehicles off the roads of England for more than thirty years, although there were a few rebellious attempts to evade the law. One of them was quite ingenious: a Mr. Carrett of Leeds built a steam-powered road vehicle with a body like a fire engine and then provided his friends with firemen's outfits. Whenever he was stopped by the police, he told them that there must be a fire somewhere and that he was on his way to find it and help put it out.

As a result of the Red Flag Laws, England was the last of the great nations to foster the development of the automobile. Meanwhile, the German-born Austrian, Siegfried Marcus (1831-1899), and the Belgian-born Frenchman, Etienne Lenoir (1822-1900), were working in the early 1860's to develop road vehicles that could be driven by some kind of power other than steam or electricity. The internal-combustion engine was as yet unknown, so Lenoir had to invent one as he went along. In 1860 he patented an internal-combustion engine that was driven by illuminating gas, and in 1863 he constructed a road vehicle powered by this engine. It had one cylinder, which developed 1½ horsepower at its top speed of 100 rpm, and the car was so slow that it took an hour and a half to go six miles.

At that time, the idea of building an engine which derived its power from explosions of petroleum spirits did not seem very promising. The oil resources of the world had only recently been discovered, and no one knew very much about refining the crude product or just what to do with some of its distillates after they were produced. The most volatile distillate—gasoline—seemed worthless. It was highly explosive when vaporized, difficult to store and handle, and had no practical use. Elaborate schemes for disposing of it were

The car Siegfried Marcus built in 1875

proposed. Kerosene was, and for many years continued to be, the most desired petroleum product, because it can be burned in lamps and stoves, and its high flash point makes it safe to handle.

Nevertheless, Siegfried Marcus went ahead with his experiments and in 1864 produced a crude automobile with a 2-cycle engine which was patterned after Lenoir's, except that it had a carburetor which could handle liquid fuel, and its explosive mixture was ignited by an electric spark. Marcus was a poor man, so his vehicle consisted only of a wooden cart with the engine attached directly to the rear wheels. The car—if it can be called that—proved to be a loud, noise-making nuisance which quickly brought complaints from the neighbors and warnings from the Vienna police. Since Marcus had little interest in his invention, he abandoned his experiments for more than ten years. In 1875 he produced another proto-automobile, the strange-looking vehicle shown on this page. It is still in existence and may be seen in the Vienna *Technisches Museum*.

In 1876, George B. Brayton, an American inventor, exhibited a 2-cycle stationary engine at the Philadelphia Centennial Exposition. It used fuel oil under compression in-

stead of gas, but it burned the oil instead of exploding it. It was a heavy, awkward, slow-running engine, but it is important because it attracted the attention of George B. Selden (1846-1922), a patent attorney of Rochester, N. Y. Selden was clever enough to see the enormous advantage such an engine might have for propelling road vehicles. He kept himself informed about European engine progress and on May 8, 1879, filed application for a basic American patent on the automobile. The patent was granted to him in 1895 and became grounds for the history-making Selden patent case, which dragged on until 1911 (see page 66).

Nikolaus August Otto (1832-1891), a German technician, had made an important advance in the development of the internal-combustion engine in 1866 when he, working with Eugen Langen (1833-1895), had invented a 2-cycle gas engine. In 1877 he built a 4-cycle engine. This had been projected in theory by Beau de Rochas in a treatise written in 1862, but Otto was the first to construct a working mechanism. The 4-cycle engine (in which the piston moves through four strokes—intake, compression, power, and exhaust—to complete a cycle of operation) is used in all American automobiles today.

The next two pioneers in automobile invention were also German born. They were Karl Benz (1844-1929) and Gottlieb Daimler (1834-1900), who worked simultaneously but independently on road vehicles driven by internal-combustion engines. Daimler's first attempt (in 1885) had only two wheels and was therefore a rudimentary motorcycle rather than an automobile. In the same year, Karl Benz constructed a three-wheeler. Although the two men did not know each other when they were making their historic experiments, their work was destined to have a lasting effect upon automotive history. In the mid-1920's, the companies they had founded were combined to form Daimler-Benz, which still makes the celebrated Mercedes-Benz.

Daimler's patents were of tremendous importance in the development of the automobile. Rights to use them were quickly obtained by various entrepreneurs throughout Europe. In the United States, William Steinway, the New York piano manufacturer, had seen Daimler engines, launches, and motor cars in operation while touring in Germany in 1888. After obtaining the American rights, he started in business selling the Daimler engine. A Daimler quadricycle was displayed at the Columbian Exposition in Chicago in 1893, where it attracted a great deal of attention and served as an inspiration to American inventors.

Benz engines were used in many early American automobiles. In fact, it was common practice in the 1890's to import a Benz or a Daimler engine from Germany for use as a power plant in American cars.

The automobile began in Europe, and its effect upon European ways of living was enormous, but it hit American civilization with even greater force. Within one life span it made sweeping changes in our transportation setup and had secondary effects of far-reaching importance. It compelled us to learn more about metals, rubber, glass, paint, and

GERMANY: 1885

Carl Benz photographed in 1925 in the car he built in 1885

# THE BEGINNINGS OF THE AUTOMOBILE

UNITED STATES: 1893

The Duryea gasoline automobile with its 4-hp one-cylinder engine with make-and-break ignition. It is now in the Smithsonian Institution

FRANCE: 1885

Bouton in his 1885 steam phaeton. Chasseloup-Loubat is at the tiller

ENGLAND: 1896

The first British-built Daimler as it was sketched in 1896

# EARLY STEAM CARS

An American self-propelled steam threshing machine of 1873

A steamer built in 1865 by Sylvester H. Roper of Massachusetts. It is in The Henry Ford Museum, Dearborn, Mich.

A steam dogcart built by Count de Dion in 1885

petroleum products. Its coming required us to build thousands of miles of highways and literally to pull the country out of the mud. The techniques developed in automobile plants taught other American industries more about production methods, management, and handling materials than they had learned from everything they had previously manufactured. The automobile industry furthered precision-building until its machinists knew how to work not only to a tolerance of 1/1000 of an inch but even to one of 1/10,000 of an inch when necessary. And then it took these precision methods far beyond the highly skilled machinist and taught the employees on the assembly line how to apply them.

In 1893, when the automobile hit the United States with such dynamic force, the mechanization of America had not progressed very far beyond the stage it had reached in Abraham Lincoln's time, a generation before. The only inventions that affected the average person's everyday life were the steam engine, the telegraph, the printing press, the camera, the sewing machine, and the bicycle, all of which had been in use before the Civil War. Newer inventions, like the telephone, the electric light, the phonograph, and the Linotype, were not yet far enough along in their development to be in general use. If one wanted to take a long journey in 1893, he could travel only by rail or ship. Then, when he arrived at his destination, he had to use a slowly moving horse-drawn vehicle of some kind to get beyond walking distance of his point of arrival. He had to travel on schedule, and he could go only where some means of public transportation was readily available.

In the late 1880's, when the safety bicycle (the kind we use today) was invented, bicycling became very popular. Bicycle clubs were formed, tours were arranged, and for a while it looked as though America was going to make a sudden transition from the horse to the bicycle. The craze lasted through the 1890's, after which the automobile replaced the bicycle. But the bicycle era had many good effects. It helped to improve our roads, and its factories supplied many of the designers of early automobiles.

Since transportation methods had improved very little

One of the first American road vehicles—a steam carriage built by J. W. Carhart of Racine, Wis., in 1871

since the coming of the railroads, the development of the nation was retarded because there was no way of moving people and freight quickly and directly to their final destinations. Yet Americans were great tinkerers and inventors, and they were remarkably ingenious in devising new ways of making machines operate. The seed that had been sowed in Europe fell on fertile ground here. American inventors eagerly seized upon the automobile idea and started to seek ways of improving what they had learned from Europe.

In Springfield, Mass., in the early 1890's, two brothers who had been trained in bicycle manufacturing, Charles E. (1862-1938) and J. Frank Duryea (1870-     ), were fitting a primitive one-cylinder gasoline engine into a carriage with high wooden wheels. Their clumsy contraption looked so much like a horse-drawn buggy that the brothers called it a "buggyaut." Nevertheless, their strange-looking self-propelled road vehicle was America's first gasoline automobile. This historic vehicle, which is now enshrined in the Smithsonian Institution in Washington, D. C., was in operation in 1893 and may have been tried out as early as 1892.

The Duryea brothers learned a great deal from building their first automobile, and they incorporated all they had learned in a later improved model. They entered this second buggyaut in the first American automobile race—the *Times-Herald* contest in 1895 (see page 208). Not only did their car win this race, but it also won the *Cosmopolitan* race from New York to Irvington-on-the-Hudson in 1896. The Duryeas also became the first Americans to engage in the actual manufacturing and selling of automobiles when they made thirteen cars from the same basic design.

Working at the same time as the Duryea Brothers was Elwood Haynes (1857-1925), a metallurgical engineer who completed his first car and made it run on July 4, 1894. It was built according to his designs in the shop of Elmer and Edgar Apperson at Kokomo, Ind. The original car had a 1-hp, 2-cycle engine, and a freely swinging front axle like that used on a buggy. This car, with some modifications that were introduced later, is also in the Smithsonian Institution.

The Paris-Rouen race of 1894 (see page 206) had a dynamic effect upon the development of the motor car in the

## EARLY GASOLINE CARS

An 1898 three-wheeled Stevens-Duryea *dos à dos*. It is in The Henry Ford Museum, Dearborn, Mich.

A runabout designed in 1894 by Elwood Haynes and built by Elmer and Edgar Apperson. It is now in the Smithsonian Institution

The first car built by F. B. Stearns who later became famous for the Stearns-Knight and the use of the sleeve-valve engine

A Benz *vis-à-vis* gasoline car of 1891-1892. It is in The Henry Ford Museum, Dearborn, Mich.

The first Locomobile, 1899

The 1900 National Electric

The first Thomas touring car, 1902

The first Knox, 1900

The first Baker Electric, 1899

The first Pierce, 1901

The 1902 Peerless

The 1903 Pope-Hartford

United States. After hearing about the successful runs made by vehicles in that widely publicized contest, American inventors went to work in earnest. It was estimated by a contemporary source that some two thousand American men were building—or talking about building—experimental cars during the early 1890's.

In 1896 a number of new cars began to appear. On March 6, Charles B. King (1869-    ) became the first person to drive a gasoline automobile through the streets of Detroit; in June, Henry Ford (1863-1947) finished the car shown on page 122; in September, Ransom E. Olds (1864-1950) completed a handmade car and drove it in Lansing, Mich.; also in September, Alexander Winton (1860-1932) finished his experimental two-seated motor carriage and operated it successfully. Nor were these the only ones. The *Times-Herald* contest of 1895 had given the automobile so much publicity that a number of manufacturing companies were being formed.

Meanwhile, in England, British-built Daimlers were beginning to be manufactured, and several projected all-British automobile companies were planning to start operation. But before the English people could hope to take up motoring seriously, they had to get rid of their restrictive Red Flag Laws, which made it practically impossible to drive an automobile on British public roads. After much controversy, the laws were finally repealed in 1896. November 14, the day on which the restrictive acts went out of existence, was called Liberty Day by Englishmen who wanted automobiles. A great celebration was held, and a "procession" from London to Brighton was staged to commemorate the occasion. Thirty-three motor cars, practically all imported from France or Germany, took part in the run to Brighton. Several American Duryea cars were present, and, as the British said, "were practically making a race of it." Since transportation by automobile was limited, a trainload of people went along to see the fun. It was a great occasion, which the new British magazine, *The Autocar,* celebrated by printing its entire issue in red ink.

The year 1896 was marked by several other memorable events. The first automobile track race in America was held at Narragansett Park, R. I. It was won by a Riker Electric which made an average speed of 26.8 mph. And it was during this year that the Barnum and Bailey Circus used a Duryea car in its street parades.

At that time there was no good reason to believe that the automobile powered by an internal-combustion engine was eventually to become so popular that it would drive all other means of mechanical propulsion from the road. Steam, which had long been used for railroad locomotives, ships, stationary engines, and mobile threshing machines, still seemed to be the most useful and flexible source of power. As a matter of fact, some people still believe that the automobile took the wrong course in its development and would have done better if the vast amount of engineering skill lavished on the internal-combustion engine had been devoted to the steam engine instead.

As far back as the 1860's, Sylvester H. Roper, a Massa-

## AMERICAN AUTOMOBILE MANUFACTURERS WHO WERE IN BUSINESS BEFORE 1900

This list does not pretend to be complete, but it does include all the better-known companies. Individuals like Henry Ford and Charles B. King are not listed. They built handmade experimental models before 1900 but they were not producing cars commercially. Of all these companies, only three continue to manufacture automobiles: Autocar (trucks), Oldsmobile, and Packard (Ohio).

American Electric Vehicle Company (Waverly), Chicago
Autocar Company of America, Ardmore, Pa.
Automobile Company of America, Marion, N. J.
Baker Motor Vehicle Company, Cleveland
Buckeye Manufacturing Company, Anderson, Ind.
Chicago Motor Vehicle Company, Chicago
Columbia Automobile Company, Hartford
De La Vergne Refrigerator Manufacturing Company, New York
Duryea Manufacturing Company, Peoria, Ill.
Duryea Motor Wagon Company, Springfield, Mass.
Electric Car and Wagon Company, Philadelphia
Electric Vehicle Company (Columbia), Hartford
Grout Brothers, Orange, Mass.
Hasbrouck Motor Company, New York
Haynes-Apperson Company, Kokomo, Ind.
Hill and Cummins, Chicago
Holyoke Motor Works, Holyoke, Mass.
Horseless Carriage Company (Salisbury), Chicago
Kensington Automobile Company, Buffalo
Lane Motor Vehicle Company, Poughkeepsie, N. Y.
Leach Motor Vehicle Company, Everett, Mass.
Locomobile Company of America, Bridgeport, Conn.
Mobile Company of America, Tarrytown, N. Y.
Morris and Salom, Philadelphia
Mueller, H. and Sons, Decatur, Ill.
Oakman Motor Vehicle Company (Hertel), Greenfield, Mass.
Ohio Automobile Company (Packard), Warren, Ohio
Olds Motor Vehicle Company, Lansing, Mich.
Pittsburgh Motor Vehicle Company, Pittsburgh
Pope Manufacturing Company, Hartford
Racine Motor Vehicle Company, Racine, Wis.
Riker Electric Motor Company, Brooklyn, N. Y. and Elizabeth, N. J.
St. Louis Motor Car Company, St. Louis
Stanley Brothers, Newton, Mass.
Stearns, F. B. and Company, Cleveland
Sturgess Electric Motocycle Company, Chicago, Ill.
Thomas Kane and Company (Pennington), Racine, Wis.
United States Automobile Company, Attleboro, Mass.
United States Motor Vehicle Company, New York
Whitney Motor Wagon Company, Boston
Winton Motor Car Company, Cleveland
Woods Motor Vehicle Company, Chicago

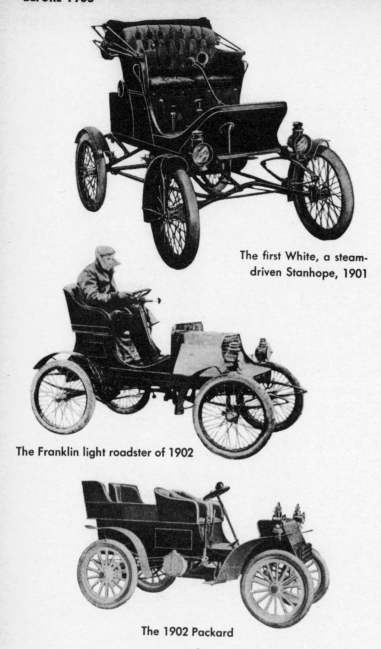

The first White, a steam-driven Stanhope, 1901

The Franklin light roadster of 1902

The 1902 Packard

chusetts inventor, had been building steam road vehicles and offering them for sale. The Grand Rapids *Herald* printed an account of a race between a horse and one of Roper's steam buggies at the Great Ocean Circus on September 8 and 9, 1864. The Roper steam car had no brakes; it was brought to a stop simply by reversing the steam.

Contemporary with Roper was Richard Dudgeon of New York, who built several road locomotives that could carry a number of people. He is supposed to have finished his first machine shortly before the Civil War. A fine example of one of his steam carriages is on display at the Belcourt Museum in Newport, R. I. It is probably the oldest mechanically propelled American road vehicle now in existence.

About 1871, Dr. J. N. Carhart and his brother, H. S. Carhart, built a primitive steam car in Racine, Wis. In 1875, the Wisconsin Legislature (which must have been the most forward-looking state governing body in the country for its day) offered a $10,000 reward to anyone who would invent a practical power-driven road vehicle that could pass certain specified requirements. A race was

staged between the only two that were built for the competition. After taking a whole week to cover the 200-mile course from Madison to Green Bay and back, one of the 6-mph steam-driven vehicles was declared the winner. The Legislature, however, awarded only half of the prize money because its members were not very favorably impressed by what the lumbering winner had actually accomplished.

During this time, power-driven road vehicles were prohibited by law from using English roads, so no progress could be expected in Britain. But in France, Amédée Bollée was building steam cars in the 1870's, and Count Albert de Dion, who was one of the great pioneers of French automobiling, was building them during the 1880's and early 1890's. In 1887, Léon Serpollet designed the first flash boiler, which made it possible to get up steam in a very short time. In 1889, Serpollet was issued what was probably the world's first driver's license.

The steam car made rapid progess in America after F. E. Stanley (1849-1918) and F. O. Stanley (1849-1940), sold their prosperous photographic supply business in 1896 in order to manufacture the famous Stanley Steamer. They built a good car, and although they did not believe in advertising, they drove their own steamers to meets and races and so obtained a great deal of publicity for their product. The Stanleys, who were identical twins, made a striking appearance, because they always dressed in matched costumes, wore the same kind of derbies, and trimmed their beards exactly alike. They were forty-seven years old when they started making steam cars, but they were so successful at it that in 1899 they were able to sell the rights to their car to the Locomobile Company for $250,000. A year later they were ready to go into business again with a newly designed steam car. When the Locomobile Company threatened to sue, the Stanleys simply abandoned the car they had built, drew an entirely new set of plans, and went into production. The Locomobile Company acknowledged defeat by turning back the Stanley patents to their original owners for a fraction of what they had cost. Locomobile then withdrew from the manufacturing of steam cars and thereafter made only gasoline-driven automobiles.

The steam cars built by the Stanley Brothers were very fast, quiet, and exceedingly simple to drive. But steamers had certain disadvantages: getting steam up took time, the boiler and flues had to be cleaned, and the water supply had to be replenished every few hours (see page 128).

In 1896 not only steam but electricity seemed to have excellent possibilities as a source of power for automobiles. In England, as early as 1888, Ratcliffe Ward had built an electric omnibus. A year later, he equipped this bus with armor plate and exhibited it as what was probably the world's first military automobile. William Morrison, of Des Moines, Iowa, is believed to have built the first American electric car. But electricity also had its drawbacks. The electric car was silent and easy to operate, but its batteries had to be recharged every fifty miles or so (see page 126). Consequently, both steam and electricity were doomed as sources of power for the automobile; by the mid-1920's the internal-combustion engine had become supreme for motor-vehicle use.

Toward the end of the century, a number of companies organized to build gasoline-powered automobiles were getting under way. In a long retrospective article published in the January 1918 issue of *Motor*, Charles E. Duryea, who was especially well qualified to discuss these early companies, wrote:

"Charles B. King was an artist and a traveler, and so was familiar with the best foreign work on the automobile. In 1895 he was making pneumatic tools and small engines. In the fall of that year, he took out a license to make Duryea engines, and with Emerson of Cincinnati built a car with one. A few years later [1902] he organized the Northern Manufacturing Company which made a runabout somewhat heavier than the Olds.

"The Autocar Company was organized in 1897; it began by making a tricycle in Pittsburgh. In 1899 it adopted a two-cylinder opposed engine of 4-inch bore and 4-inch stroke. The early Autocar used jump-spark ignition and a timer of special design. Different speeds were obtained by separate sets of gears provided with individual clutches.

"The first Packard was built in 1899; it had a single-cylinder engine and was especially sturdy in design. A particularly heavy flywheel was used; in order to quiet engine vibration, springs were built into the flywheel itself. Lubrication was taken care of by pipes to practically every bearing in the engine.

"The first Cadillac was a 'one-lunger' brought out in 1902. The cylinder, with its copper water-jacket, was distinctive. An ignition plate carrying two spark plugs was another good point in construction, because both wires ran from the coil to these plugs, so there was little chance of grounding. Planetary transmission and chain drive were used. These runabouts were heavier than most other cars. Since they were mechanically well constructed, they gave good service. In fact, some of them are still in use [in 1918].

"In 1901, two Pierce Motorettes were completed. They used one-cylinder De Dion engines and had only two speeds forward with no reverse. Tiller steering, wire wheels, and a light buggy body kept weight down to 600 pounds."

Some of the strange mechanical devices used by these early companies to solve problems of power transmission and control indicate how the automobile industry had to learn as it went along. It was a matter of trying and then trying again—and still again, if necessary—until what were colloquially known as "bugs" were eliminated from the machinery. But such things as flywheels equipped with dampening springs and individual clutches for each set of gears were relatively sensible methods of trying to solve the still little-understood mechanical problems that faced the pioneer automobile builder at every turn. Meanwhile, many inventors and manufacturers wandered off into dead-end streets and blind alleys. They wasted time and money and energy trying to drive automobiles by hand-wound springs, by compressed air, by carbonic acid, and by the

The Model A Rambler, 1900

The Peerless for 1900

The 1902 Marmon

explosions of ether, naphtha, kerosene vapor, and acetylene gas. They experimented fruitlessly with such things as the hub motor, which was a rotary engine mounted directly on each wheel so that no gears, driveshafts, or clutches were needed. This sounded like a good idea at the turn of the century, but it never got far beyond the experimental stage.

Occurring again and again in early automobile advertising was the adjective "perfect." Every manufacturer claimed to have the "perfect" car. Not until the automobile became reasonably well perfected was the word "perfect" dropped from its vocabulary.

The automobile had a long way to go before it became an efficient and dependable means of transportation. But progress was made steadily, and cars were being improved each year. By 1900, the automobile was no longer a curiosity in America, and it was technically far enough advanced to be fairly serviceable in sections of the country where the roads were reasonably good.

But horse lovers continued to scoff at it. In 1900, Colonel Henry Watterson, the doughty editor of the Louisville

The 1900 curved-dash Oldsmobile, America's first mass-production automobile

*Courier-Journal,* had nothing but scorn for the future of motoring. He said then: "The present fad in locomotion is the automobile. It is the swell thing, and the swell people must have one. But Kentuckians need not fear this new machine of locomotion. If it should displace the horse, it can be only for a time. The bicycle threatened the thoroughbreds, but where are the bicycles? Six or eight years ago the fashionable young men sold their horses and buggies and bought wheels—men's wheels, ladies' wheels, and tandems. They scorched on the boulevards, the men in their knickerbockers and the girls in their short skirts and bloomers. Where are the knickerbockers, bloomers, and bikes today? Gone down to the class of people who use them mostly for convenience. The horse and buggy has again become popular, and if the automobile is to hold sway it will be only for a time."

Colonel Watterson, as a loyal Kentuckian, was doubtless prejudiced in favor of the horse. The automobile was in a much more secure position than he was willing to admit. During the previous year, Ray Stannard Baker had made a survey of the new industry and had this to report:

"At least eighty establishments are now actually engaged in building carriages, coaches, tricycles, delivery wagons, and trucks, representing no fewer than two hundred different types of vehicles, with nearly half as many methods of propulsion. Most of these concerns are far behind in their orders, and several are working day and night. A hundred electric cabs are plying on the streets of New York, and two hundred more are being rushed to completion in order to supply the popular demand for horseless locomotion. At least two score of delivery wagons, propelled chiefly by electricity, are in operation in American cities, and the private conveyances of various makers will number well into the hundreds. A motor ambulance is in operation in Chicago; motor trucks are at work in several cities.

Thus far the automobile had been the handmade product of individual workshops, or the largely handmade product of machine shops, marine-engine plants, or bicycle factories. But aside from its utility value, the automobile's greatest contribution to our civilization is what it taught us about mass production. The first American car which sold well enough to warrant mass-production methods for its construction was the famous curved-dash Olds. Its designer, Ransom E. Olds, had been trained in his father's machine shop in Lansing. He experimented with steam-driven cars, and then in 1896 built his first gasoline automobile. It had a one-cylinder, 4-hp engine mounted beneath the carriage-like body, and was able to do 10 mph while carrying four passengers.

Olds built several other cars before 1900, but he was not very successful with them. In 1900 he completed the first curved-dash model. It weighed 700 pounds, and was sold for only $650. Just as he was about to put the car into production, in March 1901, a fire destroyed the Olds factory. Everything went up in flames except one car, which was pushed out of the building and saved. Working patterns were made from this car and production was started. The new model immediately proved to be very popular; more than 400 were built and sold before the year was over. One of them was driven from Detroit to New York in seven and a half days to be displayed at the Madison Square Garden Auto Show.

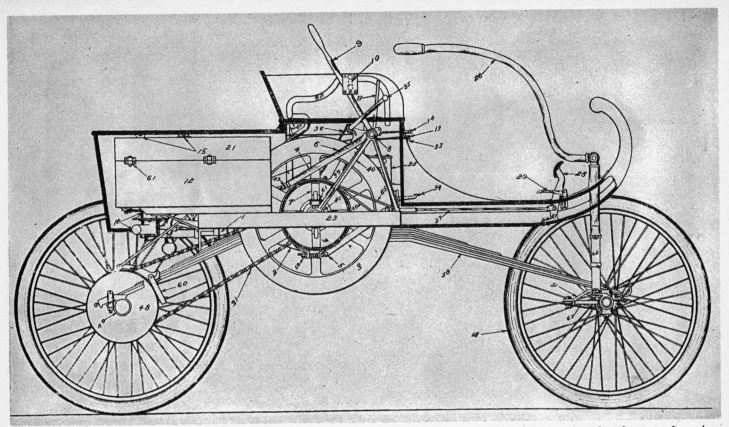

Parts diagram for the curved-dash Oldsmobile. See the diagram below for identification of numbers

After that, the car soared in popularity. There was such a demand for it that primitive mass-production methods were put into effect, enabling the company to sell 2100 cars in 1902, 3750 in 1903, 5000 in 1904, and 6500 in 1905. Then the original company stopped producing the curved-dash model and began to make higher-priced cars. But the memory of it was preserved for posterity by the most successful song ever written about automobiles—"In My Merry Oldsmobile" by Gus Edwards and Vincent Bryan.

The curved-dash Oldsmobile was a very simple car, suited to mass-production methods, and built so it could be serviced easily. Its success in the low-priced field showed the way to Henry Ford, whose history-making Model T appeared only three years after the famous little Oldsmobile had passed its peak.

The Ford Motor Company was founded in 1903. With it, a whole new era in automobile history began. The years before 1903 were the years of the pioneer and the experimenter. After 1903, automobile manufacturing became big business. Science, technology, and huge financial resources were needed to make cars, and ingenuity was no longer enough.

But in 1903, the great years of automobiling were still ahead. Millions of people, many of them as yet unborn, were to discover the pleasures of fast individual transportation —something that had never been available before. In the twentieth century, anyone who could afford to own a car could travel farther and faster than the most powerful monarchs of the past. The automobile, which had begun as a luxury for the very rich, thus helped make our civilization more democratic.

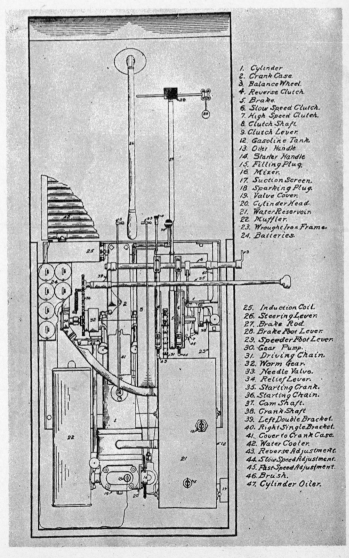

1. Cylinder
2. Crank Case.
3. Balance Wheel.
4. Reverse Clutch.
5. Brake.
6. Slow Speed Clutch.
7. High Speed Clutch.
8. Clutch Shaft.
9. Clutch Lever.
12. Gasoline Tank.
13. Oiler Handle.
14. Starter Handle.
15. Filling Plug.
16. Mixer.
17. Suction Screen.
18. Sparking Plug.
19. Valve Cover.
20. Cylinder Head.
21. Water Reservoir.
22. Muffler.
23. Wrought Iron Frame.
24. Batteries.

25. Induction Coil.
26. Steering Lever.
27. Brake Rod.
28. Brake Foot Lever.
29. Speeder Foot Lever.
30. Gear Pump.
31. Driving Chain.
32. Worm Gear.
33. Needle Valve.
34. Relief Lever.
35. Starting Crank.
36. Starting Chain.
37. Cam Shaft.
38. Crank Shaft.
39. Left Double Bracket.
40. Right Single Bracket.
41. Cover to Crank Case.
42. Water Cooler.
43. Reverse Adjustment.
44. Slow Speed Adjustment.
45. Fast Speed Adjustment.
46. Brush.
47. Cylinder Oiler.

# HOW OUR CARS GOT THAT WAY—FAMOUS FIRSTS

By Harold F. Blanchard, Engineering Consultant to Motor

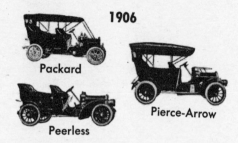

1904
Oldsmobile

1906
Packard
Peerless
Pierce-Arrow

1908
Buick

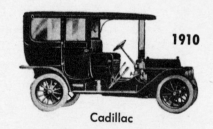

1910
Cadillac

1912
Hudson

1914
Hupmobile

During the early days of automobile development, Europe was years ahead of this country. Therefore, many of the original improvements were produced abroad.

The German Daimler company, builder of the Mercedes, came to the conclusion before 1900 that the horseless carriage should be treated functionally, with complete disregard of its horse ancestry. So Daimler lengthened the wheelbase and moved the engine up front, putting it inside a box which was soon called a hood. There was room enough here to make a real engine instead of an underseat compromise. There was now no limit to the number of cylinders which could be used, and the new location afforded ideal accessibility.

Until this time, transmissions were an unsolved problem. Planetary transmissions were popular. Individual metal-to-metal cone clutches within the transmission were also used to engage spur gears in constant mesh.

Then, in the late 'nineties, the French Panhard came through with a bright if obvious idea—the sliding-gear transmission. Behind the engine of this husky and heavy car was a large cast-metal box containing a mainshaft and countershaft with sliding gears on the former and nonsliding gears on the latter. The mainshaft was driven by the engine through a cone clutch which fitted into the flywheel. The countershaft was connected to a bevel pinion, which operated a ring gear and differential assembly which drove cross shafts fitted with chain sprockets at their outer ends. These sprockets turned the rear wheels by side chains. Drive in all speeds was through pairs of gears—from mainshaft to countershaft to rear wheels.

Sliding-gear transmissions with two, three, or four speeds were soon in use. Gears were shifted by a lever either on the steering column or at the right of the driver. Reverse was to the rear of neutral, and forward speeds were progressively engaged by moving the lever forward from neutral a notch at a time. Thus in a four-speed transmission, in order to reach fourth speed from neutral each of the four sets of gears was engaged in succession, and vice versa when the lever was moved from fourth to neutral.

The next improvement in the sliding-gear transmission was to separate the mainshaft from the clutch shaft, which is the construction used today. This new feature permitted direct drive in high gear, whereas the first sliding-gear transmissions had gears in use in all speeds. The direct-drive transmission was quieter and more durable. The selective shift, which permitted shifting directly from any gear to any other gear or neutral, was introduced about 1910.

Four-speed transmissions usually were made with direct on fourth, but a few, such as Winton and White, about

1915 used a direct third gear, while fourth gear was called an overdrive.

More recent improvements in transmissions and their dates of introduction are: four-speed transmission with silent third, 1928; synchromesh, 1928, by Thompson (who later invented the hydramatic); silent helical second gears, 1929; freewheeling, 1932; overdrive, 1934; hydramatic transmission, 1940. The first American car to have a fluid coupling was the 1939 Chrysler Imperial Eight. The device had previously been used on some foreign cars. Buick was the first American car to have a torque converter, introduced as the Dynaflow and used on the 1948 Roadmaster. A less efficient torque converter was used on prewar GMC buses, and before that on some English buses.

Both the torque converter and the fluid coupling were invented by Dr. Föettinger, a German, in 1902. He developed the torque converter as a "gear reduction" for turbine-driven steamships. A number were built and successfully operated. The fluid coupling was a logical by-product — being, in essence, a torque converter which transmitted torque without multiplying it. In his employ was a young English engineer, Harold Sinclair, who later returned home, where he adapted Föettinger's designs to automotive vehicles.

The steering-column gearshift, common at the beginning of the twentieth century, was revived by Pontiac in 1938.

The leather-faced cone clutch was the most popular type in the early years of the century, but other designs included the leather-faced multiple-disc clutch, the metal-to-metal multiple-disc running in oil, and expanding or contracting types acting on a drum mounted in the flywheel. Single-plate disc clutches came into rather general use about 1920.

Early rear axles had straight teeth on pinion and ring gear. The spiral bevel was adopted in 1912 to reduce gear noise. Hypoid ring and pinion gears, introduced in 1928, gave still quieter operation and also permitted lowering the car, because pinion and drive shaft were below center.

By 1905, most American gasoline vehicles looked like automobiles rather than horseless carriages, being characterized by such features as a hood, a tonneau or rear compartment in back of the driver's seat, and a steering wheel instead of a tiller.

The cheaper American cars, those selling for $1000 to $1500 or less, usually had a horizontal one- or two-cylinder engine under the floor, a two-speed planetary transmission, and chain drive to the rear axle. The driven sprocket was bolted to the differential; therefore, the unit was exposed to road dust because of the necessity for a chain opening in the rear-axle housing. The hood contained gasoline and water tanks, while the radiator, consisting of finned horizontal pipes, was located below the front of the hood.

The typical 1905 American car selling for more than $1500 had a four-cylinder engine, a leather-faced cone clutch, and a three- or four-speed sliding-gear transmission. Shaft drive and dust-proof rear axles with the gears within the housing, just as we have today, were employed on many of these cars, although most of the makers of the more expensive cars, not only here but abroad, were afraid to trust this newfangled rear axle and instead used noisy side chains to transmit the power from differential and jack shafts to the rear wheels. In this case, the differential housing was usually bolted to the rear end of the transmission.

A French Richard-Brasier with a single door at rear (1904)

In 1905, the highest-priced American cars sold for as much as $6000 when equipped with a limousine body, while imported cars ranged up to double this figure. Before the First World War, many wealthy people, particularly in the East, preferred foreign cars, principally French, German, and Italian, believing them more reliable and comfortable than the best American products. This was true at the beginning of the century, but as our cars improved in quality and luxury, the wealthy gradually turned to domestic machines.

In 1905, there was a landslide, both here and in Europe, to the adoption of side-entrance doors to the tonneau. Heretofore, access to this compartment was by a rear door. Runningboards were not long in arriving after this change was made.

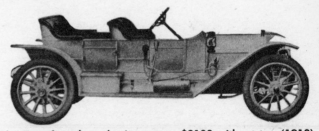

The Otto four-door demi-tonneau. $2100 without top (1910)

The same car without front doors. $2000 without top

The introduction of front doors, in 1910, was equally sudden and sweeping to the point that some of the body designs clearly show that the doors were added as an afterthought. But where bodies had been redesigned for four doors, appearance was greatly improved. This change was the first step toward the modern streamlined car.

The average dashboard carried a sight-feed oiler and a wooden box housing the ignition coils — if battery ignition was used. If the engine had magneto ignition, there might be only a switch on the dash.

Standard equipment until 1910 consisted of three oil lamps — two at the dash, and a tail lamp in the rear. Top, windshield, headlamps, and speedometer were extra. The 1910 Haynes was the first to include these essentials in the list price. The spare tire was carried on the runningboard alongside the driver. Grease cups were used to lubricate spring shackles, drag link, tie rod, kingpins, water pump, and fan.

Driving speeds were unbelievably low in 1905. Fifteen miles per hour was the average, which was exceeded only by a few. Bicycle police enforced speed laws, which usually decreed a maximum of 15 mph, although in some places the speed limit was 10 mph or less.

Maximum speed of cars varied from 25 to 35 mph for the less expensive ones, selling for $1500 or less, up to 60 mph or more for high-powered, high-priced machines. As cars improved in smoothness, power, and controllability, and roads became smoother, speed rose gradually year by year.

There was another factor that kept speed down. Traveling at the rate of 15 to 25 mph over a highway was a real thrill to people whose past experience and road judgment had been based on horse-drawn vehicles. The average man doing 25 mph was likely to feel that he was traveling entirely too fast for his safety.

Today, on the other hand, young people have been accustomed to speeds of 50 to 60 mph or more since they were born. Their eyes and judgment are unconsciously geared up to these higher speeds, so that after brief instruction in operating a car they are able to drive without effort or concern at four or five times the speed normally used by the 1905 driver.

The high-gear hill-climbing ability of some of the old cars was much better than many of the younger generation might think. There were 1910 cars which could make a very respectable showing against our latest models.

In 1910, the typical hood had rounded top panels which ran straight to a dash that was several inches wider than the hood. But in another ten years the dash was no longer visible, because hoods were broader at the rear, and cowls were rounded to meet them. This trend continued until hood and cowl formed one unbroken line.

Radiator grilles are quite ancient. They were used first about 1905 on some European road-race cars where a coarse wire mesh was placed in front of the radiator to protect it from flying stones kicked up by the car ahead. After the First World War, macadam roads in France and Italy were in very bad condition, and owners of passenger cars often installed grilles of the same type to prevent stones from damaging their radiators. Soon American accessory manufacturers were offering wire grilles as a decoration, and it was not long before car manufacturers followed suit. Then style engineers came into the picture and developed the types of grilles which are now in universal use.

Open cars, either roadster or touring, were the rule for the

first twenty years of the twentieth century, although closed bodies were available almost from the first for those who could afford them. Early closed bodies were made to order by carriage builders.

Three types of tops were used on open cars, known as folding, cape, and canopy. The cape top, when raised, protected the passengers on the rear seat. With a fixed canopy top, side curtains could be rolled down. The folding top was similar in design to tops used on some two-seated buggies, the forward portion being supported by brackets alongside the driver. It took two people to raise or lower it. This difficulty was overcome in 1910 by the general adoption of the one-man top, which had hinged braces which made the front supports unnecessary. A two-piece windshield was soon

A folding top of 1905

available for use with this top, or without it, for that matter. It had a brass frame, was bolted to the dash, and was braced by tubular struts sloping forward and downward to the frame.

Comparatively inexpensive winter tops were rather popular around 1915 for those who could not afford closed cars, which were still expensive. These tops were built by accessory makers. Ordinarily the top was solid and was equipped with detachable glass sides. Also, about this time, folding one-man tops with glass windows concealed within the body panels were introduced. When the top was up, the glass sides were raised to enclose the car. This construction was more expensive than the winter top.

Popular-priced closed cars begin with the 1922 four-cylinder Essex coach, a two-door car with a boxlike five-passenger body. It wasn't handsome according to present standards, but it was the first inexpensive closed car. It listed at $1345, or only $250 more than the touring car, whereas the four-door sedan cost $1895. It was the first closed car designed to be built on an efficient production basis.

Sloping windshields for open cars were in use before 1920, while the first closed car with a noticeable tilt to its windshield was the 1931 Reo Royale, which was also noteworthy because its windshield pillars were smoothly rounded into the roof. Graham-Paige added a new style note by adopting skirted front fenders. The Chrysler Airflow, brought out in 1934, was distinguished by a gracefully sloped rear panel, which was quickly copied throughout the industry. Safety glass, an English development, became standard equipment in the 1928 Ford windshield.

Originally, bodies had wood frames covered with wooden panels, which could be bent only in simple curves, so as to give a rounded corner where the side panel meets the rear. Probably the first car to use steel panels over a wood frame was the 1905 Maxwell, although this innovation was undoubtedly for the sake of economy, since its curves were

### THE CANOPY TOP

The canopy top was permanently fixed in place. This French Mors (1905) offers some scant protection to the passengers in the rear seat by placing a glass window behind them, but there is no windshield in front, so the driver got the wind and the rain in his face. Sometimes he used a rubber apron

### THE CAPE TOP

Also called the Victoria top. This short hood, designed for sheltering the passengers in a chauffeur-driven car, was taken over from the carriage makers. On this 1917 Cadillac it is shown with a separate tonneau windshield with adjustable sidewings. In its day this was considered the swankiest of all open-car tops

### THE ONE-MAN TOP

Few things came in for as much derision in automobiling as the so-called "one-man" top. Actually there was nothing wrong with it except the name. Two people could raise one of them in fifteen minutes or so—usually with frantic and wasteful haste because rain was falling in large wet drops

conventional. As time went on, metal panels with double curves came into vogue.

The first car to have an all-steel body was the Dodge which was introduced in 1914. And Dodge was also the first to offer an all-steel closed body, which was brought out in 1923. General Motors was the first to adopt an all-steel top for closed cars, in 1934.

Postwar changes in body styling include: fender lines running continuously from front to rear; broad, squat hoods blending with front fenders; smoother contours; fender skirts; fender aprons that partly conceal the wheels; curved one-piece windshields; blue-green tinted glass windshields to keep out hot sun rays and to reduce glare; hard-top convertibles; and steel station wagons.

Specially built radios for cars were first announced in 1929. Air conditioning was offered as an optional extra by Packard in 1940. Shortly thereafter it was adopted by Chrysler and Cadillac. After the war, air conditioning was not revived until 1953, when it was offered on some or all models by Buick, Cadillac, Oldsmobile, and Chrysler.

Until 1924, all bodies were finished with paint and varnish except for some fenders which were baked enamel. The varnish was not very durable, so the average car began to get shabby after a few years' use. But in 1924, Oakland adopted a quick-drying sprayed-lacquer finish developed by Duco; it was not long before all car makers were using finishes of this type. In addition to long life, lacquer cut down painting time tremendously, with corresponding savings in factory floor space and cost. More recently, synthetic enamels have been adopted by some of the larger car makers.

Most of the bright metal fittings on old cars were made of brass—including levers, steering column, lamps, and usually the radiator shell. Frequent polishing was necessary if the car was to be kept looking its best. Nickel plating, which became popular in the 'twenties, was more weatherproof, but still had to be polished occasionally. Chrome plating, first used by Oldsmobile in 1927, solved the problem.

The very first gasoline engines built in Europe in the 'nineties, or before, had three long-forgotten features: hot-tube ignition, an automatic-intake valve, and a mixing valve instead of a carburetor. The ignition apparatus consisted of a pilot flame enclosed in a tube driven from the crankshaft. At the right moment, a port in the tube would register with a port in the combustion chamber, and the mixture would be set on fire.

The mixing valve consisted of an adjustable needle valve which controlled the rate at which fuel flowed into the mixing chamber, where air picked up the fuel and carried it to the engine. Fuel flowed from the gasoline tank to the mixing valve by gravity. A float to regulate the level of the fuel at the jet was to come later. The downdraft carburetor was introduced in 1929, the automatic choke in 1932, and two dual downdraft carburetors on Buick 1941 models. The air cleaner was adopted in 1922, and an air silencer was added in 1930, the same year as straight-through mufflers.

The automatic-intake valve had a light coil spring just strong enough to close it at maximum engine speed, which was less than 1000 rpm. The valve was opened by engine suction during the intake stroke, was closed by its spring when compression started, and remained closed until the next suction stroke. Valve action, of course, was slow, inefficient, and somewhat uncertain. By 1905 it had practically disappeared in favor of a cam-operated valve.

Electric ignition displaced the hot tube long before 1900. There were two types: jump spark, and make-and-break. The first is merely an earlier name for spark-plug ignition, wherein a high-voltage current jumps between the spark-plug points. Low-voltage current, on the other hand, was used with the make-and-break system, which was based on the principle that when an electric circuit is broken (as by opening a switch) a spark occurs as the points separate.

The essence of the system was two contact points, one stationary and one movable, which were inserted in the combustion chamber mounted on a small plate bolted to an opening in the cylinder. The stationary point was insulated, and the wire carrying the current was connected to it. The movable point, which was attached to a small shaft that could be rotated through a small arc, was grounded by the plate. A long push rod, operated by the camshaft, broke the circuit at the proper instant to make the spark. A low-voltage magneto with only a primary coil on its armature was usually employed with this system. No distributor was necessary on multi-cylinder engines. The make-and-break system was used as late as 1910 on a number of the higher-priced foreign and domestic cars.

The first spark-plug engines used an induction coil equipped with a vibrating circuit breaker or trembler, which

Individual ignition coils for a four-cylinder motor (1904)

broke the primary circuit many times per second, thus producing a succession of sparks at the plug. The low-tension circuit was closed by a timer. There was a separate coil for each cylinder. In a four-cylinder engine, there would be four coils and four insulated metal segments on the timer. The rotating brush or roller would touch each segment successively, and current from that segment would flow by wire to the primary of its coil, while a high-tension wire would lead the sparking current from the coil to the plug.

Five dry cells, connected in series, were ordinarily used as a source of current. Since the voltage of dry cells decreases gradually when used continuously, it was customary to have two sets of cells, so one set could rest up while the other was in use.

During 1905 to 1910, a six-volt storage battery was sometimes substituted for one set of dry cells. Its capacity was vastly greater than dry cells, but it had to be removed for charging. Meanwhile, magnetos for spark-plug engines saw increasing use because they eliminated the nuisance of dry cells or a storage battery. There were two types. In one design, notably the German Bosch, primary and secondary coils were wound on the armature. Cam-operated breaker points were used to open the circuit to produce a spark, while a built-in distributor switched the high-tension current to the proper spark plug. The other type was similar, except that the armature winding was used only to generate a current which had its voltage stepped up in a separate coil that had a high-tension wire leading back to the distributor on the magneto. With this system, five dry cells feeding through breaker points, coil, and distributor could be used as an additional current source for easy starting, since some magnetos required fast cranking to generate good sparks.

At this time there was a definite trend toward magnetos as an unfailing source of ignition. However, a new development was in the offing, consisting of an electric generator and storage battery. Here was a new source of current. It was an old idea, but it first came into prominence in 1910—not for ignition, but for illumination of the lamps. The first headlamps, introduced early in the century, used acetylene gas produced by a small tank in which water dripped on calcium carbide. A major improvement occurred in 1904 when the Prest-O-Lite tank was invented. It consisted of a steel cylinder in which acetylene gas was compressed to a high pressure. Compressed acetylene, unfortunately, is likely to explode when jarred. What made the Prest-O-Lite tank possible was the discovery that high-pressure acetylene was no longer dangerous when dissolved in acetone. A gauge on one end showed when the tank was empty and had to be exchanged for a filled one. The gas was turned on by a small pocket wrench which operated a needle valve. Prest-O-Lite tanks were soon in universal use, but were gradually displaced by electric lights during the years 1910 to 1915.

In 1910, only a few of the higher-priced cars had generators and storage batteries. Therefore, ignition units, as we know them today, did not become popular until cars began to be equipped not only with generators and batteries but with starters as well.

Cadillac was the first to adopt the electric starter, in 1912. Before this, much thought and considerable development work had been put into the problem of adapting an electric motor to the business of cranking an automobile engine. Cadillac's solution was a combined starter and generator, designed by Charles F. Kettering and manufactured by his young company, Dayton Engineering Laboratories Company, or Delco for short. The unit had a single armature on which both starter and generator windings were placed. As a generator, the armature was driven from the pump shaft through an overrunning clutch. Therefore the armature was free to crank the engine when the starting circuit was closed.

Cadillac in 1912 also installed the first timing chain, similar to those in present-day use, in an American automobile.

Although electric lighting did not come into general use until later, this car was equipped with electric lights in 1907. The Apple Electric Company made the installation, obviously converting acetylene headlights and kerosene sidelights for the purpose

Changing a clincher tire was a slow, laborious process (1907)

By this time the public was becoming noise-conscious, and the chain was brought over from Europe to aid in quieting American motors.

Other starting and lighting systems quickly appeared, most of them with separate generator and starter units. An exception, however, was the single-unit device used for several years by Dodge, beginning with the first car delivered in 1915. It was a large motor-generator, permanently geared to the crankshaft by a silent chain wherein the same armature windings functioned as both starter and generator. To start the car, a switch was closed which connected the battery to the armature to crank the engine. As soon as the engine was running above idling speed, enough voltage was generated to charge the battery. No cutout relay was required with this system. And when the engine stalled, the starter came into action automatically.

Just as soon as the starting and lighting system was firmly established, magnetos began to be discarded in favor of our present-day ignition units. There was one important exception, the Model T Ford, which since its introduction in 1909 had been equipped with a magneto built into the flywheel to supply ignition to four trembler coils mounted in a box on the dash. This ignition system was used until the Model A Ford was brought out in 1928.

After the advent of electric lights, however, it was not long before accessory makers discovered that the Ford flywheel magneto had ample capacity to supply a pair of headlights. Sometime later the factory adopted this feature as standard equipment. At the same time, various manufacturers of electric units brought out starting and lighting equipment which could be installed on the Model T.

A 12-volt electric system was adopted in 1953 by Buick, Cadillac, Oldsmobile, Chrysler. It was introduced to provide a greater electrical output without increasing generator size. It also appeared to provide improved ignition for high-compression engines.

As previously indicated, the first improvement in the carburetor was the addition of a float chamber, about 1900. In a relatively short time it was discovered that the mixture became richer as air flow through the device increased. To solve this difficulty a spring-closed air valve was added which allowed extra air to enter to dilute the mixture. Carburetors with compensating jets, which made an auxiliary air valve unnecessary, were introduced about 1912.

Four-barrel carburetors were introduced during 1952-1953 because of a horsepower race between the manufacturers of some of the larger Eights. Actually, the four-barrel carburetor is of interest only to the man who wants a top speed of more than 90 actual miles per hour and increased acceleration above 70 mph.

Fuel was originally fed by gravity from a tank under the seat or sometimes in the cowl. Some of the more expensive cars, however, placed the tank at the rear and delivered the fuel to the carburetor by pressure, which was supplied either by an engine-driven air pump or by pressure bled from the exhaust pipe. The introduction of the vacuum tank, about 1915, resulted in the eventual elimination of pressure feed and made the rear tank an all but universal feature. The camshaft-driven diaphragm pump in turn displaced the vacuum tank.

Early engines were lubricated in various ways. A small tank of oil mounted on top of a horizontal engine might be used to carry oil by gravity through oil pipes leading to the cylinders, while main bearings were lubricated by grease cups. In some later engines, say around 1905, a group of small plungers within an oil tank were used to deliver oil to the individual cylinders. Many engines, on the other hand—including four-cylinder types built in 1910 and later—depended on the splashing of the oil within the oil pan to lubricate the entire engine. There was no circulating pump, nor splash troughs nor a dip stick. Oil level was determined by two petcocks on the side of the crankcase, one about two inches above the other. The crankcase was considered properly filled when oil flowed out of the upper petcock and too low when no oil would flow out of the lower one. The separate oil filter was first used as standard equipment on the original Chrysler in 1924. Crankcase ventilation was introduced by Cadillac in 1925.

The first four-cylinder engines had individually cast cylinders bolted to the crankcase. As experience in casting these intricate units increased, pair-cast cylinders appeared. And later, about 1908, foundries were able to cast all four cylinders in one piece. Not long afterward, it was found that valve noise could be subdued by enclosing the springs and tappets within chambers covered by suitable plates. The casting problem was simplified when Ford adopted the detachable cylinder head in the first Model T. The first vibration damper was an English Lanchester design adopted by Packard in 1920. Rubber engine mountings were introduced in 1927.

It was the Ford Model T that popularized left drive. The left position is much safer and more convenient when overtaking cars on the road, since left drive makes it possible to see what's ahead without pulling out so far. Why left drive was not adopted in the first place is a mystery, except that buggy drivers usually sat on the right. It was all of five years before left drive was universally accepted by American motor car manufacturers.

Knee-action, common in Europe, was introduced in this country in 1934. Coil springs in the rear were adopted by Buick for its 1938 models. The first shock absorber in general use in America was the Hartford, a friction type, invented in France. Hydraulic shock absorbers were adopted by several car makers in 1927.

Before the 1900 period, tires were of the single-tube type, the same as used on bicycles. That is, the air-holding tube, carcass, and tread were one integral piece. It was not long, however, before the clincher tire with tube and casing as separate units was developed. All cars were using them by 1905, or earlier.

Changing a clincher tire was a slow, laborious process. The process was speeded up by the introduction of rims with a quick-detachable flange. A number of designs were in use by 1910, although the more conservative makers still stuck to the old-fashioned clincher. This improvement, however, was only a stopgap. What was obviously needed was a tire and rim, or a tire and wheel which could be readily removed and replaced as a unit, thus eliminating the trouble of taking a tire apart on the road, inflating it, and installing it again. Michelin, leading French tire maker, brought out a demountable rim in 1908, but it was not until about 1915 that demountable rims (of various makes) were generally adopted in this country. Cord tires started to replace woven fabric about 1920. Balloon tires became standard equipment in 1924, and super-balloons were brought out in 1932.

It is difficult to say who made the first four-wheel brake. It was an obvious development, but there were many problems involving both brakes and operating linkage. They were seen on a few European cars before 1910. Fred Duesenberg used internal hydraulic brakes of his own design on his first Model A passenger car built in 1921. The original Chrysler Six was the first production car to have four-wheel brakes, and they were hydraulics too. By this time brakes on all wheels were quite common in Europe.

Power-operated brakes, which were used to some extent for years before the war, were offered on a number of cars in 1952-1953. Power steering was also introduced during this period on cars in all price classes from Chevrolet up. All the more expensive cars offered this feature.

Duesenberg was the first to build a straight Eight passenger car in this country, while Cadillac was the first to offer a V8 (in 1915). The French De Dion-Bouton company had brought out a V8 a year or two before, and about the same time the English Sunbeam company made a V12 racing car. For that matter, the Maxwell, predecessor of the Plymouth, built a race car about 1906 with a 750-cubic-inch 12-cylinder flat (pancake) engine.

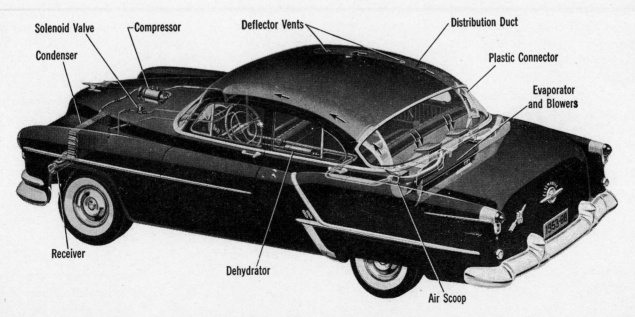

Air conditioning on the 1953 Oldsmobile

*Automobile* France
(â-tō-mō'-bil)

**Automóvil** Spain
(a-to-mo-bil)

**АВТОМОБИЛИ** Russia
(a-to-mo-bil)

**Automobil** Sweden
(a-to-mo-bil)

**Automovel** Portugal
(a-to-mo-bil)

اوتومبيل Turkey
(a-to-mo-bil)

سيّاره Egypt
(sāy'-yă-rah)

Αὐτοκίνητον Greece
(âf-tō-kī-nī'-tŏn)

موٹر گاڑی India (Hindustani)
(mō'-tar gă'-ri)

**Carrozza tan=nar** Malta
(câr'-rōz-ză tăn-năr)

মোটর গাড়ি India (Bengali)
(mō'-tar gă'-ri)

મોટોર ગાડી. Zanzibar
(mō'-tar gă'-ri)

**Automobil** Germany
(a-to-mo-bil)

**Automobili** Italy
(a-to-mo-bil)

*Automobiel* Netherlands
(a-to-mo-bil)

**Automobil** Denmark
(a-to-mo-bil)

אויטאמאביל Yiddish
(lib-om-ot-a)

# HOW THE AUTOMOBILE GOT ITS NAME

In the 1890's, when the new motor-driven privately owned vehicles were first attracting attention, no one seemed to know quite what to call them. The term "horseless carriage" was fairly popular, but even then people realized that this important new invention deserved something more positive as a name than anything the adjective "horseless" might imply.

While the first American automobile race was being planned in 1895, Mr. H. H. Kohlsaat, owner of the Chicago *Times-Herald,* the newspaper that was sponsoring the race, decided to get some publicity for the affair by running a contest to establish a definitive name for the new vehicles. When he offered a prize of $500, thousands of entries poured in. The prize was divided among three people who had proposed the word "motocycle." It was a most unsuccessful name, which sooned died the death it deserved. But it lasted long enough for the publishers of a new magazine to call their publication *The Motocycle.* That, too, was destined to have a short life.

Here are some of the early attempts to find a name for the automobile. A few of them became fairly popular, but most of them never got beyond the small circle of their inventors' friends.

| | | |
|---|---|---|
| Motocycle | Autopher | Ottomobile |
| Quadricycle | Autovic | Pneumobile |
| Autobat | Self-Motor | Steamobile |
| Autocar | Motor Wagon | Texmobile |
| Autocycle | Buckmobile | Zentmobile |
| Autogen | Farmobile | Buggyaut |
| Autogo | Clarksmobile | Ipsometer |
| Autokinet | Gasmobile | Petrocar |
| Automotor | Lancarmobile | Trundler |

British terminology for automobiles and their parts differs widely from American. For instance, in England they call a sedan a saloon; the luggage compartment is the boot; a convertible is a drophead; the hood is a bonnet; fenders are called wings; a horn is a hooter; and a windshield is a windscreen. Even the terminology of traffic differs. A detour is a road diversion; a traffic circle is a roundabout; a road shoulder is called the verge; and a divided highway is called a dual carriageway. Gasoline, of course, is petrol, and the British Imperial gallon is one-fifth larger than ours.

But the British are enthusiastic motorists. Many of them who cannot afford to own even the most miserable, aged, broken-down, and inexpensive automobile follow motoring and everything that has to do with it with avid interest.

*The foreign names for the automobile shown in the column to the left were published in the December 1911 issue of* Motor, *which shows how early the automobile became firmly established on an international basis.*

**BUICK**

**CADILLAC**

**CHEVROLET**

**CHRYSLER**

**DE SOTO**

**DODGE**

**FORD**

**HUDSON**

**KAISER-FRAZER and HENRY J**

**LINCOLN**

## THE ANCESTRY OF PRESENT-DAY AMERICAN AUTOMOBILES

**MERCURY**

**NASH**

By Harold F. Blanchard, Engineering Consultant to Motor

**OLDSMOBILE**

There are only nineteen makes of automobiles manufactured in America today. And there are only eight companies building them. General Motors makes the Buick, the Cadillac, the Chevrolet, the Oldsmobile, and the Pontiac. The Ford Motor Company makes the Ford, the Lincoln, and the Mercury. Chrysler makes the Chrysler, the De Soto, the Dodge, and the Plymouth. Kaiser-Fraser makes the Kaiser and the Henry J. This company merged with Willys in 1953. Other independent American automobile manufacturers are Hudson, Nash, Packard, and Studebaker.

**PACKARD**

**PLYMOUTH**

**PONTIAC**

In the long section that follows, Mr. Blanchard traces the ancestry of each make back to its origin. He also shows representative cars which demonstrate how that particular make of automobile was changed and improved over the course of years. Detailed specifications for three typical American automobiles — Cadillac, Ford, and Studebaker are given at the back of the book.

**STUDEBAKER**

**WILLYS**

1905 Model C. Two-cylinder engine under body. Radiator beneath hood

# BUICK

David Buick's first car was put on the market in 1903. It had a two-cylinder valve-in-head engine under the floor and a two-speed planetary transmission which was connected to the rear axle by a central chain. This car was continued without fundamental change through 1910. It was low-priced for its time, selling for $1000 to $1250. The hood, with a decorative screen at the front, contained gasoline and water tanks, while the radiator, consisting of finned horizontal pipes, was located below the hood front. As with many modern cars, the hood extended far forward of the front axle. The engine had 4½ x 5-inch cylinders, giving a piston displacement of 159 cubic inches; 22 hp was developed at 924 rpm. Wheelbase in 1905 was 86 inches, and tire size through the years was 30 x 3½.

In 1906, Buick brought out a $2500 four-cylinder car, the Model D. Cylinders were individually cast and were of the so-called T-head design; that is, the intake valves were located in pockets on one side of the engine and the exhaust valves in pockets on the other side. Each set of four valves was operated by its own camshaft. Bore and stroke were 4¼ x 4½ inches, and piston displacement was 255 cubic inches. The engine was variously rated at 24 to 35 hp during its three years of production, 1906-1908. Clutch and transmission were in unit with the engine.

A small popular-priced ($800-$1000) four-cylinder car made its appearance in 1908 and was continued through 1911. It had a 3¾ x 3¾-inch valve-in-head engine with pair-cast cylinders. Piston displacement was 166 cubic inches, and upward of 18 hp was developed. The transmission was a two-speed planetary with a cone clutch for direct. (Model 10, 1908-1910; Models 32-33, 1911.) During the years 1912 to 1915, a car in the same price class was built with the same size engine, but supplied with a three-speed sliding-gear transmission driven by a cone clutch. (Models 34, 35, 36, 24, 25, B25, C25.)

In 1908, a $2500, 2500-pound car was brought out (Model 5). The four valve-in-head cylinders were 4⅝ x 5 inches, piston displacement was 336 cubic inches, and wheelbase 108 inches. A still larger, more powerful car was built in 1909 (Model 7). Cylinders were 5 x 5 inches, wheelbase was 122, and tires 34 x 4—a popular tire size for many years.

The year 1909 saw the introduction of a 4½ x 5-inch engine, which was continued through 1912 in Models 16, 17, 38, 39, 43. A cone clutch and three-speed sliding-gear transmission was used in these cars as well as in those described in the preceding paragraph.

A four-cylinder car in the $1500 class was made from 1910 to 1913. It had a 255-cubic-inch engine. A $550 car with a two-cylinder 127-cubic-inch engine of 14 hp was marketed only during the year

1910 Model 16 four-cylinder had full-width rumble seat

1912 four-cylinder Model 43. Note diagonal windshield braces and Prest-O-Lite tank on running board

1911. From 1911 to 1913 there was a 201-cubic-inch four-cylinder car in the $1000 class, and a $1300, 221-cubic-inch model in the years 1914 and 1915.

A six-cylinder automobile with a $1500 to $2000 price was manufactured from 1914 to 1916.

Sixes were produced exclusively from 1918 to 1930, except for a 170-cubic-inch Four at $665 to $965 which spanned the years 1916 to 1924. Only eight-cylinder cars have been built since 1931.

Buick was the first to use a vacuum-operated clutch in 1932, rear coil springs in 1938, and two dual downdraft carburetors on the 1940 models. Buick was also the first to have a torque converter, introduced on the 1948 Roadmaster. This, combined with two-speed and reverse planetary transmission, was called the Dynaflow transmission. In 1952, a four-barrel carburetor was adopted on the Roadmaster. Power steering was another 1952 feature. Important changes in 1953 were a 322-cubic-inch V8 188-hp engine, a 12-volt electric system on Super and Roadmaster, optional power braking on the Roadmaster, and an entirely new concept in the design of the Dynaflow torque converter which gives much faster acceleration. Air conditioning is optional on some 1953 models.

1924 four-door five-passenger Model Six-47 sedan. Four-wheel brakes are new

1912 four-cylinder Models 28, 29 overhead valve powerplant with magneto ignition

1931 Model 8-66 two-window coupe

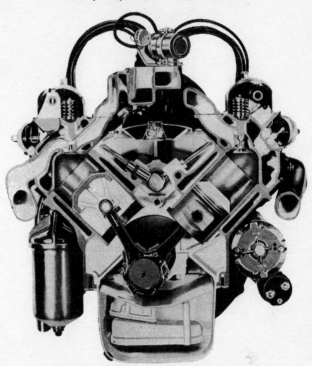

1938 Series 40 sedan

1953 Buick motor. V8 section shows cone-shaped combustion chambers and in-line valves operating from a single rocker shaft on each cylinder head

1953 Roadmaster Riviera sedan. Wheelbase has been reduced to 125½ inches

First Cadillac, the 1902 Model A

Single-cylinder 1906 Model M touring car

Price of the 1909 Model 30 was $1400

The first Cadillac Eight 1915 seven-passenger model cost $1975

# CADILLAC

Cadillac entered the industry in 1902 with a well-built single-cylinder car with a horizontal engine under the front seat. At the end of its transverse crankshaft was a two-speed and reverse planetary transmission, which drove a chain connecting to a sprocket at the center of the rear axle. With a comparatively low price of $750 to $1000, depending on the year, it was one of the most popular cars (a best-seller some years) on the market until it was discontinued in 1909; by then, a single-cylinder car was out of date. Its engine had a bore and stroke of 5 inches and a piston displacement of 98 cubic inches, and developed 7 hp in the beginning and 10 hp at the end of this period.

Even though Cadillac was very successful in the low-priced market, company interest was centered in higher-priced cars. In 1905, a four-cylinder car with a three-speed planetary transmission was brought out for the $2500 buyers. It had a 300-cubic-inch engine rated at 30 hp. This model was discontinued at the end of 1908.

A still more expensive four-cylinder with a three-speed sliding-gear transmission was offered for the year 1906 only. Its piston displacement was 392 cubic inches, and it developed 40 hp. Price was $3750.

From 1907 to 1914, Cadillac's main effort was concentrated on four-cylinder models which cost about $2000, although the 1909 car was only $1400. Their engines grew gradually in size from 226 cubic inches in 1907 to 365 cubic inches in 1914. The last of these Fours had a two-speed rear axle equipped with an electromagnetic shifting mechanism.

In 1915, the Four was discarded for a V8, the first Eight to be manufactured in this country. It developed 60 hp with a piston displacement of 314 cubic inches. This engine size was continued through 1937, while horsepower was raised to 87. The original eight-cylinder five-passenger touring car sold for $1975, which was the price of the preceding four-cylinder model. Following Cadillac's lead, numerous V8's were brought out, to be followed by several straight Eights. Some V12's also soon appeared.

In 1928, Cadillacs were provided with a new engine of 341 inches displacement. Valve-in-head V16's were built from 1930 to 1937, and similar V12's from 1931 to 1937. An L-head V16 was made from 1937 to 1940.

Cadillac adopted the hydramatic drive in 1941. The V8 engine

1933 Cadillac twelve-cylinder convertible coupe

was redesigned in 1936; this engine was used through 1948, while its horsepower, due to refinements, increased from 135 to 150. In 1949, a 331-cubic-inch overhead-valve engine of 160 hp was introduced—the first of the modern overhead-valve V8's. In 1952 its power was increased to 190, mainly because of the adoption of a four-barrel carburetor. In 1953, the horsepower was raised to 210 by various refinements, including an increase of the compression ratio from 7.5 to 8.25. Power steering was adopted in 1952 as an option, as well as Autronic Eye automatic headlamp-beam control. Optional air conditioning was introduced in 1953 on all models except the soft-top convertible. All 1953 models have a 12-volt electric system.

1902 Model A one-cylinder engine. Vertical intake valve is opened by a rocker actuated by a long push rod driven by an eccentric on a timing-gear shaft. Lever and cam under tip of the long push-rod control the amount of intake opening, thus making a throttle unnecessary.

1939 Cadillac town car with Fleetwood body

1953 El Dorado convertible with luxury styling costs $7750

The Little was bought by Chevrolet in 1912. The car shown is the 1913 Little Four which sold for $690 fully equipped.

Chevrolet 1917 V8 with valves in head. Dual carburetors are used, and exhaust manifolds are formed within the cylinder heads. Cone clutch and flywheel are exposed

# CHEVROLET

The Chevrolet was named after the late Louis Chevrolet, its first designer, who was a famous race driver in his day. The company went into production in 1912, and bought the Little car in the same year. All Chevrolet cars have had overhead valves.

In 1913, the line consisted of the Little Four priced at $690, the (Chevrolet) Little Six at $1285, and the six-cylinder Chevrolet Model C at $2100. The smaller Six was dropped at the close of the year, but the larger one was made during 1914 and 1915.

The real ancestor of the modern Chevrolet, unless you count the Little Four, was a four-cylinder model introduced in 1914 at the low price of $750. It weighed 1975 pounds, had a wheelbase of 104 inches, and tires were 30 x 3½ inches. The engine had $3^{11}/_{16}$ x 4-inch cylinders and a piston displacement of 170.9 cubic inches, and developed 24 hp. Engines of these dimensions were made right through the years until the company turned to six-cylinder cars in 1929.

In 1916 the engine was also employed in a cheaper model which was priced at $490. In 1918, the more expensive four-cylinder model, now listing at $995, was given a similar engine with the same bore but a longer stroke — 5¼ inches.

Chevrolet built a V8 with overhead valves during 1917 and 1918.

The Chevrolet V8 four-passenger roadster built in 1917 and 1918. There is a narrow aisle between the two front seats. Price $1385

1915 Model H2 Chevrolet with four-cylinder valve-in-head engine

Four-door, five-passenger sedan, 1925

The Imperial Landau was an attractive four-door car built in 1929

1938 Master De Luxe Chevrolet with four-door touring sedan body

It listed at $1285 and $1385 respectively for the two years it was made.

In 1923 the company dropped the larger-size engine in favor of the smaller, and continued with it through 1938.

Chevrolet built a V8 with overhead valves during 1917 and 1918. It listed at $1285 and $1385 respectively for the two years it was made.

Chevrolet switched to six-cylinder engines in 1929. Bore and stroke were $3\frac{5}{16}$ x $3\frac{3}{4}$ inches, piston displacement was 193.9, and 46 hp was delivered at 2600 rpm with a compression ratio of 5 to 1.

The power of this engine has been increased steadily through the years without any basic change in design. It developed 60 hp at 3000 rpm in 1932. In 1933, the piston displacement was increased to 206.8 cubic inches to give 80 hp at 3200. In 1937, the piston displacement was raised to 216.5 to provide 85 hp. Engine size remained unchanged through 1952. In 1950 Power Glide was introduced, with a 235.5-cubic-inch engine of 105 hp. In 1953, this engine was adopted for all models, developing 108 hp with a 7.1 compression for gearshift cars and 115 hp with 7.5 compression for Power-Glide cars. Power steering was introduced in 1953.

The Power-Glide torque-converter transmission was brought out in 1950. It was redesigned in 1953 with two-speed automatic shift.

A front view of the 1953 Chevrolet

1953 Two-Ten four-door sedan carries new body with low, sweeping lines

Eight-cylinder Imperial sedan, 1931

Original six-cylinder Chrysler 70 introduced in 1924

First Chrysler Airflow, 1934

1938 Chrysler Imperial sedan

1941 Chrysler Windsor club coupe

1953 Custom Imperial four-door sedan

# CHRYSLER

The original Chrysler 70 attracted unusual attention at the 1924 Automobile Show in New York because of its handsome appearance and the excellence of its design, including a number of new features such as four-wheel hydraulic brakes, oil filter, and air cleaner. The instrument board started a new trend in styling because the instruments were grouped behind an oval panel of glass.

This Chrysler was one of few cars to be designed from the ground up beginning with a clean sheet of paper and without hampering precedents. It wasn't a large car; its wheelbase was only 112¾ inches, but it was exceedingly powerful for its weight and therefore was a top performer for that year. Its engine developed 70 hp at 3500, and the weight of the $1335 touring car was only 2750 pounds.

In appearance it was a big car scaled down. Pictures of it in pre-show teaser advertisements which gave no clue as to its size suggested that it was a big $3000 car. The scaling process included smaller tires—29 x 4.50, whereas competitive cars used 31 x 4's.

The hydraulic brakes with their comparatively frictionless operation and their perfect equalization provided an entirely new standard of stopping ability. Brakes were the external contracting type connected to a supply reservoir operated by a hand valve. Internal hydraulic brakes and the self-filling master cylinder did not come into use until 1927. This brilliant new model was continued through 1928.

A low-priced four-cylinder car was built under the Chrysler name from 1926 to 1928, but the name was changed to Plymouth beginning with the 1929 model.

The Chrysler Imperial, a Six with a $3395 price tag, was brought out in 1926 and was continued until the end of 1930. Its bore was 3½ inches until 1928, when it was increased to 3⅝ inches. Two Eights were introduced in 1931, the Model CD which listed at $1525, and the Imperial Eight at $2745 which replaced the Imperial Six. At the same time the manufacture of three low-to-medium-priced Sixes was continued. At least one six-cylinder model and two or more Eights have been offered every year since 1931.

In 1930 a four-speed transmission with a silent third gear was used on Models 70 and 77. A vacuum-operated clutch, freewheeling, and floating power were features of the 1932 cars. The Airflow body was brought out in 1934, and overdrive was introduced the same year.

Chrysler was the first in this country to employ the fluid coupling. It was an optional extra on the 1939 Chrysler Imperial Eight. A four-speed semiautomatic transmission with fluid drive was a new development on 1941 models.

In 1940, a safety tire rim was adopted in order to minimize the danger when a blowout occurs, not only on Chrysler cars but also on Dodge, De Soto, and Plymouth. An overhead-valve 180-hp 331-cubic-inch V8 came out in 1951. For this V8, a torque converter was introduced, but Chrysler's four-speed two-range semiautomatic transmission was retained. Optional power steering was another 1951 feature. In 1953, a 12-volt electric system was introduced on the Crown Imperial models, and the torque converter was redesigned to include a two-speed and reverse automatic transmission.

The Airflow De Soto made its debut in 1934

# DE SOTO

De Soto made its initial bow in 1928 with a six-cylinder model which listed at $885. Its 174.9-cubic-inch engine developed 55 hp at 3000 rpm. A 72-hp Eight was brought out in 1930, but was discontinued at the end of the 1931 model year.

Downdraft carburetion was introduced in 1929. Floating power, a vacuum-operated clutch, and freewheeling were adopted in 1932. Roomy Airflow bodies and overdrive were features in 1934. The fluid coupling was an optional extra in 1940, while a four-speed semi-automatic transmission with fluid coupling was first offered in 1941.

In 1952, a 160-hp 276-cubic-inch overhead-valve V8 engine was introduced, equipped with a torque-converter transmission. Power steering was offered as an option on both V8 and Six, and both could be had with an overdrive and a standard three-speed transmission.

Four-door, five-passenger sedan, 1928

1931 De Soto six-cylinder roadster

1938 De Soto two-door sedan

1953 Fire Dome V8 four-door sedan with 160-hp engine

Original Dodge
touring car, 1915

# DODGE

John and Horace Dodge, who had become wealthy manufacturing engines for the Ford Motor Company, brought out the first Dodge Brothers car in 1915. It was a simple, reliable four-cylinder car moderately priced at $785. It used an L-head engine with a bore and stroke of 3⅞ x 4½ inches, which developed 35 hp. Piston displacement was 212.3 cubic inches, and weight was 2250 pounds. It was the first automobile to have an all-steel body. Wheelbase was 110 inches, and tire size was 32 x 3½.

The new machine was a success from the start, and was manufactured without basic changes until the end of 1928. Dodge Brothers also was the first manufacturer to adopt (in 1923) the all-steel closed body, developed by Edward G. Budd.

A novel feature of the Dodge was a combined starter and generator driven by silent chain. It was a comparatively large unit, which employed the same armature and field windings for both engine cranking and current production. To start the engine, a switch was closed on the dash, allowing current to flow from the battery to the motor-generator unit. As soon as the engine reached a speed corresponding to about 10 mph in high gear, the voltage generated by the armature was sufficient to charge the battery. No cutout relay was required with this system, and the engine could not be stalled because the device automatically cranked the engine whenever armature voltage fell below battery voltage.

Another interesting feature was a three-speed transmission in which countershaft gears did not rotate when high gear was engaged. The 1915 car had a cone clutch. A dry multiple-disc clutch was used from 1916 to 1927. In 1928, a single-plate Borg and Beck clutch was adopted.

In 1928 a popular-priced Six was brought out to take the place of the Four. It had a 3⅜ x 3⅞-inch engine of 208 cubic inches piston displacement, developing 58 hp at 3000. Tires were 29 x 5 inches. There were two models, the Standard Six at $895 and the Victory Six at $1095. This chassis was continued for the next two years as the DA, price $995.

A larger six-cylinder car was also introduced in 1928, known as the Senior Six. Its list price was $1495, and the 3¼ x 4½-inch engine was rated at 60 hp at 2800 rpm. Wheelbase was 116 inches and weight 3409 pounds. Later in the same year the engine was enlarged to 3⅜ x 4½ inches, and power increased to 68 at 2800 rpm. The horsepower of the 1929 Senior Six was raised to 78 at 3000 without changing engine size. The model was discontinued at the end of 1930.

A new Six of 189.8 cubic inches came out in 1930, for $865. A series of Sixes in the same general category was made year by year up to and including 1942, by which time the engine had grown to 230.2 cubic inches.

A straight Eight was put on the market in 1930 and was manufactured until the end of 1933. In the beginning its bore and stroke were 2⅞ x 4¼, piston displacement was 220.7 cubic inches, horsepower was 78 at 3000 rpm, and price was $1145. The engine size was increased to 240.3 cubic inches in 1931 and to 282 cubic inches in 1932-1933.

An improved four-speed two-range semiautomatic transmission was brought out in 1949. It was used in conjunction with a clutch and a fluid drive. In 1953, an overhead-valve 140-hp 241-cubic-inch V8 was introduced, and also a torque converter, which was combined with the transmission mentioned above. In 1953, overdrive was offered as optional on cars equipped with a three-speed transmission.

First closed car with all-steel body, 1923

1928 four-window coupe

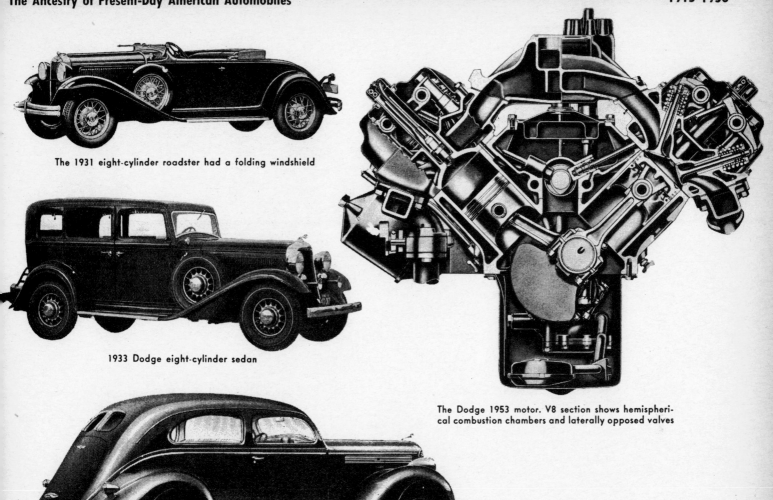

The 1931 eight-cylinder roadster had a folding windshield

1933 Dodge eight-cylinder sedan

The Dodge 1953 motor. V8 section shows hemispherical combustion chambers and laterally opposed valves

1938 two-door sedan

1953 Coronet four-door sedan. New grille retains Dodge look

1953 Coronet Sierra, a new body type for Dodge. Rear seat folds down

Side entrance doors featured the Model C built in 1905

By removing the tonneau, the 1903 Model A became a roadster

# FORD

Ford's first car was a two-cylinder model, brought out in 1903, which sold for less than $1000. Its L-head engine, with opposed cylinders, was placed under the floor, lengthwise of the frame. It had 4 x 4-inch cylinders which gave a piston displacement of 100.5 cubic inches. Eight hp was developed at 1000 rpm. Weight was 1250 pounds, wheelbase 72 inches, and 28 x 3-inch tires were used. A two-speed planetary transmission was attached to the engine. A central chain was used to transmit power to the rear axle. This model was built through 1906.

A four-cylinder air-cooled car of which little is known was announced in 1904. The same year a four-cylinder water-cooled model was brought out with 4 x 5-inch cylinders under the hood, two-speed planetary transmission, and shaft drive to the rear wheels. A $2000 four-cylinder of similar design was built in 1905.

In 1906, Ford brought out the famous Model N roadster, which was the forerunner of the still more famous Model T. The Model N was a four-cylinder car which sold at the astonishingly low price of $500. It was difficult for people to believe that even a *small* four-cylinder could be manufactured for so little money. The little car, with 134.2-cubic-inch piston displacement, a 78-inch wheelbase, and a weight of only 700 pounds, was a lively performer, and had a number of features that were continued on the Model T. The same year Ford brought out a $2500 Six, also marketed in 1907 and 1908.

In 1907, the Model N engine was enlarged from 3⅝ x 3¼ inches to 3¾ x 3⅜ inches, thus increasing the piston displacement to 149 cubic inches. Price was $600 — raised to $700 in 1908.

The Model T made its debut in 1909 with a 3¾ x 4-inch 176.7-cubic-inch engine, developing 20 hp. Engine size remained unchanged until the end, in 1927. The Model T and all previous Fords used a two-speed planetary transmission. Model T prices ranged from $950 in 1910 to $260 for the roadster in 1925.

The Model A was a brand-new design introduced in 1928, price $495. It was the first Ford to have a single-plate clutch and a three-speed transmission. Furthermore, it was the first American car to use a safety-glass windshield as standard equipment.

The Model A engine was larger than the Model T. Cylinders were 3⅞ x 4¼, piston displacement was 200.4 cubic inches, and 40 hp was produced at 2200 rpm. The line was discontinued in 1933. By this time the price had risen to $540.

In 1932, a V8 was introduced at $590, a light but powerful car developing 65 hp at 3400. Its engine size of 3¹¹⁄₁₆ x 3¾ was maintained without change through 1942. A smaller V8, the 60, with 135.9 cubic inches displacement, was built from 1937 to 1940.

After using one transverse leaf spring at front and rear for forty years, Ford switched to conventional springing in 1949, using coil springs in front and leaf springs in rear. The same year an optional overdrive was offered. In 1951, an automatic transmission consisting of a torque converter and a two-speed and reverse planetary transmission was adopted. In 1952, a brand-new 215-cubic-inch overhead-valve Six of 101 hp was introduced.

A 226-cubic-inch L-head Six of 90 hp was introduced in 1941. It was superseded in 1952 by a 215-cubic-inch Six of 101 hp.

The six-cylinder Ford Model K introduced in 1906

The first Model T came out October 1, 1908. Driver sat at left

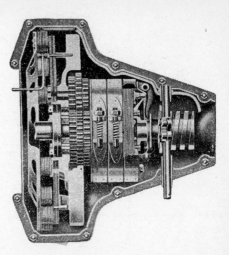

The 1906 Model N roadster sold for $500. It possessed a number of features which were used in the Model T

Flywheel and two-speed transmission assembly used on the 1909 Model T. In front of the flywheel is a magneto which supplied ignition current generated in a set of stationary coils

The Model A went into production in 1928

1946 Ford

1932 The first Ford V8, which supplanted the Model A

1953 hardtop

1953 Customline Fordor sedan. Wide new grille has horizontal bar

Original Hudson touring car, 1910. Price, $1,150. Top extra

# HUDSON

Ample driver vision featured this 1914 sedan which had a center door and an aisle between the front seats, a not unusual feature at this date

The Hudson Company was named after its principal founder, J. L. Hudson, whose department store in Detroit is said to be the largest in the world. Production began in 1910 with a neat-looking 20-hp 198.8-cubic-inch four-cylinder car which sold for $1150. Wheelbase was 100 inches, weight 2000 pounds, and tires were 32 inches in diameter.

The same engine was used in 1911 on the roadster, whereas the $1250 touring car had a larger engine of 226.2 cubic inches displacement, developing 33 hp.

The first Hudson had a cone clutch, but a multiple-disc clutch with cork inserts running in a half-and-half mixture of engine oil and kerosene was introduced in 1911. A single-disc cork-insert clutch was adopted in 1928 and has been used ever since.

A Four and a Six were brought out in 1913, both with 4⅛ x 5¼-inch cylinders. The former developed 37 hp at 1500 rpm, and the latter 54 hp at the same speed. Prices were respectively $1875 and $2450. The four-cylinder car was discontinued at the end of the year, but the Six was made during the following two years. It had a four-speed transmission with direct in third. All other Hudsons have used three-speed transmissions.

In 1914 Hudson produced a $1750, 3½ x 5-inch Six, and these cylinder dimensions were used on various engines without a break until the end of 1929. An L-head valve arrangement was employed until 1927, when a rocker-operated overhead-intake valve was placed over the direct-acting exhaust valve. In 1916 this model was called a Super-Six because it was equipped with a carefully balanced counterweighted crankshaft — the first American car with this feature. A four-cylinder Essex with the rocker-valve system just mentioned entered the field in 1919. It had 3⅜ x 5-inch cylinders, a piston displacement of 178.9 cubic inches, and a horsepower rating of 55. Price was $1600. This engine was used through 1923, when a distinctly smaller Essex was produced with six 2⅝ x 4-inch L-head cylinders with a piston displacement of only 129.9 cubic inches. Price was $850, weight 2130 pounds, and wheelbase 110½ inches. The engine was gradually enlarged until in 1933 its dimensions reached 2¹⁵⁄₁₆ x 4¾ inches. In this year the name was changed to Essex Terraplane.

The 1922 Essex coach was an innovation because it was priced at a very low figure — $1345, or only $250 more than the touring car.

In 1930 Hudson brought out a straight Eight with a 2¾-inch bore and 4½-inch stroke. The bore was increased to 2⅞ inches in 1931, and to 3 inches in 1932. The size has remained the same since.

The 1934 Terraplane was equipped with a 3 x 5-inch six-cylinder engine which was carried through 1942. A somewhat smaller Six, with 3 x 4⅛-inch cylinders, came on the market in 1938, and was continued through 1942.

A new 262-cubic-inch L-head Six was introduced in 1948, developing 121 hp, the first Hudson engine to have pressure lubrication. The car was unusually low, only 5 feet high because of a depressed floor. Hydramatic drive was adopted in 1951. The Hornet, brought out in 1951, was a larger Six (308 cubic inches) of 145 hp. The Hudson Jet, a low-priced Six with 105-inch wheelbase, was introduced in 1953. This 202-cubic-inch engine developed 104 hp. Production of eight-cylinder engines ceased in 1952.

Famous Hudson Super-Six, 1916, had an exceptionally well-balanced crankshaft

First Essex coach, 1922, started the trend toward popularly priced closed cars. It listed at $1,345, just $250 more than the touring car

1933 Hudson Super-Six sedan

1938 Hudson victoria coupe

Smart lines distinguish this 1933 Terraplane eight-cylinder convertible coupe

1953 Hornet four-door sedan with dual carburetion available

1947-1948 Kaiser four-door sedan

# KAISER-FRAZER

Kaiser-Frazer went into production in August 1946. Both Kaiser and Frazer were equipped with a six-cylinder 226-cubic-inch L-head engine rated at 100 hp. A conventional three-speed transmission was used. Overdrive was adopted in 1947, and the hydramatic drive in 1950. Production of the Frazer was discontinued at the end of 1951. The 1946 Kaiser-Frazer closed cars were the first to have a continuous fender line running from front to rear.

1953 Kaiser Manhattan four-door sedan

# HENRY J

The Henry J was a low-priced car introduced in 1951 by Kaiser-Frazer. It was a 2400-pound car with a 100-inch wheelbase, and was offered with either a four- or six-cylinder Willys L-head engine of 68 and 80 hp. A three-speed transmission with optional overdrive was used.

1953 Henry J two-door Corsair

# LINCOLN

The original Lincoln was a 1921 model with a V8 engine

Henry M. Leland resigned the presidency of Cadillac to found the Lincoln company in 1917. He was also the founder of the Cadillac company. Lincoln's first model was brought out in 1921. It was a finely built V8 which sold for $4600 as a five-passenger touring car. Cylinders were 3⅜ x 5 inches, piston displacement was 357.8 cubic inches, and horsepower was 90 to 95 at 2800 rpm.

Henry Ford bought the company at a receiver's sale in December 1922 for $8,000,000.

In 1928 the bore was increased ⅛ inch, and this engine was continued through 1932. It was rated at 90 hp at 2800 in 1928, but the same engine dimensions developed 125 hp at 2900 in 1932.

A twelve-cylinder model was introduced in 1932 with 3¼ x 4½-inch cylinders. Bore was reduced ⅛ inch in 1934. This engine size was used until the car was discontinued at the end of 1940. Prices of twelve-cylinder Lincolns ranged from $4500 for 1932 models down to $3200 in 1933 and up to $5000 or above for the later cars.

The Lincoln-Zephyr was brought out in 1936. It was distinguished by a frameless body design and was equipped with a twelve-cylinder engine. Its original price was $1320, which gradually increased to $1795 in 1942. Lincoln-Zephyr engines from 1936 to 1939 had a bore and stroke of 2¾ x 3¾, and developed 110 hp at 3800 or 3900 rpm. In 1940 the bore was increased by ⅛ inch, and by another 1/16 inch in 1942.

In 1949, the V12 was supplanted by a 337-cubic-inch L-head V8 of 152 hp. This completely redesigned car had a separate frame and conventional springs, and the torque tube was discarded. Hydramatic drive was adopted in 1949. A 160-hp 317.5-cubic-inch overhead-valve V8 engine was introduced in 1952. Its horsepower was increased to 205 in 1953 by the use of a four-barrel carburetor, larger intake valves, and higher compression. Power brakes and power steering were introduced in 1953 as options.

1931 Lincoln convertible phaeton with body by Derham

The first Lincoln Twelve, brought out in 1932

1929 Lincoln seven-passenger limousine

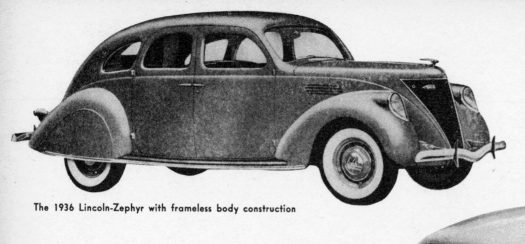

The 1936 Lincoln-Zephyr with frameless body construction

1941 Lincoln-Zephyr

The Lincoln engine for 1953

1941 Lincoln Continental cabriolet

1953 Capri hardtop with one-piece wraparound rear window

The first Mercury, 1939

# MERCURY

The Mercury made its debut in 1939. Its design was similar to that of the Ford, but it was equipped with a 239.4-cubic-inch engine of 95 hp, whereas the Ford had a 217-cubic-inch engine of 87 hp. In 1949, the engine was enlarged to 255.4 cubic inches, producing 110 hp which was increased to 125 hp in 1952. Conventional springs were adopted, coil in front and half-elliptic in rear. An overdrive was offered as an option. In 1950, an automatic torque-converter transmission was introduced.

The 1946 Mercury convertible with varnished wood body

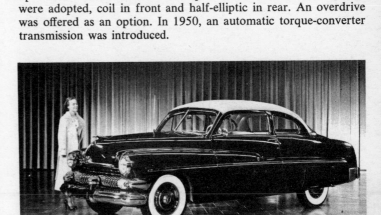

The 1951 Mercury Monterey with white vinyl-leather top

1953 sport coupe. One-piece rear window replaces three-piece assembly

# NASH

First Rambler was a buggy with single-tube tires, 1900

1909 limousine. Acetylene generator shown in front of gearshift

First Jeffery, a 1914 four-cylinder model

Nash name was adopted in 1918. The Six is shown

Nash began life in 1900 as a Rambler made by the Thomas B. Jeffery Company. In 1914 the name was changed to Jeffery, and changed again when Charles W. Nash left the presidency of Buick to buy the company in 1917.

Not much is known about the 1900 Rambler except that it was a horseless buggy with a single-cylinder engine and a two-speed planetary transmission. The 1903 car, however, had a 5½-hp engine, a 78-inch wheelbase, and 28 x 3 tires. The 1904 buggy sold for $750, weighed 1250 pounds, and was powered by a one-cylinder 5 x 6 engine which developed 7 hp. The 1905 car was similar, but the engine was rated at 8 hp. This was the last one-cylinder Rambler.

A two-cylinder car was introduced in 1904. It had 5 x 6-inch opposed cylinders, a piston displacement of 235.6 cubic inches, developed 18 hp, weighed 2000 pounds, and had 30 x 3½ tires and a 90-inch wheelbase. Price was $1350.

The engine was located under the floor. In unit with it was a two-speed planetary transmission with a cone clutch for direct. A central chain took the power to the rear axle. This car was continued without much change through 1909, although wheelbase was lengthened to 106 inches and tire size increased to 34 x 4. A smaller 4 x 5-inch two-cylinder car selling for $800 was marketed in the year 1906.

Two four-cylinder cars were introduced in 1906. Model 14 listed at $1750, weighed 2250, and had 4 x 4½-inch cylinders which gave 226.2 cubic inches piston displacement. Engine developed 20 to 25 hp, and car had 32 x 3½-inch tires, and wheelbase of 106 inches. Models 15 and 16 sold for $2500, weighed 2700 pounds, and were equipped with a 5 x 5½-inch engine of 431.9 cubic inches piston displacement which developed 35 to 40 hp. Tires were 34 x 4, and wheelbase 112. The larger car was continued through 1912.

A somewhat smaller four-cylinder car was built during the 1907-to-1913 period. Its bore and stroke were 4½ x 4½, piston displacement was 286.3 cubic inches, and price was $2000 to begin with.

One- and two-cylinder Ramblers used a two-speed planetary transmission with a cone clutch for direct. Four-cylinder Ramblers were variously equipped with three types of clutches: cone, multiple-disc, and expanding. Transmissions on four-cylinder cars were the three-speed sliding-gear type, except for the 1906 Model 14, which had only two speeds. Four-speed transmissions were used on the 1914 and 1915 Jefferys, and three-speed transmission on the 1916 and 1917 models. Cone and disc clutches were employed. All Nash cars have had a single-plate clutch.

From 1914 to 1917, Jeffery built a $1550 four-cylinder model with 3¾ x 5¼ cylinders and a 231.9-cubic-inch piston displacement which produced 42 hp. Tires were 34 x 4, and wheelbase 116.

A six-cylinder Jeffery was introduced in 1914, price $2250. Its 3¾

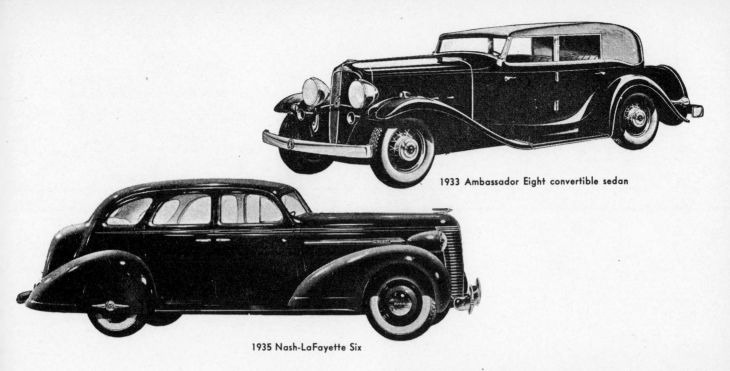

1933 Ambassador Eight convertible sedan

1935 Nash-LaFayette Six

x 5¼-inch cylinders produced 56 hp. Tires were 37 x 4½, and wheelbase was 128 inches. A 212-cubic-inch Six selling for $1650 was made in 1915 and 1916, and a 267-cubic-inch Six developing 53

The Nash-built Ajax made its appearance in 1925. It had a six-cylinder L-head engine with 3 x 4-inch cylinders which developed 40 hp at 2400 rpm. It was succeeded by the Nash Light Six in 1927. In 1928 Nash's L-head car was called the Standard Six. L-head LaFayettes were made from 1934 to 1940. In 1940 they were discontinued for the L-head Nash 600, built during 1941 and early 1942. The latter was distinguished by an integral frame and body construction, a new type of independent front-wheel suspension, and coil springs both front and rear. Nash introduced twin ignition on its overhead-valve engines in 1933, and adopted overdrive in 1935.

In 1950, the hydramatic drive was adopted, and the name of the 600 model was changed to the Statesman. The Nash Rambler was introduced, a small car with a 173-cubic-inch L-head engine developing 82 hp. Wheelbase was 100 inches. The initial body type was a two-door with a rollback top. The Nash-Healey came out in 1951, the first modern American sports car. It was a one-seat roadster weighing 2600 pounds, with a wheelbase of 102 inches. It had a hopped-up engine with two carburetors and a special camshaft. Nash adopted power steering in 1953.

1953 Rambler Custom convertible. Air scoop above grille helps ventilate engine compartment

1953 Statesman Custom Country Club hardtop, powered by 100-hp engine

Electric runabout, 1901

First Oldsmobile curved-dash runabout, 1901. Price $600. Catalogue states, "Any of our extra seats, top, or delivery box can be instantly attached"

1906 two-cycle, two-cylinder car

Light tonneau, 1904

Huge six-cylinder car with 42-inch tires, 1910

Four-cylinder car with overhead valves, 1916

# OLDSMOBILE

The Oldsmobile gets its name from Ransom E. Olds, who also founded the Reo company.

Oldsmobile made its first car in 1897, a one-cylinder buggy with tiller steering and a two-speed planetary transmission. The car continued to be built through 1907. In later years it was distinguished by the famous curved dash. Price was $650 in 1900. Cylinder dimensions were 5½ x 6 inches in 1904. Two two-cylinder models with engine under body and planetary transmission were offered to the public in 1905.

The first four-cylinder car was a 1906 model with 4½ x 4¾-inch cylinders, developing 26-28 hp — built until the end of 1909.

All Oldsmobiles of four or more cylinders used cone clutches through 1920, cone and disc clutches respectively in the two 1921 cars, and disc clutches thereafter. All of these cars were equipped with three-speed transmissions, with two exceptions: (1) 1910 to 1912, cars had four-speed gearboxes; (2) the hydramatic drive brought out in 1940 had four speeds, as did also the semiautomatic transmission that preceded it.

A $2750 four-cylinder with bore and stroke of 4¾ x 4¾ inches was a 1908 model. The first Six was a large car listing at $4200, brought out in 1908. In contrast, a small four-cylinder with a 165.6-

Six-cylinder, five-passenger sport touring, $885, 1924

1939 Series 70 and 80

Front view of 1938 Oldsmobile

Oldsmobile 96 and 98 for 1941

1953 Super 88 four-door sedan

Super 88 Holiday coupe for 1953. 165-hp motor has four-barrel carburetor

cubic-inch engine and a wheelbase of 91 inches was made in 1909 for $1200, while three other Olds models in this year were priced at $2000, $2750, and $4200.

A large Four and an even larger Six for $3000 and $4600 respectively were made in 1910, but maximum car size was reached in the 1912 Limited, which had 42-inch tires and a 706.9-cubic-inch engine. Price was $5000.

A V8 was introduced in 1916 with a piston displacement of 246.7 cubic inches, at a price of $1195. This was made until the end of 1920. A 177-cubic-inch Six was produced from 1917 to 1920. Modern Oldsmobile Sixes and Eights may be said to stem from a Six which first saw the light of day in 1928.

Oldsmobile was the first to adopt the hydramatic drive, which was introduced as an option in 1940.

A redesigned hydramatic drive was introduced in 1946. In 1949, an overhead-valve 304-cubic-inch 135-hp V8 engine was adopted. Its power was increased to 160 in 1952 by the use of four-barrel carburetors, and was further increased to 165 in 1953 by minor changes in design. The Autronic Eye automatic headlamp-beam control was introduced in 1952. A 12-volt electric system was adopted in 1953 and air conditioning and power brakes were offered.

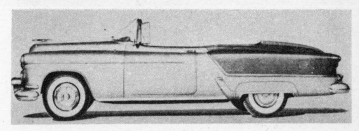

1953 Fiesta coupe. The 170-hp motor has 8.3-to-1 compression ratio

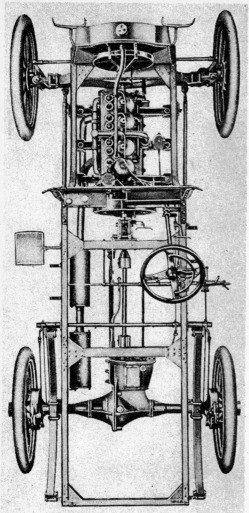

1905 chassis. L-head cylinders were cast in pairs. Expanding type clutch was used. Transmission and rear-axle housing were cast as a unit out of aluminum for a number of years. Two mufflers in tandem were used. This was one of the quietest cars of its day

Packard one-cylinder automobile built in 1900

Characteristic Packard hood lines were adopted in 1904

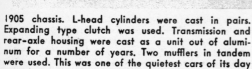

A twelve-cylinder car was brought out in 1916. The 1917 model is shown

1924 four-door, five-passenger sedan

# PACKARD

In 1899 an automobile company was started in Warren, Ohio, by two brothers, J. W. and W. D. Packard. At first their car was called the Ohio, but the name was soon changed to Packard, and the factory was moved to Detroit at about the same time. A single-cylinder model was produced from 1899 to 1904.

A car with a four-cylinder engine which delivered 25 hp at 1000 rpm came out in 1903. Its price in 1904 was $2000. In 1905 there was a larger smooth and quiet four-cylinder which had a piston displacement of 265.7 cubic inches, furnishing 28 hp at 900 rpm. Price was $3500, and wheelbase was 108 inches. The three-speed transmission on these early Fours was attached to the rear axle, and through 1909 the clutch was an expanding type. A dry multiple-disc clutch was used from 1910 through 1926, when a disc clutch with one or two plates was adopted. In 1912, the transmission on the rear

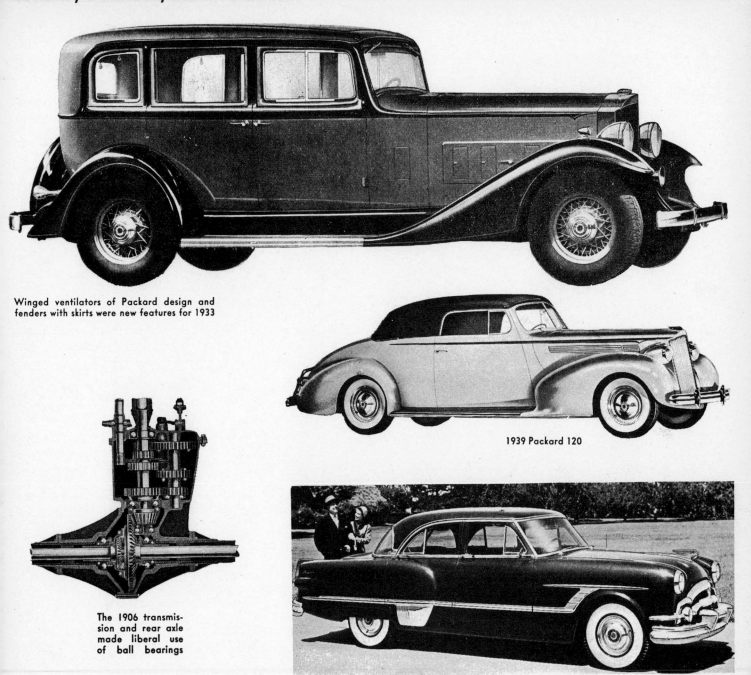

Winged ventilators of Packard design and fenders with skirts were new features for 1933

1939 Packard 120

The 1906 transmission and rear axle made liberal use of ball bearings

1953 Packard Patrician 400 four-door sedan, powered by 180-hp engine

axle was abandoned for the unit power plant construction.

The 1906 four-cylinder was increased in size and price. Its engine was 4½ x 5¼ inches, price was $4000, wheelbase 119 inches. The 1907 model was still larger. Its engine had 5 x 5½-inch cylinders, weighed 2900 pounds, and sold for $4350. Horsepower was 30 at only 650 rpm. This model was made until the end of 1912.

Meanwhile a smaller four-cylinder car, built along the same lines, was brought out in 1909 and was continued through 1912. It had a piston displacement of 265.7 cubic inches, developed 18 hp at 650 rpm, had a wheelbase of 112 inches, and was priced at $3200.

Packard built its first Six in 1912 — a large, luxurious $5000 automobile with 4½ x 5½-inch cylinders and a piston displacement of 524.8 cubic inches. Wheelbase was 133 inches. This model was continued through 1915.

In 1913, a slightly smaller Six was introduced. It had 4 x 5½-inch cylinders, weighed 3500 pounds, and sold for $4150. It was also made during 1914 and 1915.

Packard made a Twin-Six exclusively from 1916 to 1920, and also produced it up to 1923 as a running mate to a new Six. Throughout the years this Twelve had a piston displacement of 424.1 cubic inches, and 3 x 5-inch cylinders. At the start it was moderately priced at $2750, but the figure rose as high as $6000 in 1921, and then receded to $3850 in 1923.

The Single Six was introduced in 1921 — a 52-hp car with a 116-inch wheelbase, listing at $2795. Cylinder size was enlarged from 3⅜ x 4½ to 3⅜ x 5 inches in 1923, and was increased again in 1926 to 3½ x 5 inches, where it remained through 1928.

A straight Eight, selling for $3650, came out in 1924, with 3⅜ x 5-inch cylinders. Bore was enlarged ⅛ inch in 1927, and these cylinder dimensions were maintained through 1936. A smaller Eight, in the $2500 class, was made from 1929 to 1932.

A Twin-Six engine of new design came out in 1932. Its original selling price was $3745, whereas it cost $4155 the last year it was made, 1939. It had a huge engine which rose from 160 hp in 1932 to 175 hp in 1939. A popular-priced straight Eight at $1060 was brought out in 1935, and a $995 Six of similar design in 1937. A luxury car, a large Eight, instead of a Twelve, was sold from 1940 to 1942.

An automatic transmission, consisting of a torque converter and a two-speed and reverse, was introduced in 1949, called Ultramatic. The power of the large Eight was increased from 155 in 1952 to 180 in 1953, mostly by using a four-barrel carburetor. Power brakes were introduced in 1952, and power steering in 1953.

Maxwell Model H touring car, 1905.

The Maxwell Model L was built with only
one seat. The 1905 car is shown, price $700

The Model H Maxwell limousine, 1906, listed at $2,000

# PLYMOUTH

The lineage of the Plymouth runs back through the Maxwell line. Chrysler acquired the Maxwell plant in 1923.

Maxwell brought out its first two models in 1904, selling them for $700 and $1550. Both had two-cylinder opposed engines under a hood and employed the unit power plant construction.

The smaller, built only as a roadster, had 4 x 4-inch cylinders which developed 8 hp at 1000 rpm. Its transmission was a two-speed planetary type. The larger car used a 5 x 5-inch engine which produced 14 hp at 1000 rpm. A multiple-disc clutch was used, and the transmission was a three-speed sliding-gear design. The clutch was disengaged whenever the hand brake was applied. This was a common feature in that day. The car was started from rest by slowly releasing the long brake lever to give smooth clutch engagement. The clutch pedal was used only for gear-shifting. Two-cylinder models were last made in 1912.

A variety of four- and six-cylinder cars with prices from $785 to $3000 were manufactured before 1914, when the company introduced a freshly designed four-cylinder car priced at $750. It had a 185.8-cubic-inch engine which developed 25 hp; weight was 1650 pounds, and wheelbase 103 inches. A cone clutch and a three-speed sliding-gear transmission were important features. This Maxwell was one of the very first really low-priced cars to have a transmission of this type.

Its engine size of 3⅝ x 4½ inches remained unaltered down to and including the year 1926. It was this year that the name was changed to Chrysler 58. Next year, its successor, with the same bore but a 4⅛-inch stroke, was called the Chrysler 50. In 1929 it became the Plymouth. During this transition period the car was re-styled and improved in many mechanical details.

A Plymouth Four with a larger engine, 3⅝ x 4¾, came out in 1930 and was used until 1933, when the Four was abandoned for a 189.9-cubic-inch Six. This engine was increased to 201.3 cubic inches in 1934 and to 217.8 cubic inches in 1942. Floating power was first used on a Plymouth, the four-cylinder 1931 model.

Overdrive was introduced in 1952. In 1953, a torque converter was adopted, working in conjunction with a clutch and three-speed transmission. With the torque converter, practically all driving is done in high gear.

Four-cylinder, 30-hp Model G Maxwell roadster with detachable tonneau, price $1,575

This 1914 Maxwell, Model 25-4, was the ancestor of the Plymouth. It had a 25-hp four-cylinder engine, three-speed transmission, 103 inch wheelbase and sold for $750

The first Plymouth 1929

Four-cylinder Chrysler. Name was changed from Maxwell in 1926 and car was restyled as shown. The name Plymouth was adopted in 1929

The first smooth four-cylinder automobile, the 1931 Plymouth with floating power

1946 two-door sedan

1953 Belvedere hardtop carries extra-cost wire wheels. Pull-type door handles are used

The Pontiac's ancestor—the first Oakland, built in 1908

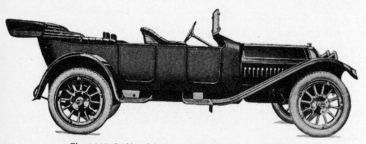

The 1913 Oakland Six was a big handsome car with a long hood. Runningboard steps were individual

1933 Pontiac eight-cylinder coupe listed at $695

First Pontiac Six was brought out in 1926

The Pontiac 1931 convertible cabriolet

# PONTIAC

The Oakland, which was the ancestor of the Pontiac, was first made in 1908 as a two-cylinder car selling for $1375. (Pontiac is the name of the town where this line of cars has always been built, whereas Oakland is the name of the county.)

The first car had a wheelbase of 96 inches, 30 x 3½-inch tires, and a 159-cubic-inch engine with 4½ x 5-inch cylinders which produced 20 hp. The transmission was a two-speed planetary type. This car was made the following year with some improvements, including a 100-inch wheelbase and 32 x 3½ tires.

Oakland brought out its first four-cylinder machine in 1909, and continued its manufacture until the end of 1916. Sixes started in 1913. The 1909 four-cylinder had a bore and stroke of 4½ x 5 inches, a piston displacement of 318 cubic inches, a rating of 40 hp, 34 x 4-inch tires, and a wheelbase of 112 inches. This model was continued through 1910 and 1911.

Two four-cylinder cars were introduced in 1912. The smaller one used a 4⅛ x 4¾-inch engine of 253.9 cubic inches displacement, rated at 40 hp. Tires were 34 x 4, and wheelbase 112. Price was $1450 the first year and $1600 the second.

The larger 1912 model was listed at $2100. Its cylinder dimensions were 4½ x 5¼, giving a piston displacement of 334 cubic

1936 Pontiac De Luxe
Eight two-door sedan

1941 Pontiac Custom
Torpedo four-door sedan

inches, which produced 45 hp. Wheelbase was 120 inches, and 36 x 4½-inch tires were used.

A new 1913 model was a $1000 four-cylinder car which developed 30 hp. Cylinders were 3½ x 5-inches, tires 32 x 3½, and wheelbase 112. Two Sixes were brought out in 1914. They were listed at $1785 and $2500, and had piston displacements of 288.6 and 446.9 cubic inches respectively. There was also a new four-cylinder at $1785, with a piston displacement of 297.8 cubic inches.

In 1916 a six-cylinder car selling for $795 was brought out. It had an overhead-valve engine of 177 cubic inches piston displacement. This model was made through 1923, at which time its price was $995. It was the only model Oakland produced from 1918 to 1923. An L-head engine of the same dimensions, $2^{13}/_{16}$ x 4¾, was used in Oakland's 1924 car.

A V8 was produced during 1916 and 1917. It sold for $1585 and had a piston displacement of 346.3 cubic inches. Oakland six-cylinder cars from $1045 to $1245 were made from 1928 to 1932.

A lively V8 weighing 3140 pounds and developing 85 hp at 3400 rpm was made from 1930 to 1932. Price in 1930 was $1145.

A new Pontiac Six entered the field in 1926 with the moderate price of $825. Its original piston displacement was 186 cubic inches. The name Oakland was dropped in favor of Pontiac in 1932.

A wholly new L-head straight Eight was brought out in 1933, with a price of $695 at the start. Its 223.4-cubic-inch engine developed 75 hp at 3600 rpm. Essentially the same engine was used in 1942, although piston displacement had increased to 248.9 cubic inches and horsepower had risen to 103 at 3500 rpm.

A six-cylinder engine of similar design was introduced in 1935. Originally it had a piston displacement of 208 cubic inches and developed 80 hp at 3600. Today this engine, with 31 inches more piston displacement, delivers 90 hp at 3200 rpm.

Multiple-disc clutches were used on Oakland cars from 1909 to 1911, cone clutches from 1911 to 1923, and single-plate disc clutches have been in use since that date. All Oakland and Pontiac cars with four or more cylinders were equipped with three-speed transmissions.

It was Oakland that first adopted sprayed lacquer finish, in 1924, and Pontiac that revived the steering-column gearshift, in 1938.

The hydramatic drive was adopted in 1948, and power steering in 1953.

A front view of the 1939 Pontiac

1953 Catalina hardtop, with longer 122-inch wheelbase, one-piece windshield

Rear-entrance Studebaker touring car with two-cylinder engine under floor, 1904

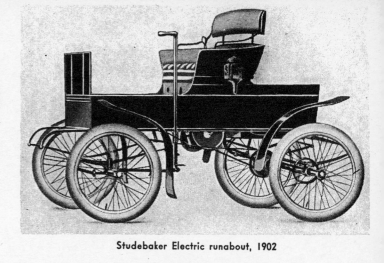

Studebaker Electric runabout, 1902

# STUDEBAKER

1906 four-cylinder, Model E Studebaker touring car

In 1904 the Studebaker Corporation, which for half a century had been famous builders of fine carriages and wagons, brought out its first gasoline automobile. This was a two-cylinder car with 5 x 5½-inch horizontal engine placed under the body, priced at $1100. Studebaker also made electrics during the early years.

A four-cylinder model for $3000 came out in 1905. From 1906 to 1908, production was concentrated on expensive four-cylinder machines running from $2600 to $4250.

Then, in 1909, Studebaker acquired the EMF, a four-cylinder machine most reasonably priced at $1250. Its 4 x 4½-inch cylinders produced 30 hp. A cone clutch was used, and the three-speed transmission was attached to the rear axle. The car was a good performer and excellent value for the price, consequently it soon was a popular buy. This EMF Model 30 was marketed through 1913.

In 1910, a small four-cylinder car called the Flanders was produced in the EMF plant. Its price was only $790.

Various EMF and Flanders models followed until 1914, when these names were dropped. Two new Studebakers were offered this year, a Four and a Six, both with 3½ x 5-inch cylinders. In 1916, engine bore was increased ⅛ inch. These dimensions were also used in 1917. The last Four, with bore and stroke of 3½ x 5 inches, was produced in 1919. Only Sixes were made from 1920 to 1927.

The President Eight with 100-hp engine came into the picture in 1928. The Erskine was a small car introduced in 1927, selling for $975. It lasted through 1929. Another small Six, the Rockne, made its bow in 1932. Original price was $585, but this was raised to $635 in 1933.

Another small Six which had been carefully designed to give maximum overall economy was the $700 Champion, which came out in 1939. It weighed only 2330 pounds, and, although its six-cylinder engine had a bore and stroke of only 3 x 3⅞ inches, it developed 78 hp at 4000 rpm.

An automatic transmission with torque converter was adopted in 1950. A V8 overhead-valve 233-cubic-inch engine of 120 hp was brought out in 1951. Power steering and striking new body designs were features of the 1953 models.

Eight-cylinder, seven-passenger Studebaker limousine, 1928

The EMF, brought out in 1909, was ancestor of modern Studebakers

Six-cylinder touring car, 1915

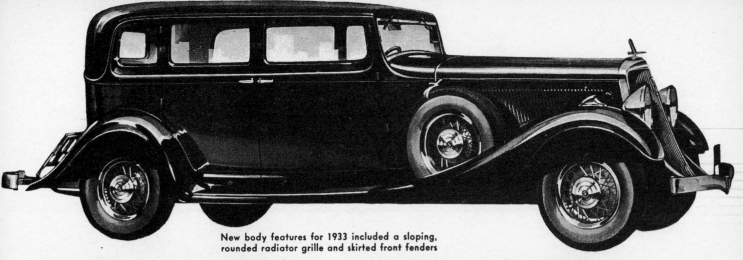

New body features for 1933 included a sloping,
rounded radiator grille and skirted front fenders

Rear view of 1946 Studebaker, first completely new postwar car

Horizontal and vertical grille identifies the Champion line for 1946

1953 Land Cruiser four-door sedan, 4¼ inches higher than
hardtops and coupes, has front-hinged rear doors for safety

1953 Champion Starliner hardtop combines low silhouette with sweeping contours

Overland Model 22 four-cylinder roadster, 1907

# WILLYS

1915 four-cylinder Willys-Knight

First four-cylinder Whippet, 1927

Six-cylinder, poppet-valve de luxe sedan 1931

The Overland, predecessor of the Willys, came out in 1902. It had a one-cylinder engine with a 3½-inch bore and 4-inch stroke, and developed 5 hp. It was priced at $595 and weighed 600 pounds. Twelve cars were produced in 1912, and the model was continued for the next two years.

Both two- and four-cylinder models were built in 1905, and the latter type has been offered ever since, except during 1931 and 1932, when Sixes and Eights were made.

A six-cylinder car was introduced for the year 1909 only. Sixes were not produced again until a Willys-Knight with six cylinders was brought out in 1915. All Overland and Willys cars have used L-head engines except for Willys-Knight models, of which the first was a 1914 four-cylinder type. Knight engines were discontinued in 1932.

Small, economical, low-priced four-cylinder cars have characterized the line during most of the years of its existence. There was a 153.9-cubic-inch car in 1905, while engines of less than 200 cubic inches have been offered almost every year since.

A 153.4-cubic-inch car for $615 came out in 1916. Another small Four of 143.1 cubic inches and an $845 list price appeared in 1920.

The Whippet was a small new four-cylinder design which was put on the market in 1927. Its 134.2-cubic-inch engine developed 30 hp at 2800. Price was $625. A newly designed engine of the same piston displacement was brought out in 1933 as the Willys 77, price $445. This car was the ancestor of the 1942 Willys Americar, which was listed at $788.

The Civilian Jeep was introduced in 1945. It was offered as a two-seat passenger car, light pickup truck, tractor, and mobile power plant. Two- or four-wheel drive was optional. Wheelbase was 104 inches. A four-cylinder 134-cubic-inch L-head engine developing 63 hp was used. In 1948, a six-cylinder 148.5-cubic-inch L-head engine of 70 hp was introduced in a newly designed chassis with both front and rear wheels independently sprung—making the Willys the first American car to have this feature at the rear.

In 1950 an F-head four-cylinder was offered. (In an F-head engine the exhaust valve is seated in the cylinder block the same as in an L-head, but the intake valve is seated in the head as in an overhead-valve engine. The latter valve is of course operated by a rocker arm.) Except for changes in cylinder head and camshaft, the engine was identical with the L-head Four. The new head increased the hp to 70. The Six was likewise optionally equipped with an F-head which raised the hp to 90. In 1952 a two-door closed car was introduced. A four-door and a hardtop were added in 1953.

Willys 77, small four-cylinder car introduced in 1933

Rear view of the 1933 Willys 77

1938 Willys four-door sedan

Universal jeep

De luxe station wagon

Four-wheel-drive station wagon

The first new Willys passenger car in ten years, 1952

1953 New Aero Eagle custom hardtop

A road test of the Selden car during the New York trial (1907)

# THE SELDEN PATENTS

*From the August 1953 issue of* Motor

Automotive historians may recognize a milestone in any one of countless incidents in the lengthening story of the automobile, but none with more justice than the long, bitter, and successful war waged by Henry Ford against the massed opposition of the industry over the Selden patent. Ford's victory in this stubbornly fought campaign freed the industry from the shackles of royalties and licensing arrangements and permitted Ford to build a car for the common people.

At the time, the Ford-Selden battles were the most engrossing topics of the day, not only within the industry, but also among the millions of people who wanted the individual transportation they could not as yet afford.

Ford's opposition sprang not so much from his dislike of the royalty, which he refused to pay, as from his unwillingness to believe that George B. Selden had actually invented the automobile. "He made no discovery and gave none to the world," Ford said later.

Selden, the son of a jurist and a patent attorney in his own right, had a flair for mechanics. It was partly this interest that took him to the Centennial Exposition at Philadelphia in 1876, where he saw the 2-cycle internal-combustion engine invented by George B. Brayton, an Englishman, then a resident of Boston. Impressed, Selden avidly read the accounts of experimental work being done in Europe on liquid-fuel engines and came to realize the limitless possibilities of a road vehicle propelled by liquid hydrocarbon.

On May 8, 1879, he applied to the U.S. Patent Office for a patent on an automobile. His claims were sweeping. He asked to be recognized as the inventor not merely of an internal combustion engine but of the automobile as a whole.

Fabulous though it might later become, a patent on the automobile in 1879 would have been worthless. No one in this country was interested in building a car, and until somebody did, the royalties which are every inventor's goal would not be forthcoming. Selden was too wary to head up this dead end. He kept his application alive, by adding improvements, for sixteen years. Meanwhile, he tried tirelessly and fruitlessly to persuade investors to back a car of his design. Then, in 1893, when the Duryea brothers built and demonstrated their gasoline automobile, Selden decided the time was ripe to obtain his patent. It was granted on Nov. 5, 1895.

Development of the infant industry was swifter than anyone had dreamed. Capital, which had been so coy a few years before, now poured into scores of back-shed shops, and new versions of the horseless carriage broke out like a rash. To Selden's disgust, the newcomers either did not know about his patent or did not care. Steps had to be taken to collect the royalties for which he had worked so long.

He found needed help in William C. Whitney, the Eastern capitalist whose Columbia and Electric Vehicle Company was industriously and profitably promoting street-railway systems. On Nov. 4, 1899, Selden assigned his patent to the company, which later became the Electric Vehicle Company. Arrangements were made to license automobile manufacturers under the patent and collect the royalties, which now seemed destined to surpass a maharajah's dream.

In 1903, the dream was disturbed by the organization of the Ford Motor Company, which from the first pointedly ignored the claims of Selden and the Electric Vehicle Company to part of its profits. The latter company had already sued the Winton Motor Carriage Company for infringement and had won its case. Winton appealed, but apparently did not have its heart in the case, for on March 5, 1903, it joined nine other royalty-paying manufacturers in the formation of the Association of Licensed Automobile Manufacturers. Ford was the chief holdout.

The payments exacted by the Electric Vehicle Company were a considerable 1¼ per cent of the retail price of every car built. The company paid Selden a share and handed two-fifths of all the money collected over to the association. Since the wholesale value of motor vehicles built in 1903 was roughly $13,000,000, they probably brought over $17,000,000 at retail, a sum that realized about $185,000 for the licensing company.

George Selden, holder of basic patent on the automobile. Despite date on side, car was not built until 1906

Henry Ford at the time of the Selden patent suit. The car is a Lenoir, built in 1907 from French patents of the 1860's

Having vanquished Winton with comparative ease, the Electric Vehicle Company and the ALAM set its sights on Ford. First it tried persuasion. The meeting was hardly a success. James Couzens, Ford's best-known associate, told Fred L. Smith, Oldsmobile and ALAM president, that "Selden could take his patent and go to hell with it." Selden did not go. Instead, with the Electric Vehicle Company and the ALAM, he took it to court, suing the Ford company, C. A. Duerr and Company, Ford's New York agent, and others for infringement of the patent.

Ton after ton of evidence was produced. Lawyers delved into the already dusty antiquity of self-propelled vehicles. Threats and counterthreats were made. Rumors kept the industry jittery. Six years passed in legal wrangling.

The case finally came to trial in June, 1909, in the U.S. District Court at New York City. Three months later, Judge Charles M. Hough handed down his decision. Ford, the court ruled, had infringed on the Selden patent. His company would henceforth have to pay the same royalty, now reduced to 0.8 per cent, as other manufacturers, and was liable for back royalties, which by this time amounted to a staggering sum. Ford refused to do either and immediately appealed the case.

If the legal bickering of the past six years had been bitter, it now became violent, a war literally to the death. The ALAM published notices that anyone selling or buying an unlicensed car might be sued for damages. Ford replied by offering to post a bond to protect every purchaser of his cars.

Interest in the case reached far beyond the courtroom and the automobile factory. The people generally took Ford's side. They got the impression that he was fighting their battle against monopoly. "Trust busting" was popular, and the people identified the Electric Vehicle Company, already in disfavor for some of its traction deals with the trusts.

Before the appeal was heard, Selden built an automobile along the lines laid down in his patent claim. It turned out to be a stubborn starter and not altogether a satisfactory per-

former in other ways. Selden blamed its balkiness on the machine shop that had made the crankshaft. The engine had three cylinders in line, and the three crankshaft throws should naturally have been 120 degrees apart. Actually, two of the throws were only 106 degrees apart, with the third 127 degrees from the other two. This, Selden complained with some heat and understated accuracy, made timing difficult.

The second trial, ending on Jan. 9, 1911, brought full vindication for Ford, although on some points the reasoning of the court was not easy to follow. In a word, the Selden patent was held to be valid, but Ford, in the court's opinion, had not infringed upon it.

Although Selden had claimed invention of the whole automobile, the engine he described was a 2-cycle type based on the Brayton engine of 1876. A note in his diary proved that he had seen the Otto 4-cycle engine and had described it contemptuously as "another damned Dutch engine." Ford's engine was of the Otto 4-cycle type.

Effects of the decision were widespread and radical. With no royalties to collect, the ALAM collapsed, to be succeeded by a trade association of all automobile manufacturers except the Ford company, which still is not a member except through its Lincoln-Mercury Division. Ford, like all other makers, was free to build as many automobiles as he could at as low a price as he could, for there was no longer the drain of royalties and the constant threat of lawsuits to hold prices up.

Selden's remaining years were spent largely in dreaming of the fortune he might have amassed had the decision gone for him instead of against him. The fortune would have been respectable. His royalties on motor vehicles built in 1911 and 1912, the last two years before his patent expired, would have amounted to about $6,656,000.

If a basic patent of this type had been licensed to all manufacturers in the single year of 1950, the same royalty rate would have produced approximately $110,000,000!

# WHICH IS WHICH?

...PRIZES...

1st—Jones Speedometer
2d—An Automobile Clock
3d—A Pair of Royal Hampers

## HOW MANY OF THESE 1904 CARS CAN YOU NAME?

Starting in its August 1904 issue, *Motor* ran a monthly prize contest based on identifying the various makes of cars then on the road. It must have been a difficult contest, for relatively few of each make were manufactured, and one could hope to see a representative lot of them only in a large city. *Motor* said: "In order that a novice may be on an equal footing with an expert, we have selected only those cars of which there are pictures *with names* in the advertising columns of *Motor* — thus making the solution simple *for the careful observer.*"

The "careful observer" who goes through the early files of *Motor* will have no trouble positively identifying half of the cars, for numbers 1, 3, 5, 6, 10, and 11 were shown in various issues of *Motor* exactly as they appear here. Number 9 also was shown, but although the gentleman at the wheel was identified as Mr. Harlan Whipple, president of the A. A. A., the car's name was not given. This, however, is not as unfair as it might seem, for this car was one of the best-known of its day. It was a great car then, and it still is.

Cars numbered 2, 4, 8, and 12 are more difficult to identify because they are not shown in *Motor* at the same angle as they appear here, but the editor is willing to hazard a pretty good guess as to what they are. However, Number 7 stumps him completely. The oddly shaped radiator would seem to make identification easy, but the car

is not shown head-on anywhere in the magazine.

Winners of the September contest were: (first prize) H. W. Longfellow, Jr., 44 Fuller Street, Brookline, Mass., (second prize) Miss Marie Boyd, 59 Meeting Street, Charleston, S. C., (third prize) F. W. Stevenson, Hewlett, L. I. Miss Boyd obviously knew her cars better than most women do now. And was H. W. Longfellow, Jr. the son of the poet?

*Motor* printed the names of many of the runners-up, but it did not identify the cars. The editors' identifications and informed guesses appear below, printed upside down, so you won't be tempted to read them without at least trying to identify some of the cars for yourself.

1. The Chainless Wolverine. (It was advertised atop a sculptured marble block bearing the slogan: "A Monument of Automobile Perfection.") 2. The radiator and rear fender make this look like a Columbia. 3. A Standard. (It was made in Jersey City.) 4. I think this is a Searchmont, but it could also be a Berg or a Mors. They all had rear fenders curved like this — and similar hoods too. 5. A Stevens-Duryea. (The Pierce Motorette looks very much like it.) 6. A Waverly Electric. 7. ???? 8. I think this is a Baker Electric. 9. A Mercedes. 10. An Orient. 11. A Buckmobile. 12. The hook-shape front of the frame makes me believe that this is a Winton.

# THOSE WERE THE DAYS!

The Clothes We Wore...The Places We Went...The Troubles
We Had...The Tools We Carried...The Cars We Drove...

# THE CLOTHES WE WORE

Since the first automobiles had no roofs, windshields, or adequate fenders, their passengers were exposed to wind and rain, the heat of the sun, and the cold air of early spring or late autumn. (The cars were usually put in storage for the winter.) As a result of this exposure to the vicissitudes of weather and to the dirt and dust of unpaved roads, protective clothing had to be designed to make life bearable for the motorist—especially the female motorist. And since the early cars were nearly all very expensive to buy and maintain, they were owned mostly by wealthy people who could afford the best of everything. Consequently, clothing for both men and women began as high-style costumes created by some of the best designers of the day. Materials were fine too; leather, fur, rubber, and cravenette of first-quality were widely used. There was nothing plebian about the early motor car; except for the popular-priced curved-dash Oldsmobile and some of the cruder high-wheeled buggy types, automobiles were not available to lower-income people until Henry Ford mass-produced the Model T in 1908.

The charm of turn-of-the-century styles has only recently begun to be appreciated. Even though it is unlikely that women can be persuaded to go back to the ground-sweeping skirts of that time, veils, big hats, scarves, and suede coats have already reappeared on the scene from time to time.

The next few pages show how styles for motoring developed until the 1920's, when the universal acceptance of the closed car made special clothing for automobiling unnecessary.

Cravenette cap and dust hood

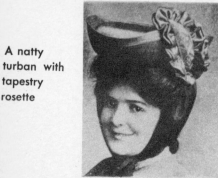

A natty turban with tapestry rosette

Mr. and Mrs. "Charley" Gates in their Mercedes at Saratoga

The Louis coat style in leather

Russian pony skin coat

Following the voluminous mode

Motor hat
with
dust curtain

A group of enthusiasts from the Daytona colony

Same hat with
curtain
arranged as
trimming

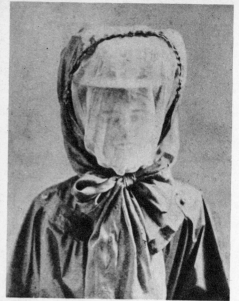

1906

1906

1903

1906

1906

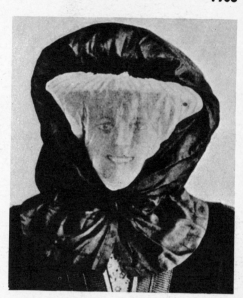

1906

1906

1907

1903

1905

1905

1905

# FASHIONS IN HATS AND VEILS

1905

1906

1906

1905

1906

1905

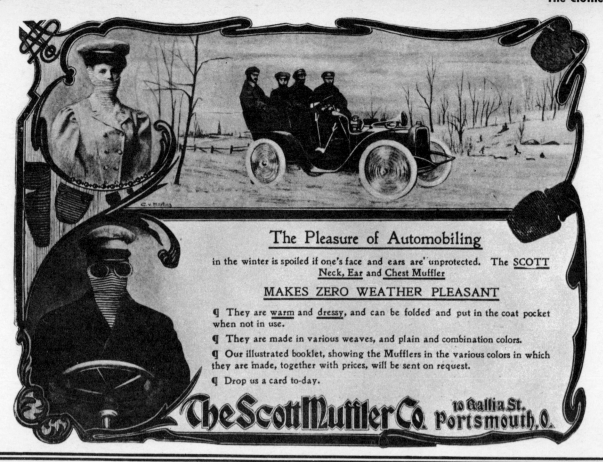

Rain hood (1907)

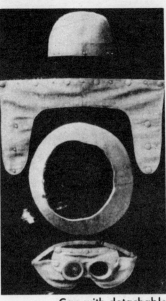

Cap with detachable flap and goggles (1908)

Rain cap (1907)

# FOR PROTECTION AGAINST DUST AND RAIN

Dust and rain were among the early motorist's worst enemies. He could avoid the cold simply by laying his car up for the winter, but dust and rain threatened him the year around. Many of the costumes and headgear designed for this kind of protection were quite ingenious, but a few of them, such as the all-enveloping muffler with goggles shown on the opposite page, seem horrifying to modern eyes.

A new style motor hood of silk rubber (1905)

A lady's rubber raincoat (1905)

A gentleman's rubber raincoat (1905)

Three winter clothing advertisements for 1904 Note the prices quoted for fur and leather garments

Combination boots
and trousers (1907)

A hooded coat
of Russian pony

Fur-lined long gloves

Australian opossum
coat with bear hat

Russian pony coat;
furlined robe

# OH THE COLD, CRUEL WINTER!

In the early part of the century, automobiles, like boats nowadays, were ordinarily laid up for the winter. Only the hardiest and most determined motorists insisted in driving their cars in the snow and slush of winter months. Most of their cars had no roofs, no windshields, no heaters, and often did not even have fenders. Those who did drive during cold weather had to dress warmly. Fortunately, fur garments were then quite cheap. Many of them could be bought for $100—or even less. But the clothing that was created for winter driving was always bulky; sometimes it seems downright fantastic as in the picture directly below.

A foot muff
(still sold in England)

Not a bee keeper,
but a lady motorist (1905)

A man's raincoat
and driving mask (1904)

Leopard, squirrel, and civet
(fur coats—not wild animals) (1907)

A woman's raincoat
and driving mask (1904)

High fashion in an automobile hansom cab (1904)

A lightweight waterproof
coat over a fur garment

The new "umbrella" rain
coat for the motor girl

A fur jacket for warmth,
an outer coat for protection

# FASHIONS FOR 1904

A variety of dust coats (1906)

Altogether
Parisian (1906)

The latest pongee
motor coat (1905)

Waterproofed
chiffon silk (1906)

A stunning design in
English blanket cloth (1906)

A brown suede coat
with jeweled buttons (1905)

An automobile coat
made of squirrel fur (1905)

1907

1907

1908

1907

1908

A child motorist's garb (1906)

Fashionable stripes and checks appear (1906)

An Auto-Silk veil (1906)

# WOMEN'S FASHIONS FOR 1905-1908

Bulkiness and protection against the weather were still characteristic of the motoring clothes of these years, but they were undergoing subtle changes. As designers learned more about the specific functions required of automobile clothing, they began to create styles which were somewhat similar to the street costumes of the time, but which were nevertheless intended especially for motoring. Anyway, the girls seem prettier in them.

Equipped for any weather (1907)

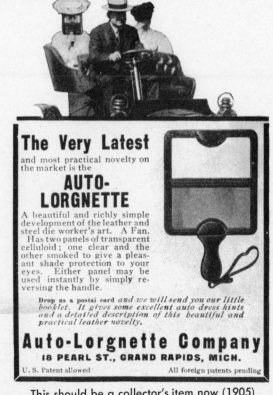

This should be a collector's item now (1905)

A waterproof motoring coat (1905)

A wedding outfit for 1912. Note the car waiting outside with its acetylene headlights and kerosene sidelights gleaming.
From an advertisement for French Auto Oil

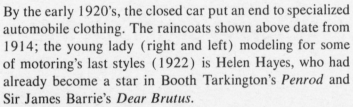

# THE LAST DECADE OF
# SPECIAL MOTOR CLOTHING

By the early 1920's, the closed car put an end to specialized automobile clothing. The raincoats shown above date from 1914; the young lady (right and left) modeling for some of motoring's last styles (1922) is Helen Hayes, who had already become a star in Booth Tarkington's *Penrod* and Sir James Barrie's *Dear Brutus*.

# MOTORING STYLES FOR MEN

(1905)

(1906)

(1906)

# TEDDY BEARS: 1905-1906

*Spring holds the robe in place*

*Heavy plush velour*

*Waterproof*

*Note separate foot pockets*

Sitting in a leather bag
lined with fur (1905)

This robe with magnificent baby bear
fur front $20.00 (1906)

Long before the raccoon coats
of the 1920's (1905)

A serviceable dust
coat in linen (1906)

# HOW TO BE STYLISH
# YET SNUG AND WARM

A Chesterfield coat
with leather lining (1906)

On the road from Boston to New York (1903)

## THE PLACES WE WENT

The early automobiles certainly got around. In no time at all they were running all over the country. The roads weren't so good, but if you went slowly enough you could get through almost anything when the weather was fair and the roads dry.

The car on the opposite page is one of the early rear-entrance tonneaus that gave way to side doors a year or so later. Notice that the car to its right has the big brass headlamps carefully hooded. It was no fun to shine all that brass, so you did your best to protect it from being splashed by mud and dirt. The same car is provided with wicker basket hampers that were then popular for carrying picnicking equipment. As you can see, interior of the car had very little room — just enough for the passengers. There were no front doors because the engine got very hot, and the driver needed ventilation for his feet.

If you look carefully at the picture of the daring young lady at the edge of the Palisades, you will see that she didn't really have such implicit confidence in her brakes. There is a rock firmly wedged under the front left wheel.

Through the Santa Cruz Redwoods (1903)

Along the Russian River, Sonoma County, California (1904)

Down a mountain gorge (1903)

Figuring out the road book (1903)

Where one must have confidence in his car. Miss Helen Green at the edge of the Palisades in her Pope-Hartford, Model G (1906)

Sometimes, of course, you came to a place that was absolutely impassable

Those who have driven only our present-day automobiles with their low road clearances would obviously never dare to try cross-country touring like this. The old cars may have been less dependable mechanically than our current ones, but they had high wheels, plenty of clearance underneath, and their drivers were so used to handling their cars on very bad roads that a hay field or a forest or a grassy slope didn't make much difference.

It was by making exploratory expeditions like these that the automobile gradually opened up more and more country and extended its range. Those were the days when driving a car was fun; there were always new places to go.

Through a country part stubble, hayfield, and grass

We shot down a bank thirty feet high

Steering was a fine art when you had to avoid trees, saplings, and underbrush

Here is an S. and M. Simplex that has just negotiated a difficult bit of terrain

Visiting a balloon race at the Indianapolis Motor Speedway (1909)

A Virginia road in 1904 when 12 mph was considered good speed

A Pope-Tribune in front of the Capitol (1905)

On the historic bridge at Concord, Mass. (1906)

The two cars shown on the Virginia road to the left finally reach Mount Vernon

W. J. Batchelder and party of Denver, Colo., visit the Garden of the Gods in a Peerless (1906)

A party from Los Angeles drive their car through an opening cut through one of the big trees near Yosemite (1904)

Mr. and Mrs. Ernest Rogers, of Brookline, Mass., out for a wintry spin (1904)

They stopped, built a fire, and cooked lunch right on the road . . .

. . . because they had been refused dinner at this inn (1907)

Turning a lonely circle in the snow to demonstrate this 10-hp, two-cylinder Autocar (1905)

Even in 1916, the passengers in a fine car like this Marmon 34 were exposed to the elements

In January, 1904, someone had the temerity to drive this primitive little vehicle across the ice bridge to the foot of Niagara Falls

Climbing to the pavilion of the Glacier des Bossons, Chamonix (1910)

The early motorists soon found out that their cars were more than interesting mechanical innovations. As the automobile became more popular, it helped to popularize all kinds of outdoor sports from hunting and fishing to the simple, naive pastimes of the day, like the English gymkhana shown in the three upper left pictures on the opposite page. The woman taking a snapshot (above) is standing next to a car with wire wheels and an initialed license plate in 1903. She is probably using an early Kodak—the kind that had to be sent back to the factory with the films still in it so it could be opened in a darkroom there in order to have its pictures developed.

A hunting party at Rangely Lakes, Maine (1903)

The start of a tire-rolling contest (1907)

A stop for beer, somewhere in California (1904)

At an English gymkahana (1907)

Removing and attaching a tire against time (1907)

A White Steamer against a scenic background (1906)

Disputing the right of way near Pasadena, Calif. (1904)

Up a steep road at historic Harper's Ferry (1906)

A stop for gas at a 1910 service station

A night scene in New York's Chinatown (1906)

An automobile club visits the White House (1910)

Motoring at night in New York's lower East Side (1906)

A fine photograph of an automobile in a rural scenic setting (1917)

A Kissel-Kar on a ferry in Washington state (1916)

On Pike's Peak with the Lariat Loop in view (1919)

After climbing a really steep hill (1905)

What's the matter with the damned thing? (1905)

Slight hindrance (1904)

# THE TROUBLES WE HAD

Looked at nostalgically, the years just before the First World War seem idyllic, a period of peace, innocence, and low-cost living. But for the pioneer motorist it was a time of tribulation. He was hated by almost everyone who owned a horse, and he was regarded as a rightful victim by farmers, blacksmiths, repair men, teamsters, and sellers of gasoline. Worst of all—his own car often seemed to conspire against him. Breakdowns were appallingly frequent and usually costly. And the bone-racking roads would pound to pieces better cars than could then be built. Water, sand, and mud—especially mud—were the motorist's worst enemies. He didn't get into dreadful traps like these because he was careless; he just couldn't help himself. The roads weren't properly marked, and what seemed to be a perfectly good highway might, in the space of a few hundred feet, turn into a hideous morass of hungry mud that threatened to swallow car and driver.

There was a low spot on the way, a bit of swamp that had never been properly drained, so the water collected and softened up the ground until it seemed as if the mud had no bottom. Horse-drawn high-wheeled buggies or farm wagons sloshed through such places without much trouble, but automobiles were trapped by them.

The motor car had to make its own way, literally forcing local and Federal governments to improve the roads year after year until they slowly began to be fit for motor travel. And by then, of course, the newly built roads were jammed by too many cars.

The next few pages show some of the terrors that were lying in wait for the early motorist. But despite his difficulties, he was extraordinarily optimistic about them. He had to be, or he would never have taken to motoring in those primitive times.

Struggling with sand on the Sierra Blanca (1909)

Fording a river (1904)

This alleged highway . . . (1904)

With the frame awash and night coming on (1910)

The perils of beach motoring in Oregon (1911)

Too little water could cause trouble—as this overheated Maxwell shows (1912)

Right through the water (1907)

A primitive ferry (1907)

Crossing the Potomac River on White's Ferry (1906)

# RAIN APRONS

O cold, wet, unhappy pioneers! (1904)

Sometimes things got in the way (1904)

Sometimes it was just mud (1904)

A Jeffery four-wheel-drive truck plows through (1914)

Even the convicts were ready to help (1903)

Struggling with a clincher rim

Sometimes the tube crept out

Fixing a broken drive chain

The country blacksmith would often help (1905)

Sometimes you just didn't know what was wrong (1919)

With hard springs and bad roads, the passengers didn't often go through the roof like this, but sometimes they did bump their heads on it (1916)

# THE PATHFINDERS

Equipped for real cross-country touring (1910)

The local motor club puts up road signs

A professional pathfinder establishing future automobile roads (1911)

Pathfinding in British Columbia—"Where the underbrush proved an impediment to rapid progress" (1911)

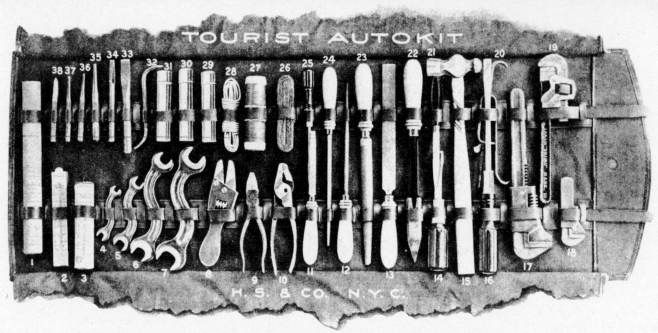

This 18-pound tool kit for motorists was offered for sale by Hammacher, Schlemmer & Co. in 1906

# THE TOOLS WE CARRIED

In the days when every man had to be his own mechanic (and his car usually broke down in some isolated place where there was no one to lend a hand or a tool), every motorist carried an outsize tool kit so he could tackle practically anything except a major repair job.

The hand tools used in automotive work are of very early origin, since they were simply taken over from various metal-working trades. In an article which appeared in the August 1917 issue of *Motor,* the following was said: "The flat wrench is the earliest form; it was used in the seventeenth century. The single-end wrench came first; then the double-end wrench. The S-wrench appeared still later to reach inaccessible nuts and bolts. From it has been evolved the straight type with offset jaws, which makes it possible to tighten a nut or bolt merely by reversing the position of the jaw after each turn.

"Long before the automobile, lifting jacks were used in factories, in railroad work, and in wagon making. Credit for the first jack intended only for automobiles should go to

the Duff Manufacturing Company, Pittsburgh, Pa., which first marketed them in 1901.

Amazingly enough, though, the hand tools of those early days have changed very little in basic design. They consisted then, as they do now, largely of devices for fastening or unfastening screws, nuts, and bolts, together with all sorts of cold chisels, files, punches, pliers, and hammers. But if the design of these tools has not changed much, the steel from which they are made has undergone enormous improvement. On the desk in front of me as I write is an old Maxwell wrench left over from a tool kit I owned years ago. Its edges are raised and scarred and out of true. No amount of wear could damage a modern wrench as badly as that; they remain in good condition even after years of use in repair shops where they undergo a lot of handling every day. The metallurgists who improved the steel is the unsung hero of the automobile industry. Few people know much about his work, but he has made things easier—and less expensive—for everyone who drives a car.

This was handy when you had to go hunting for gasoline (1913)

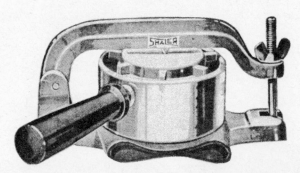

You could fix a flat on the road with this vulcanizer (1913)

## A LIST OF TOOLS AND SUPPLIES CONSIDERED ADEQUATE IN 1916

### TOOLS

2 Pair tire chains
1 Efficient jack
1 Brace wrench for changing rims
1 Efficient tire pump
1 Tire gauge
1 Valve tool
1 Small vulcanizer
1 Sheet fine sandpaper
1 Sheet fine emery cloth
All special wrenches belonging to car
2 Monkey wrenches (large and small)
1 Small set socket wrenches adapted to car
1 Small Stillson wrench
2 Screw drivers (one with all wooden handle)
1 Pair pliers with wire cutters
1 Good jack knife
1 Small vise to clamp to running board
1 12-oz. machinist's hammer

1 Punch or carpenter's nail set
1 Cotter-pin extractor
1 Large flat mill file
1 Thin knife-edged file
1 Small short handled axe
1 Towing cable
1 Oil squirt can (carried under hood)
1 Grease gun
1 Small funnel
1 Chamois skin
1 Small ball of marline
1 Pocket electric flashlight. (If car has no trouble lamp)
1 Pocket ammeter

### SPARE PARTS & EXTRAS

1 or 2 Extra tire casings and inner tubes
1 Strong two-gallon can extra gasoline
1 Strong two-quart sealable can gas-engine oil
1 Can grease
1 Small sealable can kerosene

1 Blowout patch
1 Leather tire sleeve
1 Package assorted cement patches
1 Small package raw rubber for vulcanizing
1 Small can vulcanizing cement
1 Tube self-vulcanizing cement
1 Can mastic
1 Box mica tire powder
6 or more extra tire valves
4 Extra valve caps
4 Extra dust caps
4 Extra headlight bulbs
2 Extra tail light bulbs
4 to 12 feet good insulated wire
1 Roll electrician's tape
½ as many extra spark plugs as motor has cylinders
½ as many extra porcelains as motor has cylinders
1 Ball asbestos wicking
1 Bundle waste

1 Assortment copper, asbestos, and rubber gaskets to fit car
1 Piece radiator steam hose (18 inches long)
2 Extra hose clips
2 Extra valve springs
1 Extra fan belt
1 Small sheet rubber packing (1/16 inch thick)
1 Assortment cotter pins, nuts, lock washers, wood screws, and nails

### EMERGENCY FOOD SUPPLY
(Four People)

2 Two-gallon canvas bags water
4 Pound-packages hard tack
4 Half-pound cans meat or fish
2 Pounds sweet chocolate
2 Cans fruit
Personal luggage

This is how automobile tools looked in 1917

In 1908 you needed this too

### *Here We Are—* *STUCK!*

Did it ever occur to you that the

# DAMASCUS HATCHET

would be a mighty convenient and dependable acquisition to the auto tool chest?

When the wheel drops out of sight in the mud, get out the **Damascus**, cut a pole for a lever, right things up, and then on your way again.

You would find the **Damascus** useful about the garage---or when on hunting or fishing trips in the country.

No other hatchet made that is so thin, tough and light. Weight, one and a half to two pounds.

The adjustable handle fastener is simple and convenient. "Just turn the screw" to remove or tighten the handle---no burning or wedging.

The **Damascus** is the only hatchet that will cut fresh or dry bones or hemlock knots without spoiling the edge (which is made of especially selected steel). Equipped with sheath, which can be attached to belt if desired. We guarantee he **Damascus** to be the most convenient and durable hatchet, made.

### PRICE $2.50 COMPLETE WITH SHEATH

Ask your dealer to-day about the **Damascus** hatchet. If he cannot supply you write us giving his name and the hatchet will be shipped promptly, prepaid. If not just as represented, your money will be refunded.

C. A. C. AXE COMPANY, Dept. R., 35 Congress St., Boston, Mass.

A Cadillac advertisement for 1904

# THE AMERICAN AUTOMOBILE BUSINESS GETS UNDER WAY

As soon as the manufacture of automobiles graduated from backyard to factory, the industry settled down to the serious business of making money. But just why one car was to become a lasting success while another was destined to failure is hard to analyze. Cadillac always built a good car, but so did Winton and Franklin. And the short-lived Herreshoff was designed by a man who had made a world-wide reputation for himself for building fine yachts. In those early days it was anyone's race, so they all strove manfully, competed vigorously, and tried to capture a market that was worth more than all the gold of the Indies. But of them all only the Cadillac survives.

A 1900 one-cylinder Winton photographed in modern times

1902 Franklin four-cylinder runabout with the engine set crosswise

The 1909 Premier Thirty. Price $2500, four cylinders, 30-35 hp

Notice the slogan (1906)

Designed by the famous yacht builder

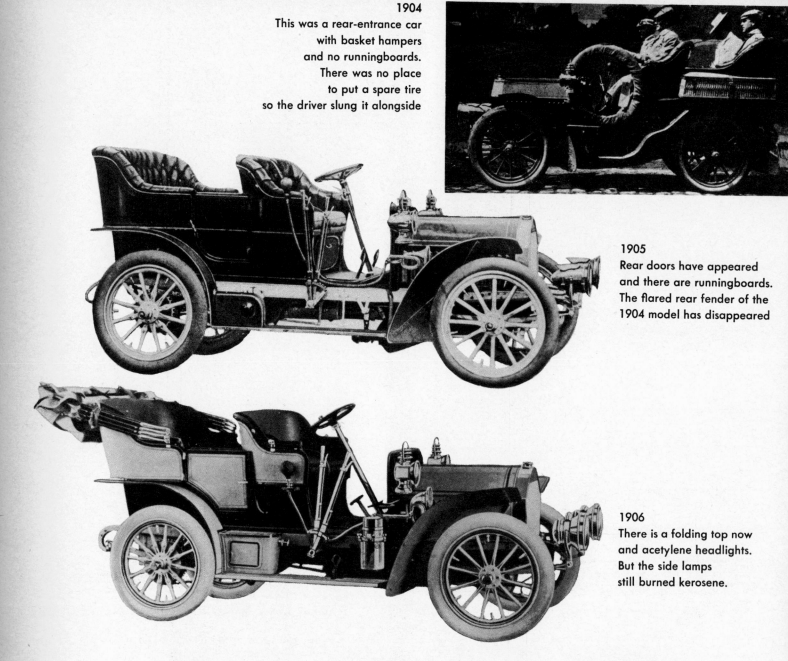

**1904**
This was a rear-entrance car with basket hampers and no runningboards. There was no place to put a spare tire so the driver slung it alongside

**1905**
Rear doors have appeared and there are runningboards. The flared rear fender of the 1904 model has disappeared

**1906**
There is a folding top now and acetylene headlights. But the side lamps still burned kerosene.

# YEARLY DESIGN CHANGE IN THE EARLY LOCOMOBILE

The first gasoline-powered Locomobile for 1902 had a four-cylinder vertical engine which had many advanced features for its day, such as a gear-driven centrifugal water pump, an electric generator, an automatic carburetor, sliding-gear transmission with direct drive on high gear, and a camshaft with integral cams. Its makers said of it: "Although this car was of the foreign type, it was in no respect a copy; it was an adaptation of the foreign type for use on our rough roads, ample clearance being provided.

"In 1905 we made one very important change—we substituted make-and-break for jump-spark ignition. There can be no doubt that the magneto will form the future method of obtaining electricity for the ignition system, and the low-tension magneto used in conjunction with make-and-break ignition we believe to be the best possible arrangement. It eliminates the coil box with its delicate moving parts, the

commutator, the spark plugs, batteries, and all heavily insulated high-tension wiring. This system of ignition is used on the best foreign cars at the present time, and those Continental firms who have adopted it have never gone back to the jump-spark system, whereas, many of those who used the jump-spark have abandoned it for make-and-break.

"A study of the Locomobile chassis shows much careful reduction of weight without any sacrifice of strength, smooth arrangement of rods and piping, elimination of unnecessary parts, and precautions taken to avoid loosening of nuts and bolts. All these were features of the first Locomobile, and have been refined from year to year. It is important to consider that the design is uniform throughout the season, the last car delivered being exactly like the first one delivered."

The 1906 Locomobile sold for $5000. It was competitive with the Lozier and the Marmon and the Darracq.

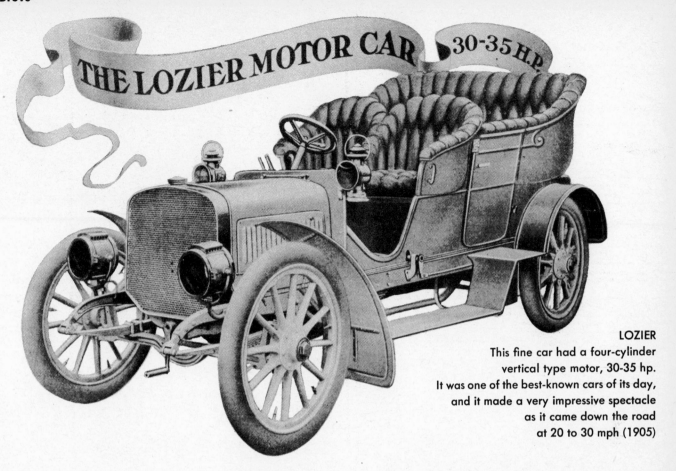

THE LOZIER MOTOR CAR 30-35 H.P.

### LOZIER
This fine car had a four-cylinder
vertical type motor, 30-35 hp.
It was one of the best-known cars of its day,
and it made a very impressive spectacle
as it came down the road
at 20 to 30 mph (1905)

### DARRACQ
This imported French car became famous
in America when it won
the second Vanderbilt Cup Race in 1905.
The car shown here
was described by its importer as:
"1904 Model Phaeton Tulip
with swinging front seat
furnished in 15-20 or 30-35 hp"

### MARMON
This famous car had a four-cylinder
air-cooled engine with the cylinders
mounted at an angle of 90 degrees.
The front fenders were slanted
from the body at a carefully
calculated angle in order
to keep mud from being thrown
in the driver's face (1905)

1911 Packard Model 30 limousine

Here are some representative cars of the decade. Most interesting is the picture of the Packard controls shown below. Notice the speedometer at the left, the bulb horn to the right, and the kerosene side lamps with handles. Right-hand drive still prevailed.

1911 Packard Model 30 runabout

How the controls looked on a 1910 Packard

Regal underslung three-passenger coupe (1911)

Hupmobile Model 32 three-passenger coupe (1913)

Chandler Six three-passenger coupe (1915)

Matheson Silent Six (1912)

King Silent 36 roadster (1911)

Franklin air-cooled two-door sedan (1916)

The famous Owen Magnetic (1917-1918), one of the first cars to adopt electric gearshift which had appeared as early as 1913

# SOME INTERESTING CARS OF THE 1920's

During the depression years, you could buy this beautiful Pierce-Arrow for $2195 (1934)

After W. C. Durant left General Motors he produced this low-priced Star for $348 (1922)

The Hudson-built Essex sedan for 1921 which preceded the famous low-priced coach

# AND 1930's THAT DID NOT SURVIVE

An Owen-Magnetic with a Brooks-Ostruk convertible custom body (1920)

The Jordan of the mid-1920's, advertised as built for "a girl somewhere west of Laramie"

When the front-drive Cord folded, Hupp used the body dies for this rarely seen car (1938)

1905

Buckboard, $375

Runabout, $475

# The Price is Lower

We have found it possible, through improvement in methods, and by added experience, to build our famous Buckboards at a price $50 lower than we were able to make them for last year.

At the same time we are making them better than last year.

There is money for you in these Buckboards—lots of it. They meet a big demand that isn't met by any other car—in other words, the Buckboards give a dealer a monopoly on three classes of buyers:

1. The buyer of small means, who can just afford to buy a Buckboard.

2. The buyer who wants to try motoring, but isn't sure he'd like it. He'll buy the Buckboard because it's so inexpensive and so simple. When he gets the "fever" he'll buy a Touring Car.

3. The buyer who has two or three cars, and wants to add a little car to run around in. The Buckboard is exactly the thing.

Better think of these things.

They mean real money.

Surrey, $450

*Catalogue if you say so*

## Waltham Mfg. Co.

*Members of Association of Licensed Automobile Manufacturers*

**WALTHAM, MASS.**

Sales Office for New York, New Jersey, Pennsylvania, Delaware, Maryland, Virginia, North Carolina, South Carolina, Georgia and Florida,

**44 Broad Street,     New York City**

Tonneau, $525

1906

*The Jewell*

8 H. P. Gasoline.

## A PERFECT CAR for $400.00

¶ The business and professional man's car.
¶ The finest runabout on the market at ANY PRICE.

THE

## Forest City Motor Car Co.

MASSILLON, O., U. S. A.

# "THE BUCKMOBILE"

*The Only Practical Motor Road-Wagon Built*

Witness our Buckboard construction—here are simplicity, durability and ease of riding.

## Light Car!
## Two Cylinder 15 H. P. Motor!

Catalog on Request

## Buckmobile Co.,
UTICA, N. Y., U. S. A.

1904

The Auto-Bug Runabout (1909)

Holsman advertised this as "The swellest high-wheeler made" (1909)

# BUCKBOARDS AND BUGGY-TYPE HIGH-WHEELERS

One of the most neglected aspects of American automobile history is the fact that motor cars with carriage or wagon-type bodies continued to be made in their original, primitive form even though the automobile itself had reached a much higher stage of development. There was need for such vehicles for farmers, mail carriers, impecunious country doctors, and traveling salesmen, especially in the Middle West, where there were few or no hill-climbing problems. Their high wheels enabled them to run on the most miserable dirt roads. The high-wheelers were not pretty to look at, but they were cheap to buy and inexpensive to maintain. They reached their peak from 1904 to 1909; then the Model T Ford took over this market.

The leading builder was the Holsman Automobile Company of Chicago. There were half a dozen other manufacturers in Chicago, four in St. Louis, and others in Ohio, Indiana, Illinois, and Iowa.

An article on the buggy-type motor car in the August 1907 issue of *Motor* said: "The industry has developed no standard form or common mechanical feature of construction. The vehicles are characterized merely by their close resemblance to horse-drawn buggies and surreys, but the types and powers of engines and transmissions used are almost as numerous as the different makes of cars.

"Taking the Holsman as typical . . . the line . . . may be divided into runabouts seating two persons and surreys seating four. The wheels are 44 inches in diameter in front and 48 inches in the rear, and are fitted with solid rubber tires not more than 1¾ inches wide at the base. The tread or gauge may be any width desired, from 56 to 62 inches, according to the standard wagon gauge prevailing in the section where the purchaser lives. The wheelbase varies in the different models from 65 inches to 75 inches. Four full elliptical springs secured to the two solid steel axles support the body, which is of the common piano-box style, except that the vehicles of longer wheelbase have a box built in

front of the dash to be used for storage. Patent-leather fenders catch the mud and water thrown up by the wheels, and the seats are of the straight back, two-passenger type common to horse-drawn vehicles. Folding victoria or extension tops are fitted when ordered. Instead of the front axle turning on a fifth wheel, the front wheels are provided with steering knuckles, marking a departure from horse-drawn carriage building common to most of this class.

"The air-cooled, two-cylinder opposed engine is rated at 10 hp. It is mounted horizontally under the body. Ignition is by jump spark from dry-cell batteries. Power is transmitted by steel cables passing over pulleys fixed to a movable cross shaft and around large sheaves secured to the rear wheels. When the cross shaft is moved forward by means of a lever at the right of the driver's seat, the cables are tightened in their sheaves and the engine can then drive the vehicle, but when this pressure is released, the cables merely slip in the pulleys as they rotate. This dispenses with the use of a friction clutch. No differential is employed, either in the rear axle or in the cross shaft, slippage of the cables being depended upon to take care of any differences in rotation of the driving wheels. Neither is there any change-speed gearing, speed of the car being controlled by the engine throttle and by allowing the cables to slip when necessary. At the extreme ends of the cross shaft are two very small pulleys. These engage the rubber tires of the rear wheels when the shaft has been moved backward sufficiently and reverse the direction of rotation of the drive wheels. Brake shoes that engage in the driving sheaves where the cables do not touch it are set and released by a hand lever on a vertical column at the driver's right."

The Waltham Buckboards shown at the top of the opposite page were also an adaptation of carriage-making techniques. Since they were intended for Eastern use, they didn't need such high road clearance and so had bicycle-type wheels.

# EARLY AMERICAN

### COLUMBIA (1903)
This, the Mark XLI, had a 24-hp motor which enabled it to reach speeds up to 45 mph. On October 1, 1903, a Columbia reached New York after traveling 1,177 miles in 76 hours without stopping for repairs except for a puncture

### WINTON (1904)
The price of this car with its canopy top and full lamp equipment was $2500, f.o.b. Ohio. Note the early sun visor and the gracefully curved combination fenders and running boards. The tonneau was entered from the rear

### THOMAS FLYER (1906)
This was a predecessor of the celebrated Thomas Flyer that won the sensational New York-to-Paris race in 1908. Model 31 had a four-cylinder, 50-hp engine and was the first car made by Thomas to use a disk clutch. Only 600 were made

# LUXURY CARS

**PIERCE-ARROW (1907)**

This was called "The Great Arrow Touring Car." It had a four-cylinder, 40-45 hp motor and was chain driven. It carried seven passengers, two of them in revolving seats. It sold for $5000. Note gear shift under steering wheel

**STEVENS-DURYEA (1910)**

Model Y, seven-passenger touring tonneau sold for $4000 f.o.b. Chicopee Falls, Mass. It had a six-cylinder, 40-hp motor; despite the fact that it carried a storage battery, it still used a bulb horn

**PACKARD (1912)**

This was Model 38; it had a six-cylinder, 60-hp motor and came equipped with electric starter and electric lights for $4050. Note the lonely, single rear seat and the fact that the factory-equipped windshield had at last arrived

# LATE AMERICAN

The 1933 Pierce Silver Arrow with twelve-cylinder 175-hp motor, power brakes, and free wheeling. Price $10,000

A four-passenger Locomobile with Healey body. It has a fold-down rear windshield and external exhaust pipes (1921)

A 1920 Brewster landaulet—one of the most beautifully built cars of its time

# LUXURY CARS

The sixteen-cylinder 1931 Marmon two-passenger coupe. It had a 200-hp motor made largely of aluminum to reduce weight

The 1933 Stutz with many advanced features for its day. The dual-valve Eight sold for $3295

A 1921 Cunningham with tonneau windshield, Victoria top, and unusual rear fender treatment

The famous Ford 999, which was the first racing car Barney Oldfield ever drove. It was steered by a cranking device instead of a wheel (1902)

The first automobile Henry Ford ever built. He made it by hand in a backyard workshop at 58 Bagley Ave., Detroit (1896)

Henry Ford's second car, a vast improvement in beauty over the first one. The flaring fenders add considerably to its appearance (1898)

The Ford Model A for 1903. It cost $800 without the rear seats; $900 as shown here. It had an 8-hp double opposed motor

The Ford Model N for 1906. It had a four-cylinder motor and was the immediate predecessor of the famous Model T

Ford's biggest car, the six-cylinder Model K, which sold for $2500 (1906)

# THE FORDS BEFORE THE MODEL T

Unquestionably the most important event in the history of American automobiling was the advent of the Model T Ford. This car, more than any other, was responsible for transforming an animal-powered America into a highly mechanized state. But the Model T did not happen overnight. It evolved over a fifteen-year period from 1893 to October 1, 1908, when the first Model T was produced. Late in 1893, Henry Ford, who was then an engineer in the Detroit Edison electric plant, began to experiment with gas engines and automobiles. By the middle of 1896 he had completed his first hand-built car, the crude-looking vehicle shown on the opposite page. In an attempt to gain publicity and public acceptance for his work, he left his job with Detroit Edison to devote all his time to building racing cars. One of them, an 80-hp monster, was driven by Ford on an ice-covered lake at the then incredible speed of 94 mph. After that, he employed Barney Oldfield, who had been a professional bicycle racer, to drive the celebrated "999." Since Oldfield was used to steering bicycles with a handlebar, Ford equipped the "999" with a two-handed steering crank, so Oldfield could keep the heavy car on the road on a sharp turn.

The fame achieved by his racing cars enabled Henry Ford to organize the Ford Motor Company in 1903. It began with $28,000 in cash supplied by twelve stockholders, all of whom were eventually to see their original investments multiplied many thousands of times.

During the period from 1903 to 1908, the Ford Motor Company was very much like any other small and struggling automobile manufacturer of the time. It brought out several models, none of which achieved any great success. In 1906, it produced the big six-cylinder Model K, which sold for

$2500. During the same year the smaller four-cylinder Model N appeared. This car had many features which were incorporated in the famous Model T and so can be considered its immediate predecessor.

It was at this time that Henry Ford was thinking about building a low-priced, mass-produced automobile. In an article which appeared in a Detroit newspaper in 1909, he explained how he had arrived at the need for such a car. "The automobile of the past," he said, "attained success in spite of its price, because there were more than enough purchasers to take the limited output of the then new industry. Proportionately few could buy, but those few could keep all the manufacturers busy, and price, therefore, had no bearing on sales. The automobile of the present is making good because the price has been reduced just enough to add sufficient new purchasers to take care of the increased output. Supply and demand, not cost, has regulated the selling price.

"The automobile of the future must be enough better than the present car to beget confidence in the man of limited means and enough lower in price to insure sales for the enormously increased output. The car of the future must be a car for the people, a car that any man can own who can afford a horse and carriage; and, mark my words, that car is coming sooner than most people expect.

"In the low-priced car dwells the future success of the automobile. Comparatively few persons can afford even a thousand-dollar car. A limited number of factories can supply all the demand for high-priced cars, but the market for a low-priced car is unlimited. The car of the future will be light as well as low in price. This means the substitution of quality for quantity, even to the use of materials not yet discovered."

So new, so shiny, and so clean! (1920)

But sometimes they looked like this (1914)

A special body and wire wheels but still a Model T (1916)

Completely disguised. The front fenders turn with the wheels (1921)

The first assembly line (1913). Henry Ford II recently said he thought his grandfather got the idea from the Waltham Watch factory

An early Model T
now in the
Henry Ford Museum,
Dearborn, Mich.

# THE MODEL T FORD

The October 1908 issue of *Motor* carried a double-page advertisement which introduced the Model T Ford to the public. It stated that Henry Ford had spent two years on design, experimenting, and research. The advertisement then said: "These experimental cars have been run under every conceivable condition. Last winter they were tried on snow- and slush-covered country roads—all summer they have worked on hills, on sand and mud roads in good and bad weather. $150,000 worth of new machinery and tools were added before we could start to build. While we do not know how many of these cars we will build in the next twelve months, the price is based on building 25,000 cars."

Eighteen years later, when the Model T was still practically unchanged, *Motor* quoted the following production figures in its May 1926 issue:

| CAR NUMBER | DATE | CAR NUMBER | DATE |
|---|---|---|---|
| 1,000,000 | Dec. 10, 1915 | 7,000,000 | Jan. 12, 1923 |
| 2,000,000 | June 14, 1917 | 8,000,000 | July 11, 1923 |
| 3,000,000 | April 2, 1919 | 9,000,000 | Dec. 26, 1923 |
| 4,000,000 | May 11, 1920 | 10,000,000 | June 4, 1924 |
| 5,000,000 | May 28, 1921 | 11,000,000 | Jan. 3, 1925 |
| 6,000,000 | May 18, 1922 | 12,000,000 | June 15, 1925 |

But by 1926, competition from Chevrolet, Overland, and other light-car manufacturers were giving the then-obsolete Model T a hard time. It had reached its peak on October 31, 1925 when 9109 cars were built in one day. By the time the Model A Ford superseded the Model T on December 2, 1927, more than 15,000,000 Model T's had been manufactured. During the last ten years of its life, half of all the cars built in America were Model T's.

During its nineteen-year career the Model T was the butt of thousands of jokes. As a result it received more publicity than any other car has ever had. But now the "Tin Lizzie" is remembered affectionately by the millions who

drove it. A good many Model T's are still around, but the early brass-fronted models are scarce. The last one was made in 1916, when the brass radiator gave way to black iron.

When it first appeared, the Model T touring car sold for $850. The price went down steadily until it reached $360 in 1917. Then war and inflation forced the price up until it reached $525 late in 1918. After that, the price was constantly reduced until it hit an all-time low of $290 on December 2, 1924.

The specifications of the original Model T were:

MOTOR. Four-cylinder, 4-cycle, 20-hp, cast in single block with removable water-jacketed cylinder head.

TRANSMISSION. Spur planetary with no internal gears.

IGNITION. Low-tension magneto generator driven directly by engine shaft.

CONTROL AND DRIVE. All forward speeds by foot pedals, reverse by hand lever (later changed to foot pedal), brake on transmission controlled by foot pedal, emergency brake on rear hubs controlled by hand lever.

WHEELS AND WEIGHT. 30-inch artillery wood wheels with pneumatic tires, 3-inch front, 3½-inch rear, 56-inch tread. Wheelbase 100 inches. Weight 1200 pounds.

The 10-gallon gasoline tank under the front seat fed by gravity to the motor. The equipment consisted only of three oil lamps and a tube horn, but the body came equipped with irons for a top. There were only two springs, both transverse, and made of vanadium steel. Splash-and-gravity lubrication slopped oil around to keep the motor functioning, but there was no oil-stick, no oil-pressure gauge, and there was, of course, no way of measuring engine temperature.

This Spartan-like car went on for nearly twenty years almost without change, but hundreds of accessory manufacturers thrived by making everything from self-starters to complete bodies to improve or dress up the Model T.

# THE ELECTRIC CAR

Of the three sources of power first used on automobiles—steam, electricity, and gasoline—electricity was by far the most reliable and the simplest. The picture of the electric chassis shown at the top of the opposite page demonstrates how starkly simple these vehicles were. But they had their drawbacks. Their speed was low, and, at the beginning, their range on a fully charged set of batteries was only about 25 miles. By 1910, this had been increased until they could go about 75 miles at 25 mph.

Nevertheless, the electrics were among the most elegant cars of their time. They reached their highest stage of development during the period just before the First World War. By then, the pattern for them had become pretty well standardized. They were usually coupes with an extra seat facing rear, so the lady driver could talk with her friend as they glided along at a sedate 15 or 20 mph.

Owners of electric cars had to have elaborate and expensive equipment installed in their garages in order to make sure their batteries were kept fully charged all the time. These charging panels had their own indicating meters, current switches, and heavy-duty cables to supply the large amount of electricity essential for the operation of these cars.

During the Second World War, a few wealthy people who had kept their ancient electrics standing for years in their capacious garages, had them overhauled and refitted so they could be used during the period of gas rationing. During wartime gas rationing in England, one manufacturer there brought out a small electric bus that would carry twelve passengers and their luggage.

Battery-operated electric vehicles still have some use as delivery trucks in urban areas, and battery-operated tractors are widely used in factories and warehouses to load and unload various kinds of merchandise.

Otherwise, the electric car as such seems obsolete. However, there is a possibility that a new type of electric may be made. It would be similar to the Diesel-electric bus and railroad locomotive. A small gasoline engine would drive a generator which, in turn, would rotate a constant torque, hydraulically stabilized, variable speed AC motor in the rear axle. Similar ideas were tried nearly fifty years ago, but they were not successful. Development work along these lines is now under way.

**A Princely Gift for Your Wife**

POPE Waverley ELECTRICS

**Model 27, Stanhope**
Open or Victoria Top, Price $1,400

Many men buy a POPE-WAVERLEY ELECTRIC "for their wives," just as many men go to the circus "because the children want to go." They generally wind up by using and enjoying the Pope-Waverley as much as either wife or children.

In the gasoline field there is some latitude for investigation and comparison—in the electric field your choice is practically narrowed down to the Pope-Waverley, whose pre-eminence is absolute, unique and unquestioned.

The more you study the electric situation the more you'll feel like owning a Pope-Waverley—no matter whether you operate other cars or not.

Anyway you'd better write for the handsomely illustrated catalogue, which will give you a graphic idea of the infinite possibilities of the Pope-Waverley from the standpoint of both pleasure and utility.

We make Coupes, Chelseas, Surreys, Stanhopes, Station and Delivery Wagons. Prices $850 to $2,250. Also Trucks on specifications.

Write for complete catalogue and name of our agent nearest you.

**POPE MOTOR CAR CO. = Indianapolis, Ind.**

Implied royalty (1905)

**THE MOST LUXURIOUS CAR EVER BUILT**

The Baker Electric illustrated was built to order for the King of Siam, and is unquestionably the most elegantly appointed automobile ever built in America.

The chassis and body are standard equipment, and its luxurious appointments far surpass any car ever built in this country.

The body and running gear are finished in ivory. The top is made of special leather, enameled in white. The dash and fenders are in white patent leather.

The side panels and front of the hood are emblazoned with the crest of the King of Siam.

This car is upholstered in a delicate pale green broadcloth, the royal color of Siam, with silver gray Persian broad lace tapestry, puff rolls and silver gray silk cord and seaming lace.

All metal parts are silver plated and it has special silver electric lamps and meter case. The lever handles are of pearl. The hood has beveled glass curtain lights at each side and in the rear.

# Baker Electrics

## The Aristocrats of Motordom

cost more than other electrics, because they are worth more—yet their low cost of maintenance makes them much less expensive than any other electric made. The first cost of an electric is not the entire cost. Cost of maintenance and repairs—should be considered.

When intelligent comparison is made between *The Baker* and other electrics, it is invariably the first choice of those who desire simplicity of control—ease of operation—low cost of maintenance—the longest mileage on one charge of the batteries—luxurious appointments—economy of current consumption—endurance and durability.

Let us tell you why *Baker Electrics* cost less for maintenance and repairs than any other electric made—why our batteries have longer life—and why *The Baker* has greater speed—longer mileage—more endurance and greater durability.

**WRITE FOR OUR HANDSOME CATALOGUE**

We want you to know why *Baker Electrics* are the *World's Standard*, by which all other electrics are judged. *Superiority is never an accident.*

**THE BAKER MOTOR VEHICLE CO.**
31 West 80th St.,                                    Cleveland, Ohio, U. S. A.

Actual royalty (1909)

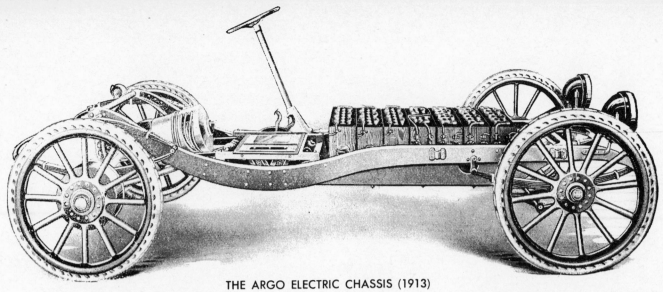

THE ARGO ELECTRIC CHASSIS (1913)

This rare picture shows what the underside of an electric car really looked like. There is a huge bank of storage batteries connected by heavy cables to a powerful driving motor mounted just in front of the rear axle. Since the car went slowly and usually traveled on paved city streets, the tires could be solid so the lady driver never had to contend with a flat or a blowout. The car itself is illustrated directly below

An early Baker electric runabout (1904)

This body style was called a Stanhope (1904)

A Rausch and Lang electric coupe (1915)

The Columbus Electric (1906)

An early Stanley Steamer (1902-1903) now in the Henry Ford Museum, Dearborn, Mich.

# THE STEAM CAR

In a retrospective article in its October 1942 issue, *Motor* said: "At the beginning of the twentieth century, steam cars were light and fragile.

"The driver had to be a pretty fair steam engineer. The boiler pressure gauge on the dash needed constant watching so steam pressure could be kept reasonably constant. When ascending a hill, the fuel valve had to be opened to increase the intensity of the fire under the boiler and closed when descending a grade. Later, this was done automatically.

"The boiler water-level gauge had to be examined frequently, and every 25 miles or so the driver had to stop to take on water, since the spent steam was exhausted into the air. Later, condensers were introduced on some cars to convert the used steam into water.

"The steam car had a number of chronic troubles. Burners became sooted and needed frequent cleaning. Boilers became encrusted with salts, and dirt deposited from the water and had to be cleaned to restore efficiency. Boiler tubes blew out and had to be replaced. The water-level glass frequently broke. Starting a fire under the boiler was a troublesome job, and after the burner was lit it took 15 minutes to half an hour before there was enough pressure to run the car.

"But in spite of its faults, early steam cars had some exceedingly important advantages over gasoline cars. They were quiet; torque was smooth; vibration was negligible; and there were no gears to shift or clutch to operate."

Nevertheless, the steam car was doomed and by the mid-1920's was extinct.

The famous Stanley Twins in one of their first cars

An early Stanley Steamer photographed in modern times

The MacDonald Steamer (1923)

The Detroit Steamer. Price $1585 (1923)

A late model Stanley Steamer which sold for $2600 (1918)

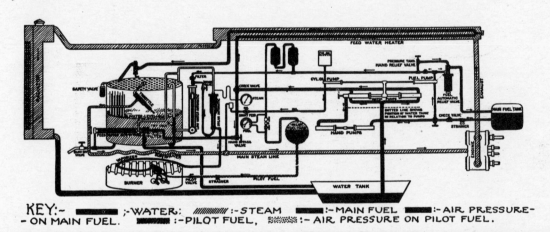

A diagram that shows in detail just how the Stanley Steamer illustrated above actually worked

The American steam car. Price $1650 (1922)

The Coats Steamer. Price $1085 (1922)

**1907 BRUSH**
This little runabout was designed by A. P. Brush,
who had designed the famous one-cylinder Cadillac.
It had a 6-hp one-cylinder motor
under the hood and sold for $500

**1914 SAXON**
The maker boasted about the streamlined body
and wire wheels for a car that sold
for only $395. What seem to be large sidelights
are actually the car's headlights

**1915 METZ**
This light car, similar
in some ways to the Saxon,
had runningboards
and real headlights

**1915 SCRIPPS-BOOTH**
This was probably the
best-known American light car
of its day. It weighed 1500
pounds, seated three people,
and sold for $775

**1953 HILLMAN-MINX**
This British-made 2100-pound four-door sedan
with a four-cylinder 42-hp motor and four-speed
transmission will cruise at 65 mph
and gets 25 to 35 mpg

**1953 FIAT**
An Italian built four-door sedan with
radiator grille and other brightwork made
of polished aluminum

# SMALL CARS—PAST AND PRESENT

Unless the Model T Ford is considered a small car (it had a
100 inch wheelbase, a 20-hp motor, and weighed only 1200
pounds), America has never had a really popular small car.
At the present time none is built here, so the market is being
supplied by European automobiles — mostly from England. In
1952, 29,000 foreign cars were brought into the United States.

Americans have always liked big, comfortable, and rather
showy cars. But as city streets become more and more congested, and parking space gets more difficult to find, a few
Americans—particularly those living in large cities—are turning
to the inexpensive small foreign cars, which can be parked in
tight places where most American cars could not get in.

**1953 AUSTIN**
The British-built A40 Somerset four-door sedan
with a four-cylinder 42-hp motor. There is also
a still smaller version, the A30 seven
with a 30-hp motor

**1953 ZEPHYR**
Built by Ford in England. The Zephyr has
six cylinders (68 hp) and is a deluxe version of
the smaller four-cylinder 47-hp Consul

A rear-engine car designed by William B. Stout in 1935

# GOING OR COMING?
## Some Radical Ideas in Automotive Design

The American automobile went through many stages of experiment and innovation during its development. Some of these experiments, like the front-drive Ruxton and the Cord (1929), and the various rear-engine cars shown here, had a great deal of basic merit but they never became popular in the United States. A three-wheeler, like the early Kelsey Motorette (1910) shown on the opposite page, also has its advantages because it can be easily maneuvered and turned in a remarkably small circle. Buckminster Fuller built one of them in the mid-1930's, which he called the Dymaxion.

Rear-engine cars are widely used in Europe, but they have been limited almost exclusively to buses in this country. In October 1943, *Motor* printed an article by a well-known engineer in which he stated the advantages of the rear-engine car. He said: "For a body of given size the car may have better visibility, increased riding comfort, easier steering, better braking, increased traction, improved fuel economy, greater luggage space, ideal accessibility — with fewer pounds of material. A rear-engine car permits the design of a combined body and frame structure that is both light in weight and economical to build. Visibility is superior because of a short hood. Inside the hood there is room for six real pieces of luggage as well as for a spare tire. And the rear-engine car is quieter because the noise of engine and fan is swept away to the rear. Heat and exhaust fumes are practically eliminated from the body compartment because they also are carried to the rear."

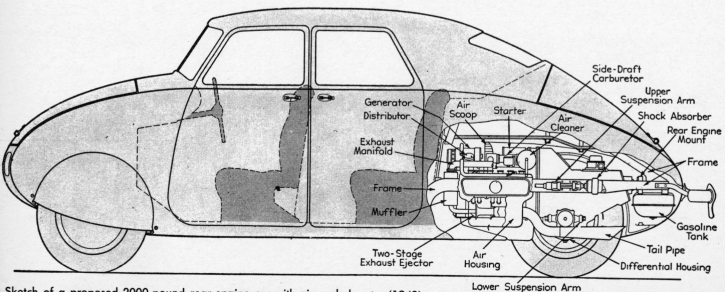

Sketch of a proposed 2000-pound rear-engine car with air-cooled motor (1943)

The experimental Briggs rear-engine car designed
by John Tjaarda   (1935)

A British rear-engine car built by Crossley in 1933

Rear view of the Briggs rear-engine car shown above

The three-wheeled Kelsey Motorette, which had a two-cylinder air-cooled opposed engine and was chain-driven (1910)

# ODDITIES

The Bi-Autogo two-wheeler (1913)

# HOW MANY WHEELS SHOULD AN AUTOMOBILE HAVE?

Although we are accustomed to seeing automobiles with four wheels, they have at various times had any number from two to eight. James Scripps Booth, who later achieved fame as the designer of a very popular American small car, built the two-wheeler shown above. Actually, it had more than two wheels because the small balancing wheels had to be kept lowered until the car got up enough speed for them to be raised. It was then steered like a motorcycle or a bicycle. It had many unusual features. First of all, it had what was perhaps the first V8 motor to be put into actual use in the United States. The cylinders were set at an angle of 90 degrees and were cast en bloc with L heads. The cooling system was really remarkable. There were 450 feet of half-inch copper tubing left exposed on the front and sides of the car. Water was pumped through the jacket to the rear tank of the radiator — thence through the top bank of tubes to small rear return tanks.

Booth began the design of his unique car in 1908 and completed it in May 1913. It cost $25,000 to build. The car may still be seen at the Detroit Historical Museum.

A three-wheeler has been shown on the previous page. Three-wheeled cars have always been rare in America, but there are a good many of them in Europe, particularly in England where their economy makes them appreciated.

The eight-wheeled Octo-Auto was designed by M. O. Reeves, of Columbus, Ind. His claims for it were that its many wheels gave it extraordinarily good riding qualities and minimized tire wear. (Of course you had to buy eight tires, but they theoretically wore out only half as fast.) The first, second, and fourth sets of wheels steered the car; the third set was used to drive it.

This car was actually offered for sale; in fact, an endorsement was written for it by Elbert Hubbard. The same designer also built a six-wheeled car which had only one set of wheels in front. But neither car was successful. The same multi-wheel principle is used today on trucks and trailers.

The Reeves Octo-Auto (1911)

### The Season's Biggest Sensation

# The 1917 Enger

### Twelve and Six—Both in One

# Twin-Unit Twelve

## $1295
*f. o. b. Cincinnati*

## $1295
*f. o. b. Cincinnati*

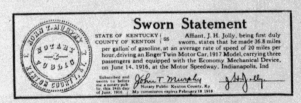

## 35 Miles Per Gallon

THE most marvelous automobile improvement yet invented!

Just move a little lever and the trick is done—the trick that is turning the automobile world topsy turvy.

One minute your car is a twelve with tremendous power for a lightning get-a-way, slow driving in crowded streets, or for hills and heavy going.

The next instant you have a six, for all normal driving—and the most economical six the world has ever seen—35 miles per gallon—read the affidavit shown below.

Just a touch of the little lever on the steering column does it all—cuts out six of your twelve-cylinders and cuts them in again—in an instant.

This Enger invention makes possible the supreme motor car combination—luxury and economy.

In other cars emergency power eats up fuel all the time—needlessly—extravagantly.

In the Enger Twin-Unit Twelve you have emergency power in abundance — but it uses fuel for **surplus** power only when called upon. The six cylinders that are idling one instant are adding extra power and push the next.

Never has a car stirred up such enthusiasm. Never was a car such an instantaneous success.

For no other car at anywhere near the price even approaches such attainments in either luxury or economy—none at any price combines them.

---

### Sworn Statement

STATE OF KENTUCKY } SS
COUNTY OF KENTON

Affiant, J. H. Jolly, being first duly sworn, states that he made 36.8 miles per gallon of gasoline, at an average rate of speed of 20 miles per hour, driving an Enger Twin Motor Car, 1917 Model, carrying three passengers and equipped with the Economy Mechanical Device, on June 14, 1916, at the Motor Speedway, Indianapolis, Ind

Subscribed and sworn to before me a notary public this 24th day of June, 1916.

*John T. Murphy*
Notary Public Kenton County, Ky
My commission expires February 18 1916

*J. H. Jolly*

---

*Write for Booklet "The Story of a Gallon of Gasoline"*

## The Enger Motor Car Company, Cincinnati, Ohio

Read this advertisement carefully. The car is stranger than it looks (1917)

The Carrm convertible body (1917). The idea
of having readily changeable bodies for
different uses occurred very early in automobile
history. The celebrated Paris-Rouen race
of 1894 was won by a De Dion-Bouton steam
tractor to which any kind of carriage trailer could
be added. The Carrm body could be made into
a touring car or a roadster as shown here.

The Dog-fish body of 1913—one of the earliest attempts to do away with runningboards and protect the spare tire from theft and weather

# STRANGE BODY SHAPES

A homemade attempt to make a multi-use car on one chassis. This Ford could be used as a touring car, a limousine, a roadster, or a coupe. And you could also lower the back of the front seat to make a bed (1920)

A novel rear-engine car designed in 1921 by Rumpler, the German airplane builder

In the early days of the automobile, when custom building was taken for granted, rich people and those who were handy with tools could indulge their whims and eccentricities. Most of their results were satisfying only to their originators. Second-hand cars of unusual design have always been hard to sell. Such cars usually end up either in museums, like the Scripps-Booth two-wheeler shown on page 134 or on the junk pile, which was doubtless the destination of many of the cars shown here. The only idea of this sort which has consistently retained some degree of popularity is the car with seats that can be converted into a bed. A car of this kind is still made by Nash.

Prince Orloff's Landaulet with extra seats for passengers at the rear and also on the top (1905)

The valveless Panhard-Levassor with original canoe body (1913)

# STRANGE THINGS PEOPLE DID WITH—OR TO—THEIR CARS

Almost as soon as the automobile was invented, people began to find novel—and sometimes freakish—uses for it just to show what their cars could do. This was all part of the ego-building instinct that played so important a part in the development of motoring. Some people took pride in the fact that their cars were expensive; others rejoiced in their cars'

beauty; and still others bought automobiles only for their high speed. But there was always a small nucleus of automobile owners who delighted in making their cars do strange and eccentric stunts. Sometimes they did this just to show off; at other times they did it for purely commercial reasons, as was true in the case of Marmon and Cadillac here.

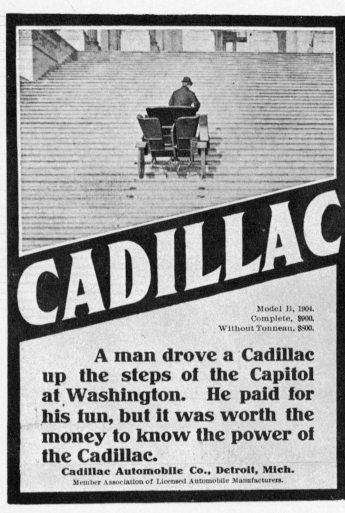

## CADILLAC

Model B, 1904.
Complete, $900.
Without Tonneau, $800.

**A man drove a Cadillac up the steps of the Capitol at Washington. He paid for his fun, but it was worth the money to know the power of the Cadillac.**

Cadillac Automobile Co., Detroit, Mich.
Member Association of Licensed Automobile Manufacturers.

We wonder just how much this man's fun did cost (1904)

Demonstrating the Cadillac's structural strength (1906)

Demonstrating the rigidity of the Marmon frame (1905)

To make horsepower graphic, this 10-hp Autocar matches its strength against real live horses (1905)

Ralph Coffin of the Washington Riding and Hunt Club puts his horse over a car full of society people (1916)

Bert Dingley drives a King on the aquaduct siphon across Bouquet Canon, Los Angeles (1914)

Just why anyone should want to invent an automobile that looked like a horse-drawn vehicle nobody knows. But in 1911 someone did—and got a U.S. patent for it. Note that the dummy horse's legs move realistically, but wheels do the actual work.

In 1908, the Carter Twin-Engine car was placed on the market. There were two sets of four cylinders, cast in pairs, 35-hp each. If one engine conked out you could get home on the other. Throw them both into action and you got full speed. (Note that there are two cranks.) The price was $5000 f.o.b. Washington, D. C.

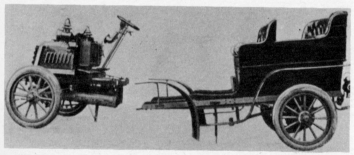

The separable motor car is a very early idea which was used even on the nineteenth-century steam-driven road vehicles. You used an engine and two front wheels as a tractor; to this you could attach any one of several bodies that you kept on hand. The same principle is used today in the tractor truck. (1904).

The car with its body raised up was built that way so as to make its working parts more accessible for repairs. Writing about it in 1905, *Motor* said hopefully: "Undoubtedly, the next few years will see much progress made in this direction."

In 1906, Alphonse Constantini invented motor-driven roller skates. They never became very popular, for as *Motor* pointed out then: "but suppose for some reason or another, one of the engines should stop. Can you imagine the motor skater on one leg, the other off the ground, with a dead motor hanging to his sole?" Still, Mr. Constantini could make forty miles an hour with both feet roaring.

A really ancient American motor vehicle—the bus section dates from 1876, but the motor tractor was photographed in 1914

An early French attempt at building an amphibian (1907)

Here it is actually going through the water like a boat

A propeller driven car owned by an American girl in Paris (1921)

An English car driven by illuminating gas during the First World War

When about to strike a victim you pulled a lever to land him safely

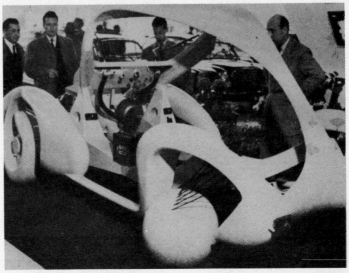

A surrealist fantasy dreamed up by an Italian designer (1952)

"Just As Easy-
As It Looks"

# TAYLOR
## Crank-Shaft
# TIRE PUMP

TAYLOR MFG. CO.
Detroit
Michigan

Advertisers did the weirdest things to attract attention (1916)

The Gabriel ten-note horn (1911)

# ACCESSORIES AND GADGETS

Some accessories were intended to be really useful; others just added to the motorist's fun—or vanity. But the ten-note Gabriel horn shown here was a beautiful thing. Its rich, round, melodious notes could be heard miles away.

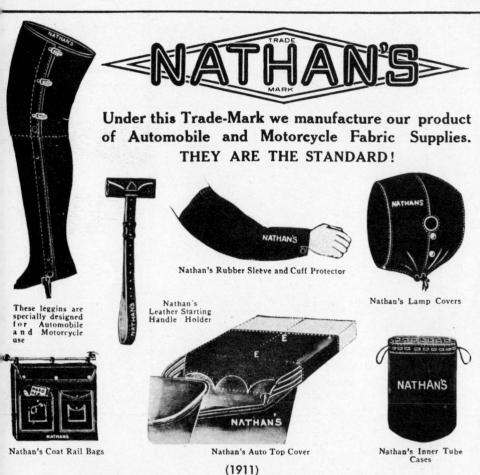

## NATHAN'S
TRADE MARK

Under this Trade-Mark we manufacture our product of Automobile and Motorcycle Fabric Supplies.
THEY ARE THE STANDARD!

These leggins are specially designed for Automobile and Motorcycle use

Nathan's Leather Starting Handle Holder

Nathan's Rubber Sleeve and Cuff Protector

Nathan's Lamp Covers

Nathan's Coat Rail Bags

Nathan's Auto Top Cover

Nathan's Inner Tube Cases

(1911)

A wheel muff to keep your hands warm while you drove an open car (1920)

A lap robe that strapped around each passenger's neck (1915)

(1911)

## Monograms

Yours is not a public car.
Get out of the crowd.
Put your monogram on your car; it is the finishing touch of refinement.
**Monograms from $2.00 up**
**THE HICKOK MFG. CO.**
32 St. Paul Street    Rochester, N. Y.

[ 143 ]

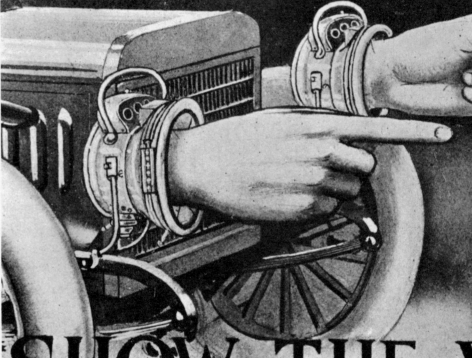

An advertising man's
conception of
tire strength (1913)

# FORTIFIED!

## PACIFIC TREADS

### Are Practically *Bullet-Proof*

Demonstrating the sturdiness of an oil lamp (1911)

## Unlimited Number of Positions

For instance: No. 1 shows upper sash in rain view position, lower sash upright. No. 2 shows normal zigzag position. No. 3 shows upper sash in straight ventilator position, lower sash in angling position. It's the

## TROY Model 32

### Combination Straight or Zigzag

Changed at will. Tension regulated at owner's discretion. Holds firmly in any position. Adjusts automatically. No thumb nuts or hand wheels.

Just one of the many new Troy Models admirably adapted to the latest foredoor cars. Send for new catalog, price list, etc.

## THE TROY CARRIAGE SUNSHADE CO.

A baby bag to keep
the baby warm (1913)

When windshields were
sold as extras (1912)

A 1908 Thomas Flyer equipped with a Stepney spare wheel. When you had a flat, you simply bolted the wheel on and kept going.

This told you your motor was overheated (1913)

The wheel pushed out of the way to make more room for getting in and out (1916)

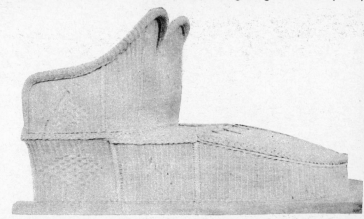

This locked the steering wheel so it couldn't be turned (1913)

A reed body advertised as light, cool, and comfortable (1906)

The isinglass in these side-curtains was purposely made small because big sheets would crack (1914)

An electric horn with diaphragm, vibrator, and battery (1905)

A spark plug—one of the few things that still looks the same

## Comfort for Your Hands

There is no way that you can keep your hands warm driving an automobile in cold weather unless you have a warm steering wheel in your hands. You cannot expect your hands to be warm holding a wheel cold as ice. No, it must be warm. That's common sense. Warm hands mean comfort, plus safety to you.

Your automobile represents a large investment which pays interest in pleasure, health, recreation and service. Don't let cold hands rob you of the interest on your investment seven months out of the year—more than half the time.

Warm Hand Wheel on
Overland Car, $12.00.

An electric hand-warmer for the steering wheel (1914)

This is how the luggage compartment began (1909)

## Dustless Motoring

**BROWN'S DUST GUARDS** absolutely eliminate the dust nuisance in motoring

Guaranteed to give satisfaction or money refunded

The following is only one of many expressions from satisfied users:

Bloomington, Illinois, June 13, 1905

W. H. Brown,
　　Chicago, Ill.
Dear Sir:
　　We herewith send you remittance to-day for your invoice———. Our customer to whom we sold these Guards told us to-day that they were worth ten times their cost. He said he would not sell them for $100.00 if he could not get another set just like them. How soon could you furnish a set of Guards for Model B Winton car——?
　　　　Yours truly,
　　　　The Keiser-Van Leer Co.,
　　　　By B. C. Van Leer,
　　　　　　Sec'y & Treas.

Made to fit any automobile. Write for booklet. Visit our exhibit at the New York Auto Show, 69th Regiment Armory, Space 30 in Gallery.

**W. H. BROWN,** 205 Lenox Building, CLEVELAND, OHIO

In 1906 fenders were sold as extras

# THE HAYNES-APPERSON CO.,
## KOKOMO, IND.

Are
Actually
Filling
Orders.

They
Have
Got the
Machine
To Sell.

Make the
Haynes-
Apperson
Double
Cylinder
Carriage
Motor

in 4, 6, 8 and 10
horse power.

Motors are
LIGHT, STRONG,
AND RELIABLE.

## MOTOR CARRIAGES,    GASOLINE MOTORS,
### AND GEARING FOR MOTOR VEHICLES.

*PROMPT DELIVERY.*    *MODERATE PRICES.*    *PRACTICAL MACHINES.*

This is one of the first American automobile advertisements to show a photograph of the actual car (1896)

## A STATEMENT.

The American Electric Vehicle Company, 447 Wabash Ave., Chicago, begs hereby to announce to possible customers that it is now, **TO-DAY,** in position to fill orders for the most advanced and artistic styles of electric vehicles. We make this statement, as many people look upon the new industry of electric vehicle manufacture as one in the experimental stage. We wish it distinctly understood that we are not only prepared to fill orders, but are ready to demonstrate on demand the simplicity and perfection of the equipment which we offer for sale. As evidence backing the above plain language we beg to state that already we have sold our electric vehicles to Montgomery Ward & Co., Chicago; Mr. H. McCormick, Chicago; Mr. Thos. B. Bryan, Chicago; Mr. W. G. Press, Chicago; and others whose names, for good business reasons, as yet we do not care to publish. Catalogue furnished on request. **COST OF OPERATION PER MILE. ONE CENT.**

An early example of testimonial advertising (1896)

## EARLY AUTOMOBILE ADVERTISING

The very first American automobile advertisements were plain, straightforward, and factual. One of their principal aims was simply to convince the reader that the company was actually in business and could deliver the car it promised. Some fly-by-night promoters had taken orders — and deposits — and had then disappeared without doing any manufacturing. Other legitimate companies couldn't build cars as fast as they thought they could, and when the cars were built they often had bugs in them that had to be eliminated by a long process of trial and error.

The two advertisements shown here appeared in 1896, which was well before the American automobile industry got under way. This meant that every car made then had to be built by hand. Each part had to be fitted, and then the finished vehicle had to be tried out to see if it would perform satisfactorily on the road. Often it didn't, and then the builder had to tear it down and start all over again.

The next spread shows some other early advertisements, but they cover a more sophisticated period (1904-1905), when automobile manufacturing was becoming a business rather than an individual machine-shop venture.

# SOME FAMOUS TRADEMARKS

Here are three of the most famous trademarks ever used in automobile advertising. The Kelly-Springfield Girl (1910) is no longer in existence, but the Fisk Time-to-Retire Boy (1912), and the Michelin Tire Man (1916) are still active.

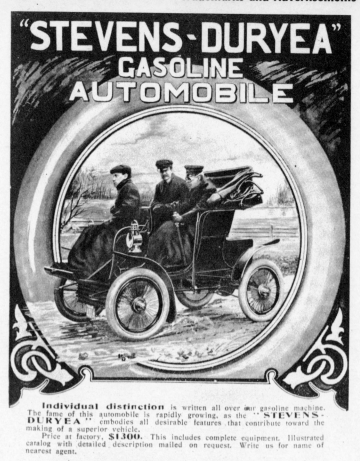

# AUTOMOBILE ADVERTISING WAS SWANKY —SOMETIMES SNOBBISH... OR DOWN-TO-EARTH AND STRAIGHTFORWARD... BUT OCCASIONALLY IT SOARED INTO THE WILD BLUE YONDER

**Ford**
THE UNIVERSAL CAR

## Buy It Because It's a Better Car

Model T
Touring Car **$550**
f. o. b. Detroit

*Get particulars from the*

## Ford Motor Co., Detroit

*The*
# PENALTY OF LEADERSHIP

IN every field of human endeavor, he that is first must perpetually live in the white light of publicity. ¶ Whether the leadership be vested in a man or in a manufactured product, emulation and envy are ever at work. ¶ In art, in literature, in music, in industry, the reward and the punishment are always the same. ¶ The reward is widespread recognition; the punishment, fierce denial and detraction. ¶ When a man's work becomes a standard for the whole world, it also becomes a target for the shafts of the envious few. ¶ If his work be merely mediocre, he will be left severely alone—if he achieve a masterpiece, it will set a million tongues a-wagging. ¶ Jealousy does not protrude its forked tongue at the artist who produces a commonplace painting. ¶ Whatsoever you write, or paint, or play, or sing, or build, no one will strive to surpass or to slander you, unless your work be stamped with the seal of genius. ¶ Long, long after a great work, or a good work, has been done, those who are disappointed or envious, continue to cry out that it can not be done. ¶ Spiteful little voices in the domain of art were raised against our own Whistler as a mountebank, long after the big world had acclaimed him its greatest artistic genius. ¶ Multitudes flocked to Bayreuth to worship at the musical shrine of Wagner, while the little group of those whom he had dethroned and displaced, argued angrily that he was no musician at all. ¶ The little world continued to protest that Fulton could never build a steamboat, while the big world flocked to the river banks to see his boat steam by. ¶ The leader is assailed because he is a leader, and the effort to equal him is merely added proof of that leadership. ¶ Failing to equal or to excel, the follower seeks to depreciate and to destroy—but only confirms once more the superiority of that which he strives to supplant. ¶ There is nothing new in this. ¶ It is as old as the world and as old as the human passions—envy, fear, greed, ambition, and the desire to surpass. ¶ And it all avails nothing. ¶ If the leader truly leads, he remains—the leader. ¶ Master-poet, master-painter, master-workman, each in his turn is assailed, and each holds his laurels through the ages. ¶ That which is good or great makes itself known, no matter how loud the clamor of denial. ¶ That which deserves to live—lives.

Cadillac Motor Car Co. Detroit, Mich.

Automobile advertising probably reached its peak of interest in the decade from 1915 to 1925. Copy ranged from the dignified Rolls-Royce advertisement (1920) at the right to the starkly simple Ford advertisement (1915) on the opposite page. The Rolls-Royce advertisement was drawn by T. M. Cleland, but it does not even hint at selling an automobile. The one below appeared in 1922 and actually mentions price. The Duratex advertisement (1917) shows how a supplier could take pride in cars using his material.

At the top of the opposite page is an illustration which appeared in 1915. Manufacturers often had people drawn slightly smaller than life-size in order to make their cars seem larger. But here the occupants look like midgets.

When Cadillac brought out its first V8 in 1915, it published its celebrated "Penalty of Leadership" advertisement. An even more celebrated advertisement appeared in the mid-1920's for the Jordan Playboy, which read in part: "Somewhere west of Laramie there's a broncho-busting, steer-roping girl who knows what I'm talking about. She can tell what a sassy pony, that's a cross between greased lightning and the place where it hits, can do with 1100 lbs. of steel and action when he's going high, wide and handsome. . . . The Playboy was built for her . . . Step into the Playboy . . . Then start for the land of real living with the spirit of the lass who rides, lean and rangy, into the red horizon of a Wyoming twilight."

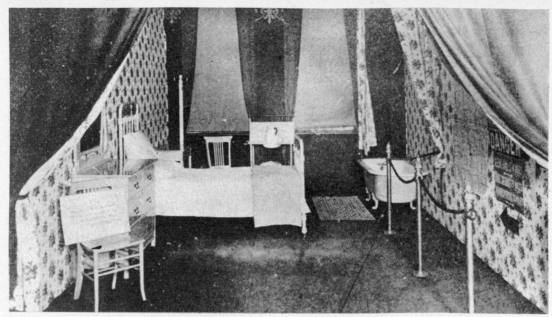

This was set up in 1907 to show how an ideal hotel bedroom should look

# FROM HOTEL TO MOTEL

When the automobile first arrived on the scene, America had many small hotels — mostly of indifferent quality, but nearly all were located close to railroad stations. As motorists opened up the country, the need for more accommodations kept increasing. Farmers and gas-station owners began building small, crude bungalows to house the traveling hordes. They soon found that many motorists would gladly pay well for a comfortable room but would turn down a poor one.

Then the motel (motor + hotel) began to flourish. More and more elegant ones were built until they began to make the older downtown hotels look shabby and out of date.

Motorists discovered that they could usually find better accommodations along the road than they could in towns or cities—and they did not have to worry about garaging their cars overnight.

Huge sums of money were invested in building elaborate motels along well-traveled routes and in popular resorts. The well-established older hotels, in order to meet the growing competition, were forced to renovate and improve, so the motorist benefited all around.

And the trailer, which had begun as a homemade affair, went professional and grew larger and larger and more luxurious, until it truly became a comfortable home on wheels.

One of the better-grade roadside inns where the early motorist could stay overnight (1904)

The sides of this trailer dropped down to make two canvas-covered sleeping compartments for four people (1920)

A really early home on wheels — heated, too (1909)

The car doubled as a dressing room in 1923

A swanky modern motel in Key West, Fla., complete with swimming pool and air conditioning (1953)

An early picture of motor camping. The smoky fire doubtless added to everyone's enjoyment (1909)

# AUTOMOBILE CAMPING

Americans have always been fond of the outdoors, so it can hardly be said that the automobile introduced them to life in the open air. But it did extend their range. Camping and picnicking grounds that were hopelessly out of reach for horse-drawn vehicles were only a relatively short run even for the low-speed cars that were in use in the early days.

Over the years the American people kept going farther and farther afield. Great National Parks that had previously been almost inaccessible for recreational purposes became easy to reach, and new ones were opened up. Because of the automobile, fishing and hunting grew even more popular with millions of people; lonely stretches of ocean beach were developed; and skiing became a widely followed winter sport.

Since people who go camping are likely to be a pretty hardy lot, handy with tools, and readily inventive, they soon found that the automobile was especially useful to them. Some of them went far beyond just making the family car do. They built special vehicles to hold their gear and to serve as shelters in which they could sleep. From these first primitive attempts the modern auto trailer evolved. (About 2,000,000 Americans now live more or less permanently in trailers.)

But the equipment used in automobile camping and picnicking has changed remarkably little. Even before any special devices were developed, clever motorists constructed special boxes, trunks, and hampers to carry camping and picnicking gear.

The car shown at the upper right of the opposite page simply has a big trunk fastened on the back, while a large umbrella is placed over the driver for protection against sun and rain. This was in 1905, when the automobile itself was still rather primitive, but the equipment in the trunk would serve perfectly well today. It consisted of aluminum utensils for four people, a folding camp stove, folding camp stools, and a large skillet into which a long wooden handle could be thrust for use over an open fire.

To the left of this picture is shown an early two-piece portable boat for fishermen. It was made of pressed steel and had flotation chambers to make it unsinkable.

However, it is not only camping and picnicking which has made the automobile so essential a recreational adjunct to millions of Americans; even more important is the use of the family car for week-ends and vacations. Instead of sitting home and snapping at one another during hot summer days, people can go outdoors and enjoy themselves.

A pioneer camper with his own trunk (1905)

A pioneer portable boat built in St. Cloud, Minn. (1906)

Fits in like a tool bag.

## Automobiling and "Evinruding" Too

When you start out on an Auto trip, assure yourself of the keenest adjunct to the sport by placing an

### EVINRUDE
DETACHABLE ROW-BOAT-MOTOR

in a corner of the car. It takes up very little room and fits in right under your feet without inconvenience. When you arrive at a lake, river or bay you can attach it in less than one minute to the first row-boat you see, even a rented one. The motor weighs but fifty pounds and is carried in a canvas case just like a satchel.

### NO AUTO COMPLETE WITHOUT IT

and the dash through the water in a motor-driven rowboat is a pleasure that is open to automobilists on every water that they visit as they can take their "power of a motor boat" right with them.

Illustrated catalog will be mailed to all who request it.

### EVINRUDE MOTOR COMPANY
**251-T Street,     Milwaukee, Wis.**
Members of Nat'l Ass'n of Engine & Boat Mfgrs.

New York City Show Room, Hudson Terminal Bldg., 30 Church Street.

Carries like a satchel.

This advertisement for an outboard motor appeared in Motor in the spring of 1913, but outboards began long before that—even before the turn of the century

What you could expect to find in the side hamper of a 1905 auto

Make your car a Traveling Hotel with the

## McMILLIN AUTO BED

Not a Hammock but a roomy, comfortable spring bed for two. Stows under the back seat in compact 12-lb. bundle, when not in use.

Note small size of Mc-Millin bed on running board.

### Price $7.50
(1916)

For Ford Cars; Other Medium Size Cars $8.50.  Give Name and Model of Car when ordering by telegraph

McMillin Auto Bed in Camp

Tourists Auto Tents $8.50 and $10.50 for camping de luxe.  Money-back guarantee on bed or tents if not satisfactory, or sent C. O. D. subject to three days' examination.

Send Today for Free Illustrated Booklet on Auto Camping.

## AUTO BED COMPANY
P.O. Box 7-M    Bellingham, Wash.

A large percentage of our inquiries and orders are coming from physicians.  They know the health benefits of outdoor life.

Luncheon a la Motor Carte—French picnicking equipment (1914)

# CAMPING
# AND
# PICNICKING

Not only did all kinds of people take to motor camping and picnicking, but as time went on they devised more and more ingenious devices to make life easier and pleasanter. From tin ovens that were heated by the exhaust to de luxe picnic equipment, the search for better living continued. Most of the equipment was home made.

Mr. and Mrs. Albert Seaman of New York covered 4278 miles in a 1910 Franklin and carried balloon-silk tents

This is an automobile oven invented by Mr. J. I. Wernette, a Grand Rapids manufacturer of heating and power-plant equipment. It consisted of a tin box lined with heavy asbestos and was so fixed that the exhaust manifold passed through it. Potatoes could be baked in this novel oven while the car was running (1917)

A picnic tender with refrigerator, stove, and folding table (1909)

A family outing in a Velie 48. The men's vests add a refined touch (1921)

Speaker Cannon's daughters in their Pope-Toledo (1904)

Chauncey Depew in a curved-dash Oldsmobile (1905)

Mark Twain enjoyed motoring too (1906)

Sir Thomas Lipton as a motorist (1903)

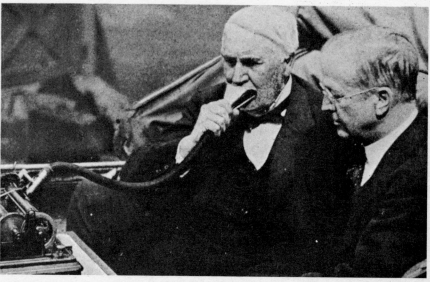

Thomas Edison dictating in Arthur Brisbane's Owen Magnetic (1916)

King Alfonso of Spain at the wheel of his specially designed sports car (1921)

## CELEBRITIES AND THEIR CARS

The fact that wealthy, distinguished, and highly placed people quickly took to motoring helped to establish the automobile at an early date. The common fear of the new contraption was allayed, and, as automobiles became more and more frequently seen on streets and highways, the public gradually began to get used to them. It was only a step from that for each family to want one for its own use. Thus it may be said that kings and emperors paved the way for the Model T Ford and for the many other popularly priced, mass-produced cars that followed it.

King Edward VII of England en route to Highcliffe (1904)

Kaiser Wilhelm of Germany entering his Mercedes (1910)

George V of England alighting from his English Daimler (1910)

President McKinley
in an early motor car

# OUR MOTORING PRESIDENTS

Calvin Coolidge, who characteristically never
wanted to go more than 15 to 18 mph

Theodore Roosevelt at the wheel of his own car.
He was the first President to learn to drive

President Taft liked motoring, but he
was always driven by a chauffeur

Woodrow Wilson photographed at the wheel while
he was still president of Princeton University

President Harding arriving at the Capitol for his inauguration. Beside him is Senator Knox of Pennsylvania; to his left is Uncle Joe Cannon of Illinois. Ex-President Wilson can be seen in the tonneau of the touring car to the right (1921)

The White House garage as it looked in 1916, when Woodrow Wilson was President. Three big Pierce Arrows are shown, but Mrs. Wilson had an electric car which she drove herself

Franklin Delano Roosevelt at the wheel of the Plymouth which had special controls so he could drive it by using only his hands. This photograph was taken at Warm Springs in 1934

Marilyn Miller (1919)

Billie Burke (1916)

# STARS OF BROADWAY AND HOLLYWOOD TOOK EAGERLY TO THE AUTOMOBILE

Ann Pennington (1919)

The Gish Sisters (1916)

Hazel Dawn (1919)

Pearl White (1916)

Julia Marlowe and her early electric buggy

Lady Ashburton of Floradora fame in her early Franklin

Rube Goldberg, the cartoonist who created complicated and useless inventions, with his custom-built Lancia (1920)

Douglas Fairbanks and Charlie Chaplin drive a motor buckboard down one of Hollywood's boulevards (1919)

Fatty Arbuckle, the movie comedian, in his custom-built Pierce-Arrow which cost more than $25,000 (1920)

Waiting for the starting signal (1906)

# THE EARLY TOURS

The owners of the early automobiles were drawn together by their common interest. They formed groups, joined clubs, and organized joint tours. Prime mover among them was Charles Glidden, a wealthy Boston paint manufacturer who won the A.A.A. tour from New York to St. Louis in 1904. His victory made him an enthusiastic motorist for life. He sponsored tours for other motorists until his name practically became synonymous with group traveling by car.

But Glidden was not the only one who organized tours. Even before his first connection with them, the New York Automobile Club had brought together the vast concourse of really early specimens shown below. Notice especially the quadricycle in the extreme left foreground. It is a hybrid between bicycle and automobile, with a folding seat for an extra passenger to ride in front. Most of the cars have exposed radiators for the motors mounted under the seats.

The Peerless shown at the bottom of the opposite page had just completed a Glidden tour of 1200 miles. The average last day's run was 124 miles at 20 mph. The three White Steamers shown above it were photographed on the St. Louis Tour which Charles Glidden won. Nine Whites entered the tour; all of them completed it.

The New York Automobile Club held a morning run to Travers Island on April 6, 1902

Americans touring in the fall or in early spring (1904)

White steam cars in the St. Louis tour (1904)

Touring from Guttenberg, N. J., Sept. 1900

A 1906 Model 14 Peerless on a Glidden tour.

A run of the Buffalo Automobile Club (1903)

Two young San Francisco chauffeuses (1905)

# CHILDREN AND AUTOMOBILES

One of the most amazing things about the early days of the automobile is the fact that people seemed to think that cars were toys to be entrusted to children. It is true that speeds were low then and that traffic was light, but just the same an enormous amount of risk was involved.

George Gould, Jr. probably maneuvered his miniature electric runabout around the grounds of his family's private estate, but ten-year-old Theron Curtis (opposite page) was allowed to drive on the public highways. He held a Massachusetts driver's license only because the state hadn't yet gotten around to setting an age limit for this privilege. The three pictures below show children playing at driving.

Finding out how it works (1904)

Ready to crank up (1904)

Ready to go (1904)

George J. Gould, Jr. driving his own electric runabout (1903)

Theron Curtis, aged ten, of North Attleboro, Mass. had a driver's license (1903)

A five-year-old drives his 4-hp specially built racer (1913)

A fifteen-year-old drives a racer in Detroit (1914)

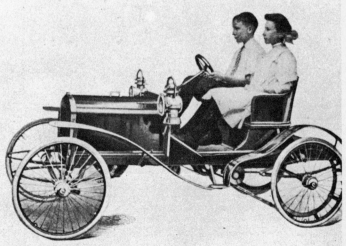

# FOR YOUR BOY

## A REAL MOTOR CAR

### BrowniekaR

## PRICE $150.00

A pleasure worth while for the youth—because instructive as well as healthful recreation.

## OMAR MOTOR COMPANY

### 29 Seigrist Street

NEWARK - - - - - - NEW YORK

You didn't have to build a car for your child, you could buy one ready made (1908)

Mrs. Alexander Pantages of Seattle at the wheel of her powerful Winton Six-Teen-Six Runabout (1908)

# WOMEN AND AUTOMOBILES

Many people have the erroneous idea that women were hostile to the early automobile. Actually, this was not so; they simply had trouble cranking the heavy engines. But they delighted in being passengers. Some of them, who could afford it, drove electric cars, which were easy to operate. And a few were hardy enough to master the gasoline-powered cars of the day, although they naturally tried to get a man to crank the motor whenever they could. Sometimes they even used their charms and appealed to strangers to turn the engine over for them.

One of the feminine pioneers in American automobiling was Theodore Roosevelt's daughter Alice (see opposite page). *Motor,* writing about her in its January 1904 issue, said: ". . . it needed only this edict from the White House completely to establish [the sport] among those whose puritanical scruples had kept them reluctant, lest in some occult manner this masculine pleasure should reflect against them.

"Washington was quite won over to the sport when Miss Roosevelt and her 'chum,' Miss Rose Wallach, showed their enthusiasm by an open indulgence of swift spins along the broad streets, whirling over country by-ways, and—whisper it, lest the vigilant ears of our pompous magistrates hear—stealthily speeding under the friendly protection of overhanging trees and dense foliage."

A lady shows her delight in automobiling (1904)

Sometimes they even drove in winter (1904)

Mlle. Chiquita and her midget car in Paris (1904)

Smith College students have their picture taken (1904)

Marguerite de Cassini, the Russian Ambassador's daughter (1903)

Miss Alice Roosevelt and Miss Sears at Newport (1903)

Most society women had chauffeurs (1910)

Will you ride with me—oh, just through the park—in my electric? (1908)

Commuters were taken to the station by chauffeurs, until women learned to drive (1908)

# THE PROTECTED AND THE UNPROTECTED

As the automobile developed, the women who had anything to do with it were divided rather sharply into two groups. The first group, which consisted of wealthy society women, had no mechanical worries. They either had chauffeurs to do the actual driving or they drove beautifully appointed cars which were turned over to them each day in perfect condition. Many of them favored the electric runabout.

At the same time, women without much money were taking to the automobile. They naturally had to learn as they went. But before long, they were doing very well and were even driving from coast to coast. In its September 1923 issue, *Motor* could say about them: "A few years ago to see women traveling alone across the continent driving their own cars was as novel a sight as to see a flapper nowadays without bobbed hair and sore-looking eyebrows. It was considered a very daring undertaking, if not a bit devilish. Certainly a very sporting thing to do; while this year there are so many women driving their own cars from the Atlantic to the Pacific coast that enterprising automobile clubs, gas stations, and tavern keepers throughout the Far West are making special plans for the handling of this class of motorist."

As time went on, women not only learned to drive; some even managed to change tires and take care of their cars. They also went off on exploring tours by themselves. These pictures, taken between 1914 and 1924, show women's gradual emancipation.

A steam car with machine gun in Washington (1900)

A Duryea with a Colt machine gun (1899)

An Austrian armor-clad car (1906)

The same car on the open road

French army officers in an "Auto de Guerre" (1903)

The British Pennington Fighting Autocar (1896)

# THE AUTOMOBILE IN WARTIME

Almost as soon as the first automobiles began to move around under their own power, military men saw the enormous advantage they would have over horses. Horses had long been a problem to the armies of the world. They not only had to be fed every day, whether used or not, but they also got tired, sick, disabled, and wounded. And sometimes in the heat of battle they became frightened and ran away.

In 1896, the British built the Pennington Fighting Autocar shown above. It was an armored vehicle mounting two swiveled machine guns. (The machine gun is of early origin; one type, known as the Gatling gun, was in use during the American Civil War.)

Military men in the United States also became interested in the automobile for wartime use. Colonel Davidson, who was a Major in the Illinois National Guard in the early 1890's, had organized a military cycle corps at the Northwestern Military Academy which, at that time, was located in Highland Park, Ill. He outfitted his cadets with rifles and shoulder packs and took them on long bicycle trips in order to demonstrate their value as a mobile military unit. He also organized a cycle corps of 100 men which was to be sent to Cuba to serve in the Spanish-American War. But the war ended before the Major and his men could sail.

The two gun carriers shown at the top of the opposite page were designed by Major Davidson. They were steam-operated, and one of them was driven under its own power from Chicago to Washington, where it was photographed in front of the Capitol.

Colonel Davidson also designed and built two mobile weapons that were precursors of our modern anti-aircraft gun carriers. They were built in 1910 and had Colt machine guns mounted on ball-and-socket joints so the guns could be swung quickly in any direction.

In 1914, Davidson built an armored car, but eight years before that, the Austrian armored car shown on the opposite page had been put through maneuvers. Its dome-shaped top mounted a machine gun which could turn a full circle.

Even before the First World War the automobile was serving in actual combat in Mexico. There, a tripod-mounted machine gun was placed on a touring-car seat and taken into battle as an effective mobile unit in the sanguinary local wars.

For wartime use the automobile began as a gun carrier; as time went on, more and more armor and heavier guns were added until the modern tank evolved out of the early primitive armored car.

A French motor convoy near Verdun (1916)

Despite the mechanization of armies, manpower was useful

A Cadillac armored car with a Colt automatic gun (1914)

An armored car in the New York National Guard (1916)

# THE AUTOMOBILE IN THE FIRST WORLD WAR

From 1914 to 1918, the automobile for military use came into its own. Great convoys of trucks carried men and munitions to the front, and at the very beginning of the war, when the German general Von Kluck was launching his swift drive on Paris, the taxis of the city were pressed into service to transport men of the French Seventh Infantry Division to the battle line. In 1923, one of the taxis that had saved the city was presented to the Hotel des Invalides.

America's entry into the war acted as a tremendous impetus to the automobile industry in the United States. The already huge automobile factories in Detroit and the Middle West worked overtime to supply trucks, ambulances, and tanks. And these same automobile factories were used to make thousands of other mechanical devices for the army. So many trucks were sent to France that thousands of them were declared surplus at the end of the war and were sold to the French government for a fraction of their value.

It was in this war that the tank was first employed as a military weapon. When the first British tanks lumbered across the battlefield, easily making their way over shell craters and open trenches, they seemed absolutely impregnable to the frightened German infantrymen who helplessly watched them advance. But counter weapons were soon invented, and the battle of one tank against another began.

One of the first pictures to be published in America of the history-making British tank of 1916

Some horses had been used in the First World War. But except for use in occasional mountain fighting, emergency service, or combat in extremely remote and primitive sections, they played no part in the highly mechanized Second World War. In this war, millions of young men in the various armies of the world received intensive training in the handling and care of power-driven vehicles. On land, on the sea, and in the air, all kinds of rapidly moving objects carried men and supplies from one place to another. Some of them had wings, others were boats, and still others moved on wheels or tracks. But they all had one thing in common -- they were all powered by the internal-combustion engine. But even during this war new means of propulsion were coming into use. The jet engine can be called an internal-combustion engine because it depends upon the combustion of fuel and air taking place inside the engine, but the power it develops does not have to be applied through drive shafts and gearing arrangements. It works direct. Rocket propulsion, however, is entirely different. It does not need ground, water, or air as a medium to operate in, and so can be used to drive vehicles even through airless outer space.

# THE AUTOMOBILE IN THE SECOND WORLD WAR

A big brother of the automobile

A scout car with rubber tracks (1941)

A scout car mounting two machine guns (1941)

The famous jeep shows what it can do (1943)

An anti-aircraft gun on wheels (1941)

A modern truck convoy (1942)

This seagoing jeep is a Ford-built amphibian that uses the same power and steering on land or water (1943)

This was a common sight in any large city in 1908

# THE PASSING OF THE HORSE

The cry "get a horse!" taunted the early motorist everywhere he went. Laws were passed to prevent him from frightening horses when he passed them. But as time went on, and as automobiles increased in number, it began to be evident that the horse was doomed as a major source of power for American transportation.

Thomas Edison once said: "The horse is the poorest motor ever made. He consumes ten pounds of fuel for every hour he works, and yet his thermal efficiency is only two per cent."

In September 1917 *Motor* said: "Even when plentifully supplied with feed, the horse soon tires and must rest at least three times the length of time he spends in actual work. The average farm horse, as government reports attest, works but 3½ hours daily and requires 27 minutes of human labor for his care a day."

In this same article it was pointed out that in 1917 there were 29,224,000 horses and mules in the United States. Three acres were then required for raising enough food to feed each animal, whereas only two and one-half acres were needed to supply a human being. This vast herd of horses was therefore consuming enough food to sustain thirty-six million more people. Also, it takes three years to raise and

train a horse for work—a period during which he is largely non-productive.

In a still earlier article (June 1913), *Motor* said: "There is still another evidence of the horse's wanton wastefulness and that is his reprehensible eagerness to die."

But the passing of the horse, oddly enough, was a good thing for all concerned, for both animals and men profited from the horse's being practically eliminated from city streets. The city horse led a miserable life; he was heavily overworked, and often badly treated. Spavined and sway-backed, he came to an unhappy end, and his carcass was then toted off to be transformed into fertilizer and glue.

The horse-and-mule population of the United States is now about one-quarter of what it was in 1917, but our animals are much happier than their ancestors were. Their numbers are dwindling yearly as the automobile takes over their work functions. Before long, the horse will no longer be used as a beast of burden in America. He will then be raised only for sport or pleasure, so he will be cared for with loving attention. The automobile he once shied at has finally proved to be his benefactor. Its iron muscles untiringly do the work of the world, while it leaves him and his master free to enjoy themselves in leisure-time activities.

# Good Bye to the Horse

**The gasolene car never took the horse's place—it created a field of its own.**

The electric car is the one to compare directly with the horse—and the horse can't stand the comparison. Wherever the Electric is introduced it's "good bye to the horse."

**Hundreds of delightful little tours, excursions and outings, beyond the horse's strength and speed, are always at command if you own an Electric Vehicle. For city traffic or suburb driving it is in a class by itself.**

A lady can drive an Electric in white suede gloves; she steps from her Electric into the theatre, the shop, the house of her friend or into Church looking as fresh and exquisitely dainty as when she made her toilette.

What delightful treats lie in store for the friends of that woman who owns an Electric. Could there be a better method of paying social scores or setting the pace? Fresh air outings—health and rest for tired nerves.

## Why the Electric Car is so Simple

### Electricity is Stored in the "Exide" Battery

Therefore there are no complications to the Electric car. Your power has been manufactured for you and stored in the "Exide" Battery. This is done at the garage, at the electric power house or at your own home. You don't have to bother with mechanic or chauffeur.

Ask any of these vehicle makers or their agents to supply you with the "Exide" Battery. They all make good electric vehicles; some for pleasure, some for business, some make both. All supply the "Exide" Battery.

Baker Motor Vehicle Co.,
Broc Carriage & Wagon Co.,
Columbus Buggy Co.,
Champion Wagon Co.,

Couple Gear Freight Wheel Co.
Electric Vehicle Co.,
General Vehicle Co.,
C. P. Kimball & Co.,
Rauch & Lang Carriage Co.,

Studebaker Automobile Co.,
The Anderson Carriage Co.,
The Waverley Co.,
Woods Motor Vehicle Co.

### Over 90% of all Electric Vehicles made use the "Exide" BATTERY

# THE ELECTRIC STORAGE BATTERY CO.
### PHILADELPHIA, PA.

A horse takes a look at his successor (1909)

# AUCTION
## 52 HORSES — 15 WAGONS

TWENTY OF THE FIFTY HEAD OF HEAVY HORSES

## SATURDAY, JAN., 31, at 10 a.m.

In Our Stable Yard 1920 North Main Street, We Will Sell All Our Horse Equipment, Consisting of the Following:

50 Head of Heavy Draft Horses
2 Light Carriage Horses
5 Two-Horse Platform Wagons with Stakes
1 Three-Horse " " " "
5 Keg Wagons
5 One-Horse Wagons, Express Bodies
5 Buggies
7 Double Heavy Team Harnesses
5 Single " Harnesses
5 Single Buggy Harnesses

The above will positively be sold to the highest bidder, as we have purchased a complete fleet of White Gasoline Trucks from the Pioneer Commercial Auto Company, Alameda at Main Street.

TERMS: 2 per cent Cash — Secured Paper Six Months at 7 per cent

## Los Angeles Brewing Company
### 1920 North Main Street,      Los Angeles

A brewing company changes from horses to motor trucks (1914)

Fifth Avenue in 1900 with one automobile in sight

Trucks—horse-drawn and motorized (1904)

Delivery wagons, horse-drawn and motor-powered (1904)

A millionaire's garage in 1913. C. K. G. Billings' estate, Fort Tryon Hall in upper New York City

The repair shop in the Billings garage

The tire room in the Billings garage

# GARAGES FOR RICH AND POOR

When automobiles first appeared on the American scene, they were kept in carriage houses, barns, and stables. Many such old buildings shelter automobiles to this day.

But as time went on, special quarters had to be designed for the automobile. Those who had plenty of money led the way by having elaborate garages built complete with repair shops, tire-storage rooms, and special equipment which the average person could not afford. The Billings garage shown above housed about twenty cars. Six chauffeurs and four helpers were kept on the payroll.

When the Payne Whitney estate was appraised in 1928, part of the assets were 29 automobiles, valued as follows:

| | | | |
|---|---|---|---|
| 1921 Rolls-Royce | $3000 | 1926 Lincoln | $3600 |
| 1920 Rolls-Royce | 3500 | 1926 Stutz | 2000 |
| 1925 Lincoln | 2500 | 1926 Reo | 800 |
| 1915 Rolls-Royce | 750 | 1916 Ford | 60 |
| 1920 Rolls-Royce | 2500 | 1922 White truck | 400 |
| 1914 Crane | 100 | 1924 Lincoln | 1200 |
| 1924 Lincoln | 1800 | 1925 Nash | 400 |
| 1925 Nash | 400 | 1925 Nash | 700 |
| 1925 Nash | 750 | 1927 Nash | 1100 |
| 1922 Ford | 25 | 1926 Lincoln | 2800 |
| 1922 Packard van | 1000 | 1926 Reo | 1300 |
| 1918 Packard | 100 | 1926 Nash | 1000 |
| Nash | 1200 | 1927 Ford | 450 |
| 1926 Ford | 300 | 1925 Buick | 750 |
| | | 1926 Nash | 1500 |

The two middle-class garages on the opposite page show how little this type of construction has changed.

The line-up of cars in another millionaire's garage (1904)

The line-up of cars in the Billings garage (1913)

Some of the cars from the garage shown above (1904)

A middle-class garage (1906)

The machine shop in the garage shown above (1904)

Another middle-class garage (1906)

A well-equipped garage in Plainfield, N. J. (1909)

A turntable on which you could swing your car around (1909)

The world's first fatal automobile accident. Scott Russell's steam carriage blows up on the road near Glasgow, killing five people (1834)

# ACCIDENTS, COLLISIONS, AND WRECKS

Railroads and then the automobile have opened up the modern world so that practically every part of it is easily accessible. Mechanized transportation has been a potent civilizing force, but like every great benefit, it has had its price. From the very first fatal accident of 1834, automobiles have killed and injured several million people. But it was not the automobile that was to blame. It is a responsive mechanism subject to its driver's control. By itself, an automobile has never hurt anyone. But in the hands of reckless, irresponsible, drowsy, drunken, or careless drivers, it is a juggernaut.

The modern car is about as safe and foolproof as any mechanism can be, but vigilant maintenance and plain common sense are needed to handle it. The fault now lies not with the automobile, but with its human masters. To remedy it, they must build better and safer highways, teach their teen-agers the responsibilities of driving, and see to it that their cars are always in the prime condition required for the proper operation of any machine. A British expert has said: "A driver must be good enough to deal with any situation, admitting no excuse for failure."

This Packard was wrecked in 1904 when its lights went out

An unhappy street scene in New Jersey (1917)

New York traffic on 42 Street between Fifth and Sixth Avenues in 1917. Look closely and you will see several horse-drawn vehicles

# THE TRAFFIC PROBLEM

Ever since the Model T got started in 1908, American automobiles have bred like rabbits. No matter how fast traffic improvements are made, there are always more cars ready to run on the new streets The problem is at its worst in the older cities of the nation, where the streets were planned for pedestrian and light horse-drawn traffic. Because of high real-estate values, most of these streets are still as narrow as they were when they were first laid down. In the business areas of cities like New York, Philadelphia, Boston, and Baltimore traffic congestion is a nightmare, and parking—

even when you are willing to pay for it—is often impossible.

Oddly enough, the present-day program of building super-highways merely adds to the problem of traffic congestion in the cities, because the new highways bring more cars into areas which have remained fixed in capacity for years.

The problem can be solved only by spending billions of dollars—or perhaps, by tearing down our cities and rebuilding our civilization in small, widely scattered centers where not only our automobiles, but our people will have space enough to move about freely.

Even one-way streets don't help much in rush hours

The parking problem: where to put them when you don't want them

A traffic cop on Fifth Avenue in 1913 when the long lines of cars were beginning to thicken

A really early cop-and-driver picture (1904). They look like twins!

Perhaps they got the idea for the Keystone cops from this (1906)

The automobile carries no lamps, but it is broad daylight. The policeman is probably warning them to be home before dark (1906)

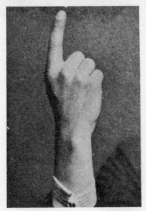 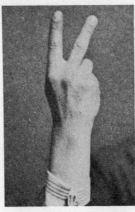 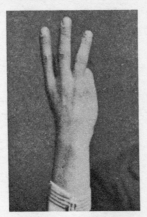 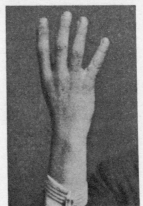 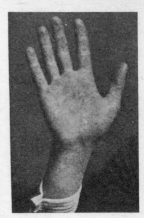

In 1920, someone proposed this elaborate system of sign language for motorists. See below for explanation

## THE TRAFFIC COP FRIEND OR ENEMY?

Almost as soon as motoring began, the driver learned to look apprehensively over his shoulder for a possible pursuing policeman. It was this threat of arrest, often justified, but sometimes run as a sort of legal racket by small towns, that made the average motorist look upon the traffic cop as his natural enemy. Yet he is an essential part of modern traffic control. His is a lonely, thankless job, particularly when he has to stand all day on his feet in rain, storm, or burning sunlight. Except for his immediate superiors, nobody appreciates him, and every driver who passes by looks at him with the suspicion long bred in motorists.

*Explanation of the hand signals shown above:* (reading from left to right) 1. You have a flat shoe. 2. Stop and inspect your car. 3. Am I on the best road to the next town? 4. Look out; danger ahead. 5. I'm in trouble. Please stop and help. *Editor's note:* The signals were never adopted.

Signal lights for New York traffic cops (1921)

Bridgeport, Conn., traffic cops wore white belts so they could be seen (1921)

In 1912 the Detroit Police Department bought a Regal roadster which could do 60 mph

A farmer scraped a dirt road with a horse drag . . .

Now there are too many cars for ordinary roads

Then tar was spread on it from a sprinkler . . .

And you had an elegant paved road like this

More super-highways like this New Jersey one are needed

The traffic problem was simple then

# ROADS AND STREETS

In its November 1952 issue *Motor* said: "After the Second World War, a top authority in the automobile industry estimated that by 1960 vehicle registrations would hit 45,000,000. This proved ten years too conservative because there were 45,000,000 vehicles registered in 1950. The same expert then predicted 53,000,000 registrations by 1960. This time, his forecast was eight years too conservative.

"The most authentic guess about the future of motor vehicle registrations came recently from the President's Materials Policy Commission — 85,000,000 vehicles by 1975. Yet there has been no real highway building boom for thirty years. The average road surface is twelve years old, and the age of the average roadbed is seventeen years."

All this points to the need for more and better highways and for a radically new approach to the handling of traffic on narrow, obsolete city streets. In the early days of the automobile, roads could be considered paved when they had a layer of tar poured over their dirt surface. But life is no longer so simple, and the problem now will have to be tackled from a national point of view so far as major arterial highways are concerned, and from a local point of view for traffic leading into and through tens of thousands of villages, towns, and cities.

It is estimated that more than 40,000 communities are without train or plane service and so are completely dependent upon cars, trucks, and buses for transportation. Three-quarters of all traveling between cities, towns, and farms is by car or bus, and two-thirds of our freight is moved by truck at least part of the way. All this makes our obsolete highway system national and local problems of first magnitude. Unless something is done about this problem soon and in a big way, the automobile must inevitably continue to choke up our roads and streets.

Cars choke urban streets everywhere . . .

Except in towns built for the automobile age

In those days you had to have your license plate made to order

# STATE MOTOR CAR LAWS IN 1906

*In its February 1906 issue,* Motor *summarized the motor-car laws of 35 states—all that then presumably had any legislation dealing with the automobile.*

ALABAMA. Registration: probate judge of resident county. Fee: 25¢. Numbers: none required. Lamps: no mention. Speeds: 8mph throughout state. 4mph at dams and causeways not over 20 feet wide.

CALIFORNIA. Registration: Secretary of State. Fee: $2. Numbers: 3 in. high at rear with abbr. name of state at least 1 in. high. Lamps: 2 white front lights with number; 1 red rear light. Speeds: reasonable; 10mph populated districts; 15mph other incorp. municipalities; 4mph at dams, bridges, sharp curves, and steep descents; 20mph elsewhere.

CONNECTICUT. Registration: Sec'y of State. Fee: $1. Numbers: 4 in. high with initials of state front and rear. Lamps: none required. Speeds: reasonable; 12mph in cities; 15mph in country.

DELAWARE. Registration: Sec'y of State. Fee: $2. Numbers: 3 in. high at rear. Lamps: 2 white front lights; 1 red rear light showing number. Speed: reasonable; 4-7mph cities, towns, etc.; 10mph sharp curves and intersections in open country; 20 mph elsewhere.

DISTRICT OF COLUMBIA. Registration: Board of Examiners. Fee: none. Numbers: 3 in. high at rear, initials D.C. at least 1 in. high. Lamps: 2 in front at sides and 1 red and white rear, 1 hour before sunrise and 1 hour after sunset. Speeds: 4mph corner turns in city; 6mph at cross streets with car tracks; 12mph if no car tracks; 15mph in country.

FLORIDA. Sec'y of State. Fee: $2. Numbers: 3 x 2 in. at rear; must carry certificate. Lamps: 2 between sunset and sunrise. Speeds: reasonable except 4mph at sharp curves, bridges, fills, and intersections.

ILLINOIS. Registration: no state provision, consult local authorities. Fees: no provision. Numbers: no provision. Lamps: no provision. Speeds: 15mph subject to local laws.

INDIANA. Registration: Sec'y of State. Fee: $1. Numbers: 4 in. high at rear; abbr. state name 2 in. high. Lamps: no provision. Speeds: reasonable; 8mph in built-up sections; 15mph other parts of municipalities; 20mph elsewhere.

IOWA. Registration: Sec'y of State. Fee: $1. Numbers: 3 in. high with initials of state at rear at least 2 in. high. Lamps: at least 1 front white, 1 red rear. Speeds: reasonable; 10mph built-up sections; 15mph thinly built-up sections; 20mph country.

KANSAS. Registration: no state provision, consult local authorities. Fee: no provision. Numbers: no provision. Lamps: at least 1 white light 1 hour after sunset to 1 hour before sunrise. Speeds: reasonable; 10mph pop. districts; 20mph elsewhere.

KENTUCKY. Registration: no state provision, consult local authorities. Fee: no provision. Numbers: no provision. Lamps: front white light and red rear when necessary before sunrise and after sunset. Speed: reasonable; 15mph except 6mph at crossings, bridges, curves, and descents.

MAINE. Registration: Sec'y of State furnishes 2 number plates. Fees: $2. Numbers: 4 in. high; word "Maine" 1 in. high front and rear. Lamps: lighted lamp 1 hour after sunset and 1 hour before sunrise. Speeds: reasonable; 8mph in cities, towns, etc. unless greater speed is permitted; 15mph elsewhere.

MARYLAND. Registration: Sec'y of State. Fee: $1. Numbers: 3 in. high in conspicuous place. Lamps: 2 white front lights, 1 red rear. Speeds: 10mph except 6mph at sharp curves, intersections of prominent crossroads in open country, and highways passing through built-up portions of a city.

MASSACHUSETTS. Registration: Mass. Highway Commission furnishes license for operator and registers cars. Certificates must be carried. Fees: $2 for registration; $2 for license; 50¢ for renewal. Private operator's license continued indefinitely; chauffeur's license good for 1 year. Numbers: 1 front and 1 rear 4 in. high. Lamps: 1 white light each side showing number. Speeds: reasonable; 10mph in cities; 15mph in country; 8mph at curves and intersections.

MICHIGAN. Registration: Sec'y of State issues seal and certificate. Fees: $2. Numbers: 3 in. high conspicuously displayed; name of state full or abbr. 1 in. minimum. Lamps: 2 white front lights, 1 red rear. Speeds: reasonable; 25mph except 8mph in business portions in corporate limits of cities and 15mph other portions.

MINNESOTA. Registration: State Boiler Inspector issues licenses. Fees: $2. Numbers: 4½ in. high at rear. Lamps: at least one. Speeds: 25mph except 4mph at crossings and 8mph at built-up sections.

MISSOURI. Registration: License Commissioner or County Clerk. Fees: $2 per annum. Numbers: conspicuously placed. Lamps: 2 front lamps with numbers 3 in. long. Speeds: 9mph.

MONTANA. Registration: no state provision, consult local authorities. Fees: no provision. Numbers: no provision. Lamps: no provision. Speeds: 20mph except 8mph city limits, fire districts, thickly settled, or business parts of towns.

NEBRASKA. Registration: Sec'y of State. Fees: $1. Numbers: 3 in. high at rear; initial and terminal letters of state at least 2 in. high. Lamps: 1 or more white front lights 1 hour before sunrise and 1 hour after sunset; 1 rear red light. Speeds: reasonable: 15mph in cities, towns, and villages except 10mph in built-up sections; 20mph elsewhere.

NEW HAMPSHIRE. Registration: Sec'y of State furnishes 2 number plates; certificate must be carried. Fees: registration fee $3; $1 for operator's license for 1 year. Numbers: 2 numbers 4 in. high, front and rear, followed by N. H. Lamps: 2 with number at least 1 in. high. Speeds: 20mph except 8mph in business districts, built-up sections of cities and towns.

NEW JERSEY. Registration: Sec'y of State. Fees: $1 for each car used; dealer's license fee $10. Numbers: 4 in. high front and rear. Lamps: 2 front lights with number at least 1 in. high and 1 red rear 1 hour after sunset to 1 hour before sunrise. Speeds: reasonable; 20mph.

NEW YORK. Registration: Sec'y of State. Fee: $2 for owners, chauffeurs, and manufacturers. Renewals $1 for owners and chauffeurs; 50¢ for manufacturer's duplicates. If car is sold, certificate must be returned. Numbers: 3 in. high at rear; state initials at least 1 in. high. Lamps: 2 white front lights with number at least 1 in. high; 1 red rear. Speed: reasonable; 10mph in business and built-up parts; 15mph where houses average less than 100 ft. apart; 20mph in country; 4mph at curves, bridges, and steep descents.

NORTH DAKOTA. Registration: no state provision, consult local authorities. Fees: no provision. Numbers: no provision. Lamps: at least 1 during hours of darkness. Speeds: 8mph in city or village; 15mph outside city or village; 4mph at crossing or crosswalks if person is upon same.

OHIO. Registration: no provision, consult local authorities. Fees: no provision. Numbers: no provision. Lamps: at least 1 front white light and 1 red rear light 1 hour past sunset to 1 hour before sunrise. Speed: reasonable; 20mph except 8mph in business and closely built-up sections of municipality; 15mph in other parts of municipality.

OREGON. Registration: Sec'y of State. Fees: $3. Numbers: preceded by Ore. 3 in. high at rear. Lamps: at least 1 front white with number and red rear. Speeds: 8mph in thickly settled or business sections of village or cities; 8mph in country within 100 yds. of horse-drawn vehicle; 4mph at crossing if person is upon same; outside of cities and villages 24mph.

PENNSYLVANIA. Registration: State Highway Dept. issues license. Fees: $3 per year. Numbers: 5 in. high at front and rear. Lamps: Rear number illuminated 1 hour after sunset; 1 white front light, 1 rear red. Speeds: 10mph in cities, boroughs, counties, and townships; 20 mph outside such areas.

RHODE ISLAND. Registration: Sec'y of State issues certificate which must be carried. Fees: $2 for owners; $10 for manufacturers and dealers. Numbers: 3 in. high at rear. Lamps: such lights as the Sec'y of State approves. Speeds: none stated; but car must always be operated at safe speeds. Stop motor if necessary to prevent accidents.

SOUTH CAROLINA. Registration: no state provision, consult local authorities. Fees: no provision. Numbers: no provision. Lamps: white front light and red rear at night and in fog. Speeds: reasonable; 6mph at intersections, bridges, curves, and descents; otherwise 15mph.

SOUTH DAKOTA. Registration: Sec'y of State. Fees: $1. Numbers: 3 in. high at rear; letters S.D. at least 2 in. high. Lamps: 1 white front light, 1 red rear; number at least 1 in. high. Speeds: reasonable; 20 mph except 10mph closely built-up parts of cities or towns; other parts 15mph.

TENNESSEE. Registration: Sec'y of State. Fees: $2 to Sec'y of State for certificate and $1 to County Clerk for filing same. Numbers: 3 in. high. Lamps: no provision. Speeds: 20mph; municipalities have authority to reduce speed.

VERMONT. Registration: Sec'y of State. Fees: $2 per year. Numbers: 4 in. long plainly displayed. Lamps: such lights with numbers as the Sec'y of State prescribes. Speeds: 10mph in city, village, thickly settled districts, or fire districts; outside, 15mph; 6mph at intersections and curves.

VIRGINIA. Registration: no provision, consult local authorities. Fees: no provision. Numbers: no provision. Lamps: no provision. Speeds: 15mph; 4mph passing if preceding car stops.

WASHINGTON. Registration: Sec'y of State. Fees: $2 per year; $2 renewal. Numbers: 4 in. high on rear preceded by Wn. Lamps: 1 white front light with number; 1 red rear. Speeds: reasonable; 12mph in thickly settled or business portions of city or village; 24mph in country; 4mph at crossings.

WEST VIRGINIA. Registration: State Auditor furnishes tags. Fees: $1 per year. Numbers: front and rear. Lamps: no provision. Speeds: no provision.

WISCONSIN. Registration: Sec'y of State issues certificate in duplicate; 1 must be carried. Fees: $1. Numbers: 3 in. high followed by W at rear. Lamps: At least one front lamp. Speeds: 12mph in corporate limits of city or village; 25mph in country.

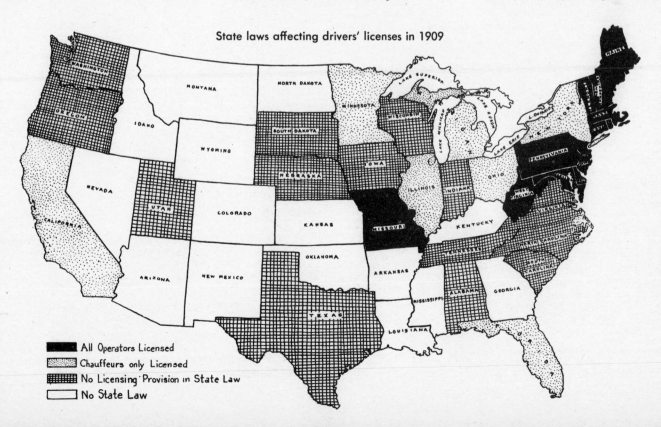

State laws affecting drivers' licenses in 1909

All Operators Licensed
Chauffeurs only Licensed
No Licensing Provision in State Law
No State Law

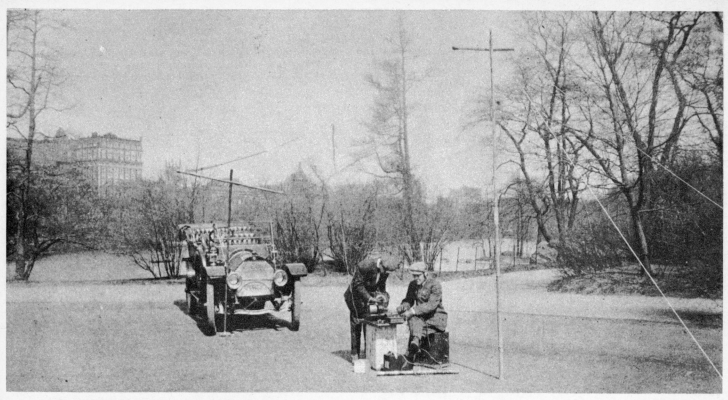

Chalmers Motor Company experimented with wireless in 1910

A portable radio set of 1923, complete with one tube and earphones. Advertised for automobile use

# WIRELESS AND RADIO IN AUTOMOBILES

Although experimenting with wireless and radio for automobile use started early, radio did not get very far until the 1930's. Only the real radio fans could use instruments that required a knowledge of the Morse Code, and even the portable battery-operated radio set shown at the left had to be taken out of the car and attached to a temporary aerial before it could be used. But once radio for automobiles became established, it caught on quickly and became enormously popular. Drivers who had to travel alone most of the time found that radio kept them awake and entertained; young people insisted on having radios in their cars; and soon everyone except those who did not like them or could not afford them had automobile radios.

This country now has more than 100,000,000 radios; about 25,000,000 of them are installed in automobiles.

A U. S. Army wireless telegraph car with its aerial uncoiled (1906)

An early car-telephone installation in Los Angeles (1911)

A police car in Oakland, Cal. equipped with two-way radio (1922)

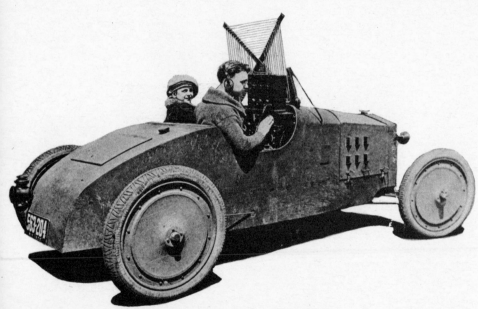

Homemade body, homemade radio, homemade aerial, (1924)

A primitive aerial installation
for automobile use in 1919

A two-way telephone system installed in a touring car in 1919

This doctor installed his own wireless (1921)

# THE EVOLUTION OF DESIGN

Once the basic problem of making a motor drive a wheeled road vehicle had been solved, a new problem arose. What should the new contraption look like? Like a carriage, a four-wheeled cycle, a steam locomotive, or what? Since the automobile was the hybrid product of the carriage and bicycle trades, it clung for a long while to its ancestral traits.

This was especially true of the terminology used to describe body types. The modern automobile, which has nothing else in common with the carriage it made obsolete, still uses ancient carriage-trade terms like sedan, coupé, phaeton, and limousine.

Horse-drawn vehicles had never gone fast enough for their designers to have to worry about wind resistance. But racing cars were doing better than 100 mph shortly after the turn of the century. At high speeds, wind resistance becomes a serious matter, so cars had to be smoothed out as driving speeds for the average car constantly increased.

Yet, as the endpapers of this book show, it was only after the Second World War that the American automobile became the low-to-the-ground, sleek, and smoothly streamlined beauty that it is today. Runningboards, separate headlights, rear trunks, and outside spares lingered on through the late 1930's—long after custom builders and innovators like Cord and Duesenberg had shown how unnecessary—and how ugly—all protruding objects are on an automobile.

The automobile has gone a long way from its carriage-trade origins, so long, in fact, that most of the people who drive cars today do not know what a landaulet or a brougham actually was. All these early body styles and terms were derived from the carriage builder, who, over the course of centuries had made his craft a true art.

The next few pages from the early files of *Motor* show how the automobile evolved from its carriage-trade background.

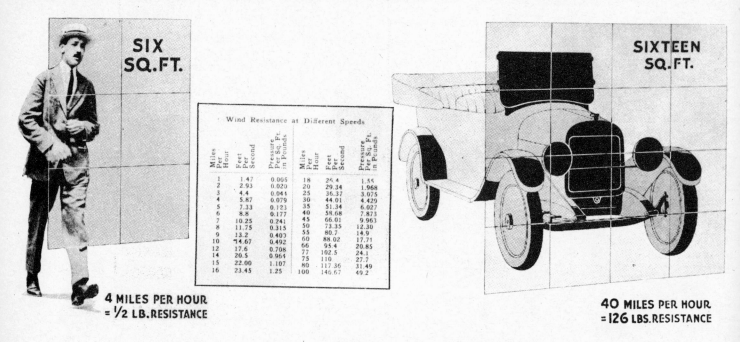

SIX SQ.FT.

SIXTEEN SQ.FT.

| Wind Resistance at Different Speeds | | | | | |
|---|---|---|---|---|---|
| Miles Per Hour | Feet Per Second | Pressure Per Sq. Ft. in Pounds | Miles Per Hour | Feet Per Second | Pressure Per Sq. Ft. in Pounds |
| 1 | 1.47 | 0.005 | 18 | 26.4 | 1.55 |
| 2 | 2.93 | 0.020 | 20 | 29.34 | 1.968 |
| 3 | 4.4 | 0.041 | 25 | 36.37 | 3.075 |
| 4 | 5.87 | 0.079 | 30 | 44.01 | 4.429 |
| 5 | 7.33 | 0.123 | 35 | 51.34 | 6.027 |
| 6 | 8.8 | 0.177 | 40 | 58.68 | 7.873 |
| 7 | 10.25 | 0.241 | 45 | 66.01 | 9.963 |
| 8 | 11.75 | 0.315 | 50 | 73.35 | 12.30 |
| 9 | 13.2 | 0.400 | 55 | 80.7 | 14.9 |
| 10 | 14.67 | 0.492 | 60 | 88.02 | 17.71 |
| 12 | 17.6 | 0.708 | 66 | 95.4 | 20.85 |
| 14 | 20.5 | 0.964 | 77 | 102.5 | 24.1 |
| 15 | 22.00 | 1.107 | 75 | 110 | 27.7 |
| 16 | 23.45 | 1.25 | 80 | 117.36 | 31.49 |
| | | | 100 | 146.67 | 49.2 |

4 MILES PER HOUR = ½ LB. RESISTANCE

40 MILES PER HOUR = 126 LBS. RESISTANCE

This diagram shows how a 1920 sixteen-cylinder Duesenberg racing car was streamlined to reduce wind resistance

Landaulet

Demi-limousine

Landaulet

Full limousine

Extension-front landaulet

Brougham

Extension-front landaulet

Extension-front brougham

Extension-rear landaulet

Bridal brougham

# CLOSED BODY TYPES—1907

# FOUR DECADES OF MOTOR-CAR EVOLUTION

FRONT

REAR

INSTRUMENTS

FENDERS

SPRINGS

STEERING WHEEL

**1919**      **1929**      **1939**      **1949**

# BODY TYPES AS DEFINED IN 1921

In May 1921 *Motor* ran an article on automobile body types in order to straighten out the confusion that still existed in terminology. As an example, the then recently developed sedan with a movable window behind the driver was called by Brewster "double-enclosed drive," by Lancia a "sporting limousine," by King a "limoudan," by Cole a "tourisine," by Packard a "salon brougham," and a "suburban" by the stock-car field. As a result, *Motor* had these drawings made to show just what the body types were.

Nearly all these elaborate terms have vanished; the roadster with its rumble seat, the landaulet, and the touring car have been replaced by the modern soft-top convertible; the limousine and the town car are seldom seen nowadays, although they are still made as luxury cars. The sedan and the coupe are still with us; the hardtop and the all-steel station wagon are the new body types of our era.

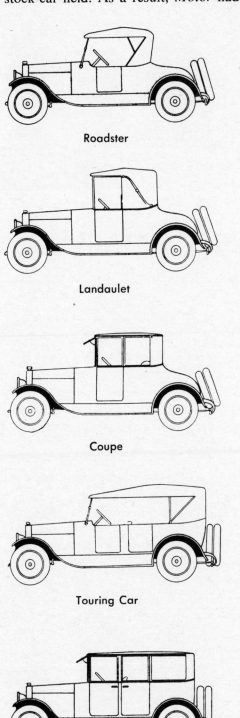

Roadster

Landaulet

Coupe

Touring Car

Sedan

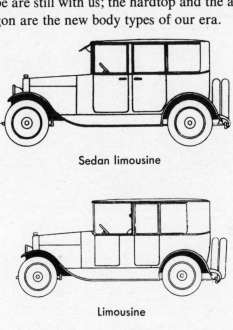

Sedan limousine

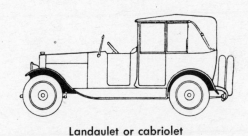

Limousine

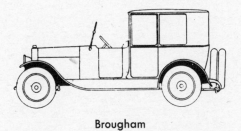

Landaulet or cabriolet

Brougham

The true brougham

A general view of the First National Auto Show at Madison Square Garden, New York (1900)

# THE FIRST NATIONAL AUTOMOBILE SHOW: 1900

Although automobile historians regularly report that the first American automobile show was held in New York at the old Madison Square Garden in 1900, Boston really deserves the honor for the first exhibit. There, on October 10, 1898, the Motor Carriage Exposition of the Massachusetts Charitable Mechanics' Association, opened at the Mechanics' Building on Huntington Avenue. Four exhibitors appeared: The Pope Manufacturing Company, The Riker Electric Motor Company, J. W. Piper and G. M. Tinker, and Kenneth A. Skinner, the American agent for De Dion and Bouton of France. Three other exhibitors straggled in later. The show was opened by a parade of motor vehicles through the streets of Boston, and a race along the Charles River track was staged as part of the show.

The New York show, which was a much bigger affair, was described in the February 1916 issue of *Motor* by John Brisben Walker who said: "Around the Garden was built a track 20 or 25 feet in width. Bridges at either end gave access to the arena in which the cars were tastefully grouped. The speedway was crowded with cars of many shapes and kinds. The doubting Thomases and Thomasesses, with whom the world of that day was principally inhabited, were invited to sit in a car and take a few laps around the Garden to prove that these handsome cars really could move.

"At this first Madison Square show the steam car and the electrics were 'it.' The one and two-cylinder gasoline cars stood panting at the curb or moved, with a loud chug-chug, a jerky motion, around the track inside the building. The steam car, light, attractive, moving rapidly and noiselessly,

responding instantly to every speed desired, and under the most absolute control, with a slight motion of the throttle lever, was undoubtedly the favorite. The large, elegantly built electrics which, upon a level track, exhibited none of the idiosyncrasies incident to rough roads and steep grades, met with a most favorable reception.

"A contract was made to erect a plank runway starting from near the center of the roof garden and winding around the edge of the building to a small platform high up against the side of the tower. Calculations proved that the cars could do this climb. But it had never been done in practice. The next day, Joseph H. McDuffee made his first climb. Steam in the boiler was brought up to a pressure of 300 pounds. More than a dozen men were placed at intervals along the climbing platform to catch the car if it refused to take the grade. McDuffee started slowly up the grade. Spectators expected momentarily to see the car stop, perhaps start backwards. The men stationed along the runway stood tense, ready to grab the car. Up, up, up it went, until finally it stood at the very top of the platform built against the tower. Then McDuffee maneuvered his car until it finally was turned, and the journey down, a much more dangerous one than the climb up, began. A sigh of relief went up when car and driver reached bottom safely . . . .

"Although there were eighteen firms exhibiting gasoline motor-cars, as against eight companies having steam cars and six showing electric vehicles, the business done by electrics and steam cars of that period was about six to one of the gasoline motor type."

This shows the track on which the vehicles gave actual demonstrations

A Winton raced through mud to reach the show

Putting a car through its paces on the show track

Demonstrating a car on a steep incline built on the roof of Madison Square Garden

# THE BEGINNINGS OF THE AMERICAN AUTOMOBILE

## By Charles E. Duryea

*In its March 1909 issue,* Motor *ran an important historical survey of the beginnings of the American automobile industry written by the pioneer inventor, Charles E. Duryea. Charles Duryea, with his brother Frank, built the first practicable American gasoline-powered automobile—the primitive motor-driven buggy shown on page 15. Since the Duryea Brothers also were the winners of the first American automobile race (the* Times-Herald *contest of 1895), they were both widely known in American automobile circles. Charles Duryea was therefore able to make an authoritative report on what happened in those early days. .*

It is manifestly impossible to show all the lines of work and the many experiments that led up to the motor car, so [we start] with the year 1895, which really marks the beginning of the successful use of automobiles in America by others than the experimenters themselves. The writer was considering the possibilities of self-propelled vehicles and was writing about them in 1882. He had carefully considered the various types of motors then in practical use with reference to their being adopted to motor-vehicle service, and had selected the gasoline engine . . . electrically ignited by batteries or some other source of electricity carried on the vehicle, as early as the summer of 1886, thus antedating foreign practice by twelve to fifteen years. He assisted as consulting engineer in designing a steam-motor buggy in 1888, but did not engage in actual productive work until 1891, because he did not believe the public was yet ready for this type of vehicle. Realizing that some years must be spent in development, experiments with motors were begun, and drawings for a complete carriage were completed during the summer and fall of 1891, followed by actual work that winter. Many experiments were made with almost every part of this first vehicle to reduce it to a practical form, with the result that the first motor carriage was finished in the fall of 1892. This vehicle was of the phaeton type with irreversible steering, employing inclined steering knuckles and single-lever control by which the steering and speed changing were manipulated as easily and certainly as a horse could be driven. It had disk-and-drum friction transmission, much resembling modern friction-drive devices; used a balance gear in the cross shaft with two chains to the rear wheels, a spray carburetor of the constant-level overflow type, and make-and-break electric ignition, supplied by a battery of wet cells. My brother joined me in this work in March 1892.

This first vehicle proved underpowered and was dismantled to provide a more powerful motor, but this attempt at rebuilding was quickly abandoned, and a complete heavier design begun along the same lines, which was then finished in the fall of 1893. It ran many miles with speeds up to 10 or 12 mph, and demonstrated that the auto of the future would be so far superior to the horse vehicle that instead of being sold to the poorer classes, unable to afford horses, it would be purchased by the wealthy and supersede their horse-drawn outfits.

This new view of the invention necessitated a different design to meet the higher price believed obtainable. Instead of attempting to build a vehicle to sell for $350 to $500, as had been thought, $1000 to $2000 was considered possible, and a more elaborate design was begun. The experimental work connected with this went forward during the fall and winter of 1893, resulting in the adoption of a three-speed-and-reverse spur-gear transmission with individual clutches, a double-cylinder, 2-cycle motor, with water circulation supplied by pump from a water tank in front, where it was exposed to the cooling air, artillery wheels, a live rear axle, and a number of other features that are standard today. The experiments were completed and actual work was begun in the spring of 1894. But owing to failure to secure enough flexibility from the 2-cycle motor, it was soon abandoned, and the 4-cycle type, formerly used, but double cylinder, was continued. This vehicle was finished late in the year 1894, and nicely painted and upholstered, went into almost daily service in the spring of 1895. The solid tires with which [it was] first equipped, proved too small for durability, so it was fitted with single-tube pneumatics, the first use of these tires on motor vehicles. After a most successful summer, it entered and won the Chicago *Times-Herald* contest on Thanksgiving Day, 1895, covering a distance of 70 miles over a course covered with snow 12 to 18 inches deep. It defeated the best foreign vehicles and was the only one of more than 80 entries to cover the course and return to its garage that day. This victory was repeated on Decoration Day, 1896, in the *Cosmopolitan* race at New York, and also on November 14, 1896, in the London to Brighton run of 52 miles. These later contests were won by Duryea vehicles, made and entered by the Duryea Motor Company, which was organized in the fall of 1895.

balanced engine. This engine also had some parts made of aluminum, now common in auto-engine construction, and was the first example of the use of this material in auto work. Haynes' experiments were afterwards carried on by the Haynes-Apperson Company.

Henry Ford began work in the early 1890's on a bicycle motor which he finished in [1896] as a small four-wheeled, self-propelled auto. It ran many miles through the streets of Detroit and frequently went into the country, sometimes carrying two people. Its successful completion, before the formation of the Ford Motor Company, entitles Henry Ford to rank as an early pioneer.

Frank Duryea in the 1895 model

Elwood Haynes in his first car

To Elwood Haynes, of Kokomo, Ind., belongs the distinction of being one of the earliest pioneers in the industry. He began actual work on his first vehicle in 1893 and had it sufficiently finished to permit a first trial ride on July 4, 1894. It had small steel wheels with cushion-rubber tires and a 2-cycle engine such as was used for launch propulsion. It also had two speeds forward by separate chains, but no reverse. The drive was on a single wheel with no differential or balance gear. As at first used, the engine had no starting crank, so it had to be started by pushing the car with the clutch thrown in. A light buggy body was mounted above the mechanism on the framework below.

This vehicle was followed soon after by one with an engine of the two-cylinder opposed type. Mr. Haynes was undoubtedly the originator of this kind of engine which afterwards became so popular for automobiles, although he was not the first to use multiple cylinders. His second car, finished late in the fall of 1895, had steel wheels and the mechanism on the chassis was boxed in. The body, seating four *dos-a-dos,* was mounted above the mechanism. This vehicle steered by a short crank, like a bicycle crank, mounted at the top of the steering post, but with the axle around which the crank turned lying parallel to the vehicle axis. Small sprockets and a bicycle chain transmitted the steering effort downward to the floor and to the front wheels. This car, although entered, did not compete in the *Times-Herald* contest, but was exhibited and awarded a prize for its well-

Alexander Winton began the construction of his first automobile in 1895 and had it running as early as May 1897. It was a bulky-looking affair with wide seats, *dos-a-dos.* The details of the mechanism were not made largely public, if at all. This first car was soon after followed by the large single-cylinder phaetons with engines of five-to-six-inch bore and stroke, with large heavy flywheels, and with heavy bob-weights mounted on eccentrics to balance piston vibration.

At the Columbian Exposition in Chicago, 1893, there was shown a six-passenger electric brake, the product of Harold Sturgess. This was one of the only two self-propelled vehicles exhibited. The writer had made an entry, but he did not exhibit, because he was unable to fill orders. The other exhibit was a German Daimler quadricycle with steel wheels and a single-cylinder engine rather like the early Ford. The Sturgess vehicle was shown again at the *Times-Herald* contest in which it covered a dozen or more miles of the course, in spite of the condition of the roads. At this same contest was exhibited one of the original Woods' electrics, marking the beginning of the Woods Electric Vehicle Company and two Morris and Salom electric vehicles, one of which was a steel-wheeled skeleton with pneumatic tires; while the other was a more pretentious brake with wooden wheels and solid rubber tires. This was steered by a vertical lever moved forward and back to give right and left motions to the steer-

Reading from top to bottom: the first Winton automobile of 1898; the 1903 National; the 1899 Autocar with rope tires; the 1899 Packard; Charles B. King of Detroit in his first car

ing wheels. This vehicle was awarded a gold medal because of its ease of control, smooth running, and other typical electric-car features. These cars became the nucleus from which the Electric Vehicle Company was formed. The energies of these able workers were devoted to commercial rather than pleasure vehicles, with the result that electric public-service cabs appeared in New York and other cities, some of which, many times rebuilt, are still in service [1909].

While these developments were taking place in gasoline and electric vehicles, the steam engine as a method of propulsion was not neglected. In the latter part of the 1880's, L. D. Copeland fitted several small steam engines to Star bicycles, Coventry tricycles, etc., and produced operative light vehicles; while the H. B. Smith Machine Company applied steam to a larger three-wheeled car. These early vehicles, illustrated in the widely circulated cycle publications, undoubtedly did much to popularize the motor-vehicle idea, as well as to influence Duryea and Winton, who were then engaged in the bicycle business, and also others, like Whitney and the Stanley Brothers, who took up the work later.

About 1896, George E. Whitney built a light steam carriage, which he operated with considerable success in Boston and neighboring cities. This vehicle contained practically all the features of the little steamers so popular a few years later and was probably their direct predecessor. Some work of a Mr. Rand, living in or near Portland, Me., was also done along these lines, and with Whitney's successful efforts did much to influence the designs so successfully shown by the Stanley Brothers at Charles River Park near Boston, Mass., in the fall of 1898. The light weight, small size, neat appearance, simple action, and low price, together with the phenomenal stunts of which these steam carriages were capable, made them public favorites at once. Orders for them flowed in, and a big business seemed in sight. At this time, John Brisben Walker, then proprietor of *Cosmopolitan* Magazine, purchased the Stanley rights for $250,-000. He retained half of the rights to start the Mobile Company of America, but sold the other half to the Locomobile Company of America. Backed by ample capital, splendidly equipped factories, and large advertising expenditures, these little vehicles jumped into instant popularity, and steam-vehicle makers sprang up on every hand. Everybody was acquainted with steam, and having been shown how to make every part of almost toy-lightness, mechanics had no trouble in duplicating these little vehicles. But the makers had reckoned without the roads. The light structures, built and tested on the beautiful roads near Boston, quickly shook to pieces on the miserable trails, called roads, in most other parts of the country. The buying public suddenly ceased buying, and the business in light steamers stopped even more quickly than it had started. The public, jumping to conclusions, had jumped wrong, and since it was disappointed, it was slow to jump again. The over-exploited electric companies also failed to pay dividends, but in spite of all this, some progress had been made.

The first real automobile show, held in Madison Square Garden in the fall of 1900, was a great educational force. There the public first began to grasp the good and bad points of gasoline vehicles for American use. The little Knox air-cooled three-wheeler, which Harry Knox had been developing for at least four years, proved its ability to run and keep cool in almost continual performance on the track. Here, too, was exhibited at least one vehicle, the predecessor of a recognized leader of today, which was resplendent in paint and varnish, and upholstered to the height of the carriage-makers' art, but it was utterly without any propelling mechanism. Yet it was admired by many, and was the ladies' delight.

About this time, the famous curved-dash runabout of R. E. Olds was placed on the market at a popular price. It found instant favor because it met the need the little steamers had failed to satisfy. Olds had been a gas-engine builder for years, and had built at least one steam vehicle in the latter part of the 1880's. His early production did much to create a typical American light runabout.

Air cooling was seen mostly on the smaller engines of foreign manufacture, which, however successful they may have been on the good roads of Europe, were underpowered in America. Here they were worked to the limit and were often badly lubricated, so they naturally gave trouble and were condemned. But Harry Knox and the H. H. Franklin Manufacturing Company, which began in 1902, built air-cooling systems that actually cooled. They were kept on the market in spite of the general acceptance of the water-cooled engine.

The two-cylinder engines of the 1894 Duryea and the 1895 Haynes cars were followed by three- and four-cylinder Duryea engines in 1897 and later. As more power was needed, cylinder sizes were increased until 1907 saw quite a number of eight-cylinder cars offered to the public. Multicylinder engines will probably continue to be used in luxury cars, but less complicated motors will have to be produced at prices within reach of large masses of people.

Particularly among more expensive cars, the American automobile industry has been led and for a time was practically dominated by foreign designs and construction methods. Wealthy buyers, who spent their vacations in Europe, used these new vehicles on splendid foreign roads and then brought them to this country as examples of superior design. But these cars frequently failed to meet American road conditions as well as American-built vehicles — a fact that was recently proved by the victory of the Thomas Flyer in the New York - Paris Race [1908].

The immediate future will doubtless continue to show an increase in the number of makers, with wider variety in the nature of the product, and a still wider range in price. As the market grows, increased production will permit better value to be offered for a given amount of money, and the distrust of the public shown in the past before many more years will turn toward acceptance and appreciation of the merits of the self-propelled vehicle, which is destined to supplant the horse as other mechanical devices have supplanted muscles in the past.

Reading from top to bottom: the original Cadillac Model A of 1902; the first Pierce-Arrow, 1900; the Stanley Steamer of 1897; the 1899 Oldsmobile; the Model B Buick of 1904

Mayade in the 4-hp Panhard
won the 1896 Paris-Marseilles

De Knyff in the 8-hp Panhard
won the 1898 Paris-Bordeaux

# AUTOMOBILE RACING
# BEFORE 1903

Levegh in his 24-hp Mors that won the
Paris-Toulouse Race in 1900

Fournier in the 60-hp Mors that won the
Paris-Berlin Race in 1901

Girardot in the 50-hp Panhard that won the
1901 Gordon-Bennett Race

M. Farman in the 40-hp Panhard, winner of the
1902 Circuit du Nord

Edge in the 40-hp Napier that won
the 1902 Gordon-Bennett Race

H. Farman in the 70-hp Panhard that won
the Paris Vienna Race in 1902

Renault's winning 16-hp Renault,
Paris-Vienna (light cars) 1902

Jarrott in the 70-hp Panhard that won the
1902 Circuit des Ardennes

Gabriel in the 70-hp Mors that won the
Paris-Madrid Race in 1903

Renault's 30-hp Renault, winner 1903
Paris-Madrid Race (voiturette)

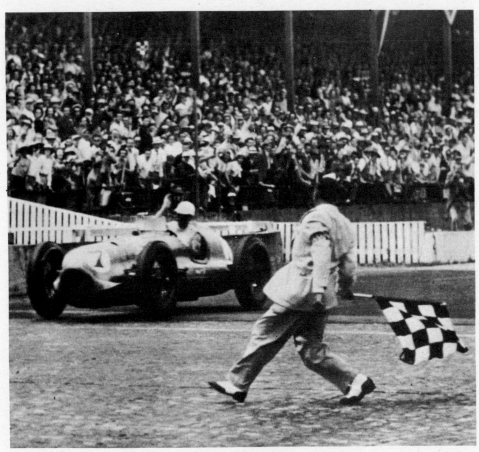

Indianapolis, 1949

# AUTOMOBILE RACING

The De Dion-Bouton steam tractor drawing a Victoria carriage. Bouton is at the tiller; Count de Dion in left front seat

# THE PARIS-ROUEN RACE: 1894

To understand the importance of the Paris-to-Rouen race, which was the first organized automobile race ever to be held anywhere in the world, one has to know how the development of the automobile then stood. (See pages 13 to 23 for the early background.) Benz and Daimler had been building automobiles for some time in Germany. An enterprizing young Frenchman named Sarazin had obtained the Daimler patent rights for France, but in order to maintain their validity he had to have some motors manufactured in France. He approached Emile Levassor of Panhard and Levassor in 1886. This machinery manufacturing firm agreed to make the motors, and work was started on them. But Sarazin fell ill and died before they were finished. His widow decided to carry on. She obtained an extension agreement from Daimler and worked closely with Levassor in building the motors. In 1890 she and Levassor were married.

Levassor then built an automobile. He was the first to realize that it was a completely new kind of vehicle and not merely a motor-driven carriage, so he put a vertical motor in front, under the hood. In 1892 he issued his first catalog. His cars then came equipped with iron-shod wheels, but rubber tires could be had as extras.

In France, meanwhile, Count Albert de Dion had backed George Bouton, a brilliant young steam-engine builder, and the two men had been making steam-driven road vehicles since 1883. Armand Peugeot was also building cars, and other French pioneers like Amédée Bollée and Leon Serpollet were busy experimenting with various kinds of power-driven road vehicles. When *Le Petit Journal* announced early in 1894 that it would hold a road competition for cash prizes, the newspaper received 102 entries, although Benz, Daimler, De Dion-Bouton, Panhard-Levassor, and Peugeot were the only automobile firms anywhere in the world that were then in a position to build finished cars.

Among the 102 entries were five cars driven by springs, five by compressed air, thirty by gasoline, twenty-eight by steam, and five by electricity. A preliminary contest was held in which all but twenty-one cars were eliminated. The race then began at 8:30 A.M., June 22, 1894, at Neuilly on the outskirts of Paris. The course to Rouen was about eighty miles; it led through Mantes, where the contestants had to arrive by noon and leave by 1:30 in order to qualify. (Mantes is about thirty miles from Neuilly.)

A large crowd watched the send-off. People realized that they were going to see something new; many of the spectators were afraid one of the cars might blow up; others looked forward hopefully to seeing a fatal accident.

The winning car (if it can be called that) was the steam-driven De Dion tractor shown above. It reached Rouen in five hours and forty minutes. One of the six gasoline-driven Peugeots arrived five minutes later; another came in right after it. Four Panhard-Levassor entries arrived anywhere from fourth to thirteenth. Fifteen cars finished the race; the last one straggled in eight hours and fifty minutes after it had started.

There was considerable confusion about awarding the prizes, because the jury refused to accept De Dion's steam tractor as a true self-propelled horseless carriage. Its dual nature—half steam tractor and half conventional Victoria—made them unwilling to qualify it. Consequently, the jury divided the first prize of about one thousand dollars into two equal halves, one of which they gave to Peugeot and the other to Panhard-Levassor. De Dion was awarded the second prize of four hundred dollars. Fortunately, he was a wealthy man, so the money did not mean much to him.

M. de Bourmont and M. Archdeacon in a gasoline driven car

A steam-powered wagonette

The Panhard-Levassor which came in eighth

A Panhard-Levassor which came in fourth

Alfred Vacheron in a car with a real steering wheel

The Peugeot which came in twelfth

# THE FIRST AMERICAN AUTOMOBILE RACE: 1895
## The Times-Herald Contest in Chicago

The Paris-Rouen Race had a catalytic effect throughout the world. Inventors and mechanics everywhere began building experimental cars. The Chicago World's Fair in 1893, at which a Daimler car was exhibited, also increased interest in the automobile in America. William Steinway, the piano manufacturer, obtained the Daimler rights for this country. He built Daimler-engined automobiles and launches for several years, but lost more than half a million dollars on the venture.

In Chicago, H. H. Kohlsaat had recently purchased the *Times-Herald* and was looking for ways to promote his newspaper. One of his employees, Frederick Upham Adams, suggested that Kohlsaat hold a contest for the new horseless carriages. Adams' persuasiveness won Kohlsaat over, and a public announcement was made, stating that a race was to be held in Chicago on July 4, 1895. A $5000 purse was offered, $2000 of which was to go to the winner, with the rest to be divided among the runners-up. More than eighty applications were received from all over the country, but it soon became evident that most of the American automobiles which were then under construction would not be finished by July, so the race had to be postponed until early November and then again to Thanksgiving Day, November 28.

Word arrived from France in June of the 700-mile Paris-to-Bordeaux-and-return race which had been won by a Panhard with three Peugeots as runners-up. In order to keep up public interest for his forthcoming Thanksgiving Day race, Kohlsaat offered a prize of $500 for a new name for horseless carriages (see page 32).

On Thanksgiving Day eve, an eight-inch fall of wet snow blanketed the whole Chicago area.

*The Motocycle,* a new and short-lived automobile magazine gave a contemporary account of the contest: "On the evening before the race, eleven competitors declared they would start, but when the motocycles were sent on their fifty-four mile run, only six had appeared at Jackson Park and Midway Plaisance [at 8:30 A.M.] They were:

"Duryea Motor Wagon Company, Springfield, Mass.
"De La Vergne Refrigerating Machine Company, New York. [Benz motor]
"Morris and Salom, Philadelphia, electric.
"H. Mueller and Company, Decatur, Ill. [Benz motor]
"R. H. Macy Company, New York. [Benz motor]
"Sturgess Electric Motocycle, Chicago, electric.

"Haynes and Apperson, of Kokomo, Ind., started for Jackson Park early in the morning. In making a turn to avoid a street car, the forward wheel of the motocycle was smashed, so they had to give up the race. A. Baushke and

Brother, of Benton Harbor, Mich., failed to get their wagon [to Chicago] in time. Something snapped in the steering gear of the wagon belonging to Max Hertel of Chicago. A. C. Ames of South Chicago and George W. Lewis of Chicago could not get ready in time.

"Along the route and at the turning corners from Jackson Park to Evanston hundreds waited. The boulevards were crowded with rigs and cutters, dashing up and down over the snow, looking for the horseless carriages.

"'Ready!'" shouted Judge Kimball, as he stood, watch in hand, at the side of the Duryea wagon. J. F. Duryea leaped into the wagon, followed by Arthur W. White, the umpire. At 8:55 o'clock the word 'Go' was uttered, and the motocycle passed through the crowd. A minute later the Benz wagon of the De La Vergne Refrigerating Machine Company started. The Benz motor proved unequal to getting over the bad road from the starting point to Fifty-Fifth Street. The wheels slipped around in the snow, but failed to go forward. So the wagon was shoved over the deep snow to a better part of the road.

"Macy's wagon started in good shape at 8:59 o'clock. The Sturgess electric motocycle left at 9:01; the Morris and Salom electric wagon left a minute later. The Mueller gasoline motocycle did not start until 10:06.

"In the parkway every drive was filled with swell turn-outs, occupied by capitalists who may wish motocycles for next summer, and inventors who were skeptical of the ability of the machines to overcome the slush and snow of the bright day.

"The run through South Park was uneventful for all the machines, but the snow made the De La Vergne people quit the contest to await a more favorable time. There were a thousand people on Fifty-Fifth Boulevard to cheer the motors as they headed for Michigan Avenue. About 10,000 people stood on the walks between Fifty-First Street and the Auditorium Hotel on Michigan Avenue.

"The judges had come to the Leland Hotel where they saw the Duryea pass. The Macy . . . overtook the Duryea at Rush and Erie, where the latter temporarily broke down. After passing through Lincoln Park, the Duryea was still behind the Macy motocycle, but it was making quick time to pass its rival. At Evanston the Macy machine was slightly in the lead. After they had turned north on Forest Avenue, the Duryea was pressing the leader hard, and in accordance with the rules of the contest, the Macy drew to one side to allow the faster competitor to pass. People along Forest Avenue applauded the unusual sight of one horseless carriage forging ahead of a rival.

"While coming back, the Macy carriage met a hack which would not give the right of way. The tire of the motocycle slipped, and its left front wheel collided with the rear

The Duryea Brothers in their tiller-steered auto-buggy that won the race

wheel of the hack. Four spokes were badly chipped, and the steering gear was bent so as to be almost useless. By keeping on the car tracks, it managed to reach the second relay station a mile farther on. The Mueller wagon passed the Macy while the New York machine was delayed for repairs.

"After passing the second relay station at Grace and North Park Streets, the Duryea wagon ran smoothly along the car tracks at a high rate of speed. At Lawrence Avenue, the operator mistook the direction of the hand on the guide post and went along Clark Street instead of Ashland Avenue. He went two miles out of his way, but struck the regular course again by going west on Diversey. But he managed to keep ahead of his rivals.

"A few minutes before 6 P.M., when the Duryea motor came through Douglas Park, laboring over the bad road, there was no one to greet it but a representative of the *Times-Herald*. On the first approaches to Western Avenue, the roadbed was comparatively hard, and the motor made magnificent time, traveling at the rate of eight mph with ease.

"Not fifty people saw the last stages of the finish or knew that the Duryea had established a world's record. It was just 7:18 when Frank Duryea threw himself out of the seat of the motor and announced the end."

The Duryea Motor-wagon that won the *Times-Herald* Race marked an advance over the earlier motor-buggy shown on page 15. It had two parallel cylinders, so arranged that one could operate independently if the other went out of commission. The cylinders drove a main shaft running down the center of the wagon. At one end of the shaft was mounted a beveled gear and flywheel. The beveled gear drove a cross shaft on which three friction clutches of different diameter were mounted to give speeds of four, eight, twelve, and sixteen mph. The second shaft was connected by spur gears to a drive shaft equipped with a sprocket wheel. This was connected by chain to another sprocket on a rear wheel. An epicycloidal gear regulated the wheels when the wagon turned.

To start the engine, gas was pumped into a mixing chamber; then a crank at the end of the cross shaft was used to turn the engine over.

The total weight of the vehicle was 1208 pounds; it had a 57½ inch wheelbase with wheels approximately 55 inches high.

# EARLY AMERICAN RACING CARS

These sparse, gaunt-looking, pioneer racing cars mark the first step of the transition of the automobile from the primitive horseless-carriage to the high-speed vehicles of today. The two streamlined cars shown here were not streamlined because their builders had studied the problems of air resistance scientifically; they were merely groping empirically toward an as yet unknown shape. It is interesting to compare these very early racing cars with the radically streamlined, modern record-breakers like Eyston's *Thunderbolt* and Cobb's *Railton*.

The cars illustrated here are representative of the pre-Vanderbilt Cup era. They were made to be raced on the smooth Daytona-Ormond Beach or on closed-circuit race tracks; they were not intended for the spectacular sport of road racing, which was to develop a more advanced type of high-speed automobile.

Ross racing a Stanley Steamer at Daytona Beach, Fla. (1904)

Charles Schmidt piloting the *Gray Wolf* (1904)

The streamlined Ross steamer called the *Tea-Kettle* and W. K. Vanderbilt in his 90-hp Mercedes at Daytona in 1904

Barney Oldfield driving the Winton 1903 racer in which he made 83.7mph at Daytona in 1904. The engine consisted of two four-cylinder motors bolted together to form a straight Eight with the cylinders lying in a horizontal plane

Hastings at the wheel of the streamlined Baker electric *Torpedo Kid* (1904)

Fred Marriott in the Stanley Steamer in which he made 127mph in 1906 on Daytona Beach

Otto Nestman driving the Stevens-Duryea Skeleton at Daytona (1904)

Herb Lytle making the Jericho Corner at high speed in his 24-hp Pope Toledo (1904)

# THE VANDERBILT CUP RACES: 1904-1937

No one did more to further automobile progress in America than William Kissam Vanderbilt, Jr., the millionaire sportsman who donated a huge silver cup as an award in the historic races that carried his name from 1904 to 1916. The first race, held on Long Island on Saturday, October 8, 1904, was attended by the leading figures of American society who expected the event to become as exclusive as the Horse Show or a polo match. But horse shows and polo matches can be held in a small enclosed area; whereas a road race requires lots of territory. People flocked to the race course by thousands to watch the exciting event.

In 1904, the automobile was just emerging from its horseless-carriage stage of development to become a high-speed vehicle. There were eighteen entries in the first race, six from France, five from Germany, two from Italy, and five from the United States. The race began at six o'clock in the morning, when sixteen of the eighteen entries finally got away from the starting line to cover the 28.4 mile course for ten laps. One of the German Mercedes turned over when its American driver had a blowout. The mechanic was killed and the driver injured. There were other accidents before the race was won by a French Panhard with George Heath, an American driver, at the wheel.

In a contemporary description of the first Vanderbilt Cup Race, *Motor* said: "For seven hours the cars chased one another around the triangular course with its doubtful surface and risky turns. Here the man counted as much as the mechanical monster he guided. A steady arm and an unfailing eye were required. The stakes being played for were not alone for possession of the cup of silver with its gold lining; the [automobile] makers of two worlds were fighting for the American motor-car trade."

The 1904 race gained wide publicity for the second race, which was held on October 14, 1905. Thousands of people started early on the night before to find a good place from which to watch. There was much drinking and merriment during the night while people waited in their cars for the race to begin. The crowds were even thicker than they had been the year before, and the success of the first race had attracted many top-flight foreign drivers like Lancia, Chevrolet, Hemery, Nazarro, Sartori, Szisz, Wagner, and Jenatzy. It was won by Victor Hemery in a French Darracq; he did an average of 60.72 mph for the 283-mile course.

The most spectacular of all the Vanderbilt Cup races was the third, which was held on October 7, 1906. Half a million spectators saw France win the cup for the third successive time when Louis Wagner drove a Darracq across the finish line. The course was slippery and treacherous; a dense fog hung over the road and the attempt of 800 deputies to patrol the highways could hardly be called successful. Again the spectators took rash and foolish chances. One of them was killed, and several were injured.

The 1906 race had so many accidents that no race was held in 1907. In 1908, part of the privately owned new Motor Parkway was used as a section of the course. This race was the first won by an American, when George Robertson drove his Locomobile to victory. An American won again in 1909 and 1910, when Harry Grant twice brought his famous Alco in first. The last race on Long Island was held in 1910. Later races were staged in Savannah, Ga., Milwaukee, Wis., San Francisco, and Santa Monica, Cal.

The 1916 Santa Monica race was the last of the original series. George Vanderbilt staged two cup races at the Roosevelt Raceway in 1936 and 1937.

Hawley's swing at Bethpage Corner (1904)

Sartori skids his Fiat through loose dirt (1904)

Heath in his winning 90-hp Panhard (1904)

The Vanderbilt Cup. Now in the Smithsonian Institution

Spectators, their cars, and the debris they left (1904)

Waiting for the second Vanderbilt Cup Race to begin (1905)

Weischott at the starting line in his Fiat

The bonfire at the Peerless Camp

Lancia finishes in second place in his Fiat

A pre-dawn breakfast while waiting

Cagno driving an Itala in the home stretch

Lining up to get a good place from which to see

Changing tires on Duray's car on its eighth lap

Buying "sleeplessness in liquid form"

Teamwork does it

The early Vanderbilt Cup Races were a peculiarly American institution, and they were characteristic of their time. People went to them because they were gaudy carnivals, gladiatorial combats, demonstrations of daring driving and great mechanical skill, sports competitions on which bets could be made, and, above all, because they were huge end-of-season picnics to which the whole family could go. No admission was charged except for the exclusive grandstand seats, so everybody went free.

And people thronged to them by the hundreds of thousands. Local residents and farmers, who at first had opposed the idea of holding speed contests at their front doors, cashed in as they merrily charged the city slickers all the traffic would bear. The annual affair became so popular that a musical comedy called *The Vanderbilt Cup Race*, starring Elsie Janis and Barney Oldfield (who actually drove a Peerless Green Dragon onto the stage), ran for two years on Broadway, while several road companies cleaned up from coast to coast.

After the passing of the Vanderbilts, road racing died out in America, although it continued to be popular in Europe.

Hemery and his 80-hp Darracq that won the 1905 race

Barney Oldfield in the Broadway play based on the race

Harry Grant and his mechanic in the Alco that won the 1909 race

The Thomas Flyer that won the race

# THE NEW YORK-TO-PARIS RACE: 1908

Perhaps the most thrilling event in the early history of the automobile was the race from New York to Paris by way of Siberia. Sponsored jointly by *The New York Times* and the Paris *Le Matin,* this great contest began on February 12 1908, when six cars started from Times Square, New York, to cross the United States, originally intending to go through Alaska and then be sent by ship to Vladivostok. Three cars from France, one from Italy, one from Germany, and an American Thomas Flyer entered the race. Only three were to finish—the Thomas Flyer, the Italian Zust, and the German Protos.

Montague Roberts drove the Thomas to Wyoming, where he turned it over to another driver who took it on to Seattle and then by steamship to Valdez, Alaska. However, it was impossible to proceed because of the spring thaw. The Thomas was returned to Seattle by steamship after losing two weeks time. Its foreign competitors had already been shipped across the Pacific to Vladivostok, but they were ordered to wait there for the Thomas.

It was a complicated race. The Thomas was allowed fifteen days over the Zust because it had lost that much time going to Alaska. And the Protos, which mistakenly had been shipped by rail from Pocatello, Idaho, to Seattle, was penalized fifteen days.

On their arrival in Vladivostok, the Thomas thus had a lead of fifteen days over the Zust and thirty days over the Protos.

To cross the North American continent in 1908 was a heroic achievement, but even to attempt to cross the frozen wilderness of Siberia required superhuman fortitude. Nevertheless, three cars went on. In an article in *Motor,* the Russian phase of the race was described as follows: "The crossing of the eastern end of Manchuria was the most difficult part of the entire journey; it put the crews of the various cars to a severer test than any automobile contest ever held has previously exacted. Yet the American and German cars arrived in Irkutsk within twenty-four hours of each other. The Italian Zust was far behind them. At Pogranitchnaya, 144 miles west of Vladivostok, the Thomas broke the teeth of its driving gear and was held up for five days. It gradually wore down the long lead the German Protos had gained in that time and was only a few hours behind it at Irkutsk. The American car overtook the German at Lake Baikal, but did not arrive in time to get the steamer crossing the lake and so had to wait a day to follow. After a chase of nearly 500 miles, the Thomas finally passed the German car. Again the Thomas broke the teeth of its driving gear; by the time its crew had repaired it, the Germans were only thirty miles away."

The 1907 Thomas Flyer that won the race was one of the most celebrated cars of its day. The original automobile that went from New York to Paris still exists and is now on display at the Long Island Automotive Museum in Southampton. It has never been restored and is in dilapidated condition. Montague Roberts, who drove it on the first lap of its long journey, visited the ancient car in the spring of 1953. When he saw it again he said: "I felt I had the best car in the world in 1908—this Thomas car."

The Italian Zust, one of the three cars to finish the race

The foreign cars leave Paris for the start in New York

The Thomas Flyer (right) is met in Iowa by Capt. Hans Hansen

Montague Roberts smiling at his triumph over snowdrifts

The Italian Zust with its drivers in cold-weather dress

The French De Dion which withdrew from the race in Siberia

The Thomas Flyer in its heart-breaking struggle with primitive Russian roads

# AUTOMOBILE RACING COMES OF AGE

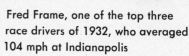

Fred Frame, one of the top three race drivers of 1932, who averaged 104 mph at Indianapolis

The driver came out of this alive

After the automobile had become a precision-built machine rather than something put together by hand in a workshop, motors became vastly improved and speeds kept going upward. Racing developed into a thrilling sport, and spectators got their money's worth as daring drivers put on an exciting show at the various tracks that were built throughout the country.

A dramatic photograph of one of the most memorable incidents of these memorable years is shown in the center of the opposite page. In the 1912 Indianapolis race, Ralph de Palma, who was at the wheel of a German Mercedes, was far in the lead. On the 198th lap out of 200, his engine went dead. De Palma and his mechanic pushed the car the rest of the way and across the finish line, still ahead of his nearest competitor. But he was disqualified because his car did not come in under its own power.

Many of the things that have made the modern automobile a dependable means of transportation were developed or improved on the race track. This was especially true of tires, gears, axles, and steering knuckles, all of which had to stand up under the terrible strains imposed upon them by high speed, sharp turns, and hour after hour of constant going, which was as hard on the car as it was on the driver.

Louis Strang in his 1911 driver's helmet

Mulford driving the big Lozier which won the Elgin National in 1910

Lancia, driving a Fiat in the first Vanderbilt (1904)

Louis Chevrolet driving a 32.4-hp Buick in 1909

Four

great

race drivers

of the

great years

of

auto racing

Ralph de Palma pushing his car across the finish line in 1912

Sir Malcolm Campbell, who did 254 mph at Daytona in 1932

# FASTER AND FASTER...

In the early 1930's, the search for ever greater and greater speed left the race track and moved to the flat beds of dry lakes in Utah and Southern California. On these ideal level surfaces, new records were made, and speed laboratories were set up there to see how fast a wheeled vehicle could be driven.

The ultra-high-speed cars that were developed under these circumstances soon began to resemble airplanes rather than automobiles. Their completely streamlined bodies and highly specialized motor equipment made them usable only for the one thing for which they were created — to set a new speed record. They could no more be driven on a highway than an airplane could.

Future development probably lies with the gas-turbine-powered car, or, even more likely, with the atom-powered car described on page 232. Meanwhile, tremendous speed on land has been achieved by the Air Force with a rocket-powered sled on tracks. This sled, which has very hard metal runners that create a minimum of friction, is driven by a 50,000-pound rocket engine that can move it from a dead start to more than 1500 mph in less than five seconds. After a 10,000-foot run, it is brought to a stop in 300 feet by having a scoop underneath the sled dip into a water trough located between the rails. The rocket engine burns a combination of alcohol and oxygen.

This astounding sled, which has far surpassed all records ever established by ground vehicles, does not have the problems that confront an automobile moving at high speed. It has no wheels or bearings, it does not have to be steered, and above all, it has no pneumatic tires to wear down or blow out. In fact it is more like a railroad locomotive than an automobile.

The third car ever to beat 200 mph. Keech in the 1928 White Triplex

Major H. O. D. Segrave in the 1929 Irving Napier

Eyston's Thunderbolt which did 357.5 mph in 1938

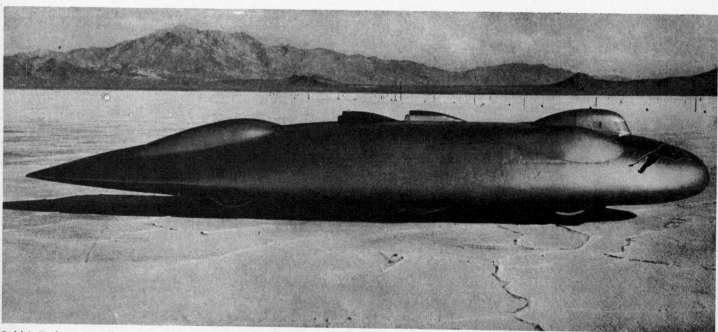

Cobb's Railton, the all-time record holder which did 394.2 mph in 1947

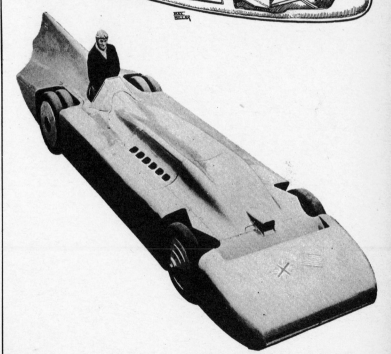

A cutaway view of Captain George Eyston's 7-ton car with twin Rolls-Royce twelve-cylinder engines (1937)

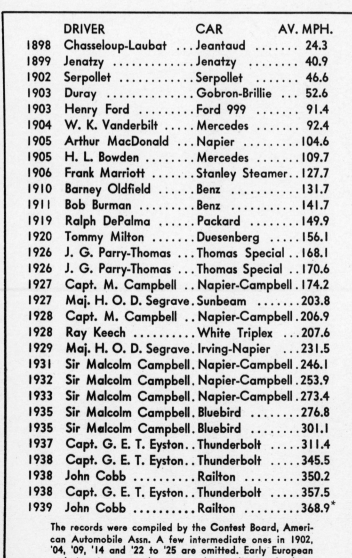

| | DRIVER | CAR | AV. MPH. |
|---|---|---|---|
| 1898 | Chasseloup-Laubat | Jeantaud | 24.3 |
| 1899 | Jenatzy | Jenatzy | 40.9 |
| 1902 | Serpollet | Serpollet | 46.6 |
| 1903 | Duray | Gobron-Brillie | 52.6 |
| 1903 | Henry Ford | Ford 999 | 91.4 |
| 1904 | W. K. Vanderbilt | Mercedes | 92.4 |
| 1905 | Arthur MacDonald | Napier | 104.6 |
| 1905 | H. L. Bowden | Mercedes | 109.7 |
| 1906 | Frank Marriott | Stanley Steamer | 127.7 |
| 1910 | Barney Oldfield | Benz | 131.7 |
| 1911 | Bob Burman | Benz | 141.7 |
| 1919 | Ralph DePalma | Packard | 149.9 |
| 1920 | Tommy Milton | Duesenberg | 156.1 |
| 1926 | J. G. Parry-Thomas | Thomas Special | 168.1 |
| 1926 | J. G. Parry-Thomas | Thomas Special | 170.6 |
| 1927 | Capt. M. Campbell | Napier-Campbell | 174.2 |
| 1927 | Maj. H. O. D. Segrave | Sunbeam | 203.8 |
| 1928 | Capt. M. Campbell | Napier-Campbell | 206.9 |
| 1928 | Ray Keech | White Triplex | 207.6 |
| 1929 | Maj. H. O. D. Segrave | Irving-Napier | 231.5 |
| 1931 | Sir Malcolm Campbell | Napier-Campbell | 246.1 |
| 1932 | Sir Malcolm Campbell | Napier-Campbell | 253.9 |
| 1933 | Sir Malcolm Campbell | Napier-Campbell | 273.4 |
| 1935 | Sir Malcolm Campbell | Bluebird | 276.8 |
| 1935 | Sir Malcolm Campbell | Bluebird | 301.1 |
| 1937 | Capt. G. E. T. Eyston | Thunderbolt | 311.4 |
| 1938 | Capt. G. E. T. Eyston | Thunderbolt | 345.5 |
| 1938 | John Cobb | Railton | 350.2 |
| 1938 | Capt. G. E. T. Eyston | Thunderbolt | 357.5 |
| 1939 | John Cobb | Railton | 368.9* |

The records were compiled by the Contest Board, American Automobile Assn. A few intermediate ones in 1902, '04, '09, '14 and '22 to '25 are omitted. Early European and American records were made on dirt tracks, later mileages on the beach at Daytona, Florida, and the final top speeds on the salt beds near Salt Lake City, Utah

*Cobb bettered his own record in 1947 when he made 394.2 mph

Sir Malcolm Campbell's 1933 Bluebird

The future of racing may lie with the atom-powered car or perhaps with the gas-turbine powered car. This little British Rover gas-turbine car did 141.756 mph in 1952 with Peter Wilks driving it at Ostend

This tremendous Eight-in-line French-built Bellamy developed 200 hp. It was owned by Miss Hockenhull, an American girl in Paris (1904)

# EARLY AMERICAN SPORTS CARS

The sports car developed early. It came into being because the first automobiles were so expensive that only the rich could afford to buy and maintain them. Since they were in a position to indulge their whims, they either had their cars built to order or they patronized the daring innovators who were designing cars intended to appeal to the sporting instincts of wealthy young men and women.

These cars were built to go fast. They were not primarily racing cars, but they were very close to them in power, speed, and appearance. Some of them, with slight modifications, appeared on professional race tracks, where they made a reputation for their makers. This was particularly true of the Mercer and Stutz, both of which established themselves in public esteem by their remarkable race-track performance.

The finest material, the best workmanship, and the most advanced design went into the making of sports cars. They have always been luxury articles created for the few people who appreciate something different and radically new—and can afford to indulge their taste.

A 60-hp Pope-Toledo being driven on the open road, although it was really designed for racing (1904)

**AMERICAN**
This car with its big single spotlight
had a 40-50-hp four-cylinder motor
and was priced at $3250 (1907)

**CRAIG-TOLEDO**
The Craig-Toledo sold for $4000
and was considered one of
the finest cars of its time (1907)

**MERCER**
The very first Mercer, the Briarcliff,
announced in June 1909.
It has a mother-in-law seat
on the side

**HUDSON**
This was the Hudson Twenty
announced in September 1909.
It sold for only $900

**GEARLESS**
This long-hooded car had a six-cylinder
75-hp motor which could drive it at 75 mph.
It sold for $4000 (1907)

A Crane-Simplex with a custom body built on nautical lines. The car cost $33,000 in 1915

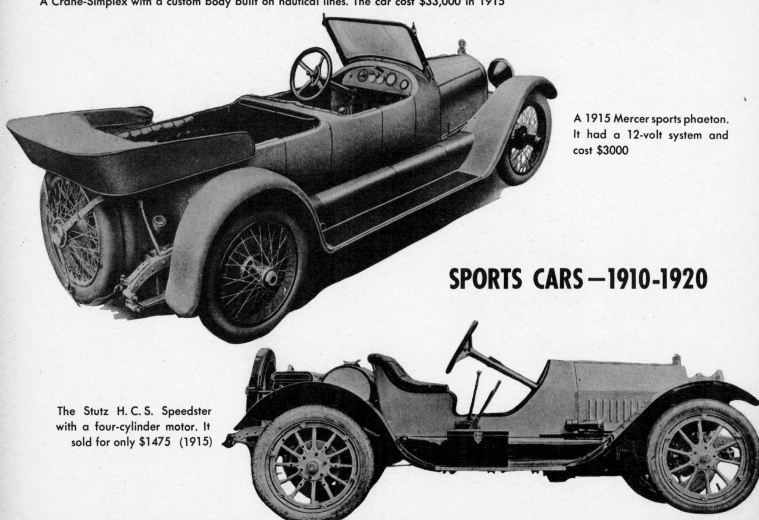

A 1915 Mercer sports phaeton. It had a 12-volt system and cost $3000

# SPORTS CARS—1910-1920

The Stutz H. C. S. Speedster with a four-cylinder motor. It sold for only $1475 (1915)

A 1912 Simplex which is now in the Smithsonian Institution

A six-cylinder Alco designed by William K. Vanderbilt Jr. for his personal use (1912)

A 1914-1915 Thomas Flyer. From The Henry Ford Museum, Dearborn, Mich.

A late Duesenberg Model SJ speedster with 320-hp supercharged engine. From the Henry W. Uhle Collection

A 1931 front-drive Cord convertible

# LATE AMERICAN SPORTS CARS

During the 1920's, the American automobile industry perfected its mass-production techniques and cars rolled off the assembly lines by the millions. Throughout most of that prosperous decade large sums of money were spent by individuals for elaborate custom-built cars, but the sports car was under a temporary eclipse. Mercer went out of business in 1925. Stutz lingered on until 1936, but the company concentrated on luxury cars rather than on the sports models that had made it famous.

Yet it was during this period that two of America's finest cars were built. The Duesenberg and the Cord were both far ahead of their time in both engineering and design. The Duesenberg got its name from the celebrated race-track

driver and self-educated pioneer automotive engineer, Fred Duesenberg. Although he had been in the industry since 1900 and had been responsible for the Mason automobile, the production cars bearing his name did not appear until the early 1920's. The finest materials and workmanship were used for cars that had to meet racing standards. Model A had a 100-hp engine and would do about 85 mph. Model J came out in 1929. It had a 265-hp engine with dual carburetion. The chassis alone cost $8500.

But Fred Duesenberg's masterpiece — and one of the landmarks of American automobile history—was the world-famous Model SJ. Only a few were built, but they were so good that most of them are still running, and they are

A 1931-1932 Duesenberg Model SJ double-cowl phaeton with body by Brunn. From the Henry W. Uhle Collection

A 1936 front-drive Cord sedan with headlights that disappeared into the fenders

highly prized by their owners. The SJ's supercharged engine developed 320 hp at 4750 rpm; it enabled the car to do 130 mph in high and 104 mph even in second gear. The car could accelerate from a standing start to 100 mph in seventeen seconds. The engine was a straight-Eight with bore and stroke of 3¾ by 4¾ inches, giving it a piston displacement of 420 cubic inches. Each cylinder had four valves operated by two overhead camshafts. The chassis cost $11,750, but it came equipped with a 150-mph speedometer, a 5000-rpm tachometer, an altimeter, and an elaborate set of oil, temperature, and ignition gauges.

Fred Duesenberg was killed in an automobile accident on a Pennsylvania mountain road in 1932. In an obituary article on him, *Motor* said: "Besides his pioneering of the supercharger for automobiles, four-wheel brakes, and his straight-Eight engines, Duesenberg's use of many new engineering ideas was noteworthy throughout his life. He was the first to use hydraulically controlled four-wheel brakes,

heat-treated molybdenum-steel frames, and balloon tires on standard-production cars."

Duesenberg's company had been bought by Auburn-Cord in 1926, but he had been given a free hand there to build his finest cars. The president of the Auburn Automobile Company, E. L. Cord, was also a remarkable man. Like Fred Duesenberg, he built unusual quality cars that were noted for their beauty of design. When the front-drive Cord first appeared in 1929, *Motor* said of it in its July issue: "The Cord is obviously distinguished by the fact that it is the first really new automobile design to appear on the market for many years."

But it was the 1936 810 Cord that made history in American automobile design. It was a short-lived car, for the company went out of business a year later, but it was perhaps the most beautiful automobile of its day. Strictly speaking, it might not be considered a true sports car, but it appealed to the sports-car crowd.

A Bristol sports coupe

An MG roadster

The Jaguar XK-120 convertible

A Sunbeam Alpine sports car

# MODERN BRITISH SPORTS CARS

The Austin-Healey 100

An Alvis convertible

A Riley four-door sports sedan

A Sunbeam-Talbot 90

A Spanish Pegaso

A German Mercedes 300SL

An Italian Ferrari

A German Taunus

An Italian Maserati

# MODERN CONTINENTAL
# SPORTS CARS

A French Delahaye coupe

A German Porsche

In 1911, an English artist drew this picture of what he thought an automobile would look like in 1961

# THE CARS OF THE FUTURE

The English artist who drew the picture shown above was evidently thinking about buses rather than private cars. But predicting what the car of the future will be like has long been a popular pastime. Over the years, *Motor* has run many pieces indicating new trends in automobile design. For instance, in January 1924, Charles F. Kettering, who was then president of General Motors Research Corporation, wrote an article entitled "The Car You'll Drive 10 Years From Now." In it he said: "Experiments at our laboratories indicate that it is possible to develop bearings which . . . will run for thousands of hours without the addition of any lubricant other than that used when the bearing was installed." He also said: "We have produced certain material which can be added to gasoline that will change the nature of the combustion taking place in the cylinder, and by the use of this new material, we can absolutely eliminate the knock from a motor. My prediction is that every car weighing more than 2500 pounds will have four-wheel brakes; later, all cars will have them. I am not willing today to say that balloon tires are a success, because they are too new yet, but I know that the use of balloon tires on the present-day car will produce only ten per cent of what is possible if the whole car is designed to ride on balloon tires."

In October 1943, when passenger-car building had been suspended during the Second World War and people were looking forward to the post-war car, Harold F. Blanchard said: "It is probable that within a few years transparent plastics may replace glass at a considerable reduction in weight, and colored opaque body panels which require no paint may be used instead of steel. With plastic tops, a windshield wiper is rarely required because raindrops spread out into an even film over the surface. If ice collects on the plastic, it can be knocked off by tapping with the hand. A windshield wiper, however, might be needed to sweep off sticky snow. If plastics do replace glass, rounded windshields with exceptional visibility may become a fact within

a few years. . . . A number of commentators believe that fenders should be eliminated by making the body the full width of the car."

All these predictions have come true—or are on the way to becoming true. Automobile bodies that will not dent or rust or lose their color and which will be stronger than steel yet lighter than aluminum can be made from resin-laminated glass fiber. In fact, most bodies on the experimental cars shown on the following pages are made of glass fiber. Magnesium also is coming to the fore as body material. It weighs less than one-quarter as much as steel and so would lighten the load the engine has to drive. It is interesting to note that in 1914 the French had developed a material they called "Fibromonolithe" made from shredded wood and granulated cork with a secret binding compound that made it possible to mold bodies even then.

But it is predictions for the automobiles still ahead of us that interest most people. In the May 1953 issue of *Motor*, L. H. Middleton, Auto-Lite's vice president in charge of engineering predicted: "Electric-hydraulic brakes on two cars in 1954 . . . at least one gas-turbine car by 1955 . . . four engines in 1954 with 9-to-1 compression ratios . . . fuel injection on gasoline engines . . . heat-pump summer-winter cooling and heating of passenger cars instead of the heater-and-cooler adaptation now in use . . . colored gas-vapor headlights to silhouette persons and objects on the road, cut glare, and increase safety of night driving . . . sparkplugs tailored to individual engines . . . windshields bent two ways, horizontally and vertically."

The gas-turbine-powered car is drawing increased attention from automotive engineers. It has low weight per horsepower, develops maximum torque and power immediately, and can operate on low-cost fuel. At present, however, its fuel consumption is considerably higher than it is in conventional gasoline engines. Even more interesting than the gas-turbine car is the possible atom-powered car. In an ar-

The General Motors Y-Job of 1938—one of Detroit's first attempts at forecasting future trends by building a handmade car

ticle in the November 1946 issue of *Motor,* John J. O'Neill, noted authority on atomic energy, said: "The atomic energy car will have a fuel supply built in at the factory adequate to operate the car for 1000 years or more. It will be powered by a new type of atomic energy fuel totally different from that used in atomic bombs.

"Atomic energy fuel sources in the new era will be based on a safe kind of atom harnessed in a power-production system devised by the author. The source of energy will be lithium atoms contained in lithium hydride, which can produce energy without producing radioactive by-products or showers of dangerous particles.

"The basic process of producing atomic energy from lithium is simple. The lithium atoms are bombarded by hydrogen atoms. A hydrogen nucleus enters the lithium atom, causing it to become unstable and explode and break itself into two helium atoms. When the lithium atom explodes, it has a temperature of several million degrees. This energy is transferred to the two newly formed helium atoms, which come out of the explosion with speeds higher than 20,000 miles per second. They collide with other atoms and these

in turn with many others, thus distributing their energy throughout the mass of the lithium and raising its temperature to heat a boiler in which water will be changed to steam to operate the ordinary type of reciprocating steam engine or a small turbine. The latter would be simpler.

"In the boiler, a nuclear gun, which will supply the stream of hydrogen nuclei, will activate the lithium.

"In the direct-lithium engine, when a sufficient number of lithium atoms are exploded, they will convert the compound to a vapor of high temperature at high pressure. This vapor will pass through a turbine (which is like tandem windmills in a tube), causing the windmills to turn at high speed, thus producing power. After passing through the turbine, the lithium vapor will be condensed back to a liquid and put through the process continuously.

"Many scientific and engineering problems remain before atomic energy can be made available [for automobiles], but they are problems that can be solved."

And then, in May 1953, the Ford Motor Company revealed that its laboratories were actually working on the development of an atomic car.

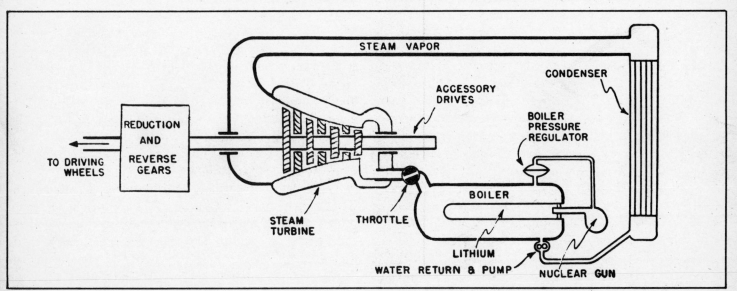

This diagram shows how an atom-driven car might work

These cars are experimental models that indicate General Motors' ideas on future design. This is *Le Sabre,* their first postwar model

The Buick *XP-300* powered by a 335-hp supercharged V8 engine. It has two carburetors, one uses methyl alcohol to prevent knocking

Pontiac's *Parisienne.* This jet-black landau has a modern version of the Victoria top. The windshield has transparent wind deflectors

Cadillac's *Le Mans* with 250-hp engine. The "memory" seat slides back as the door opens and returns when the door closes

The Oldsmobile *Starfire* convertible with a 200-hp engine. The experimental body, fenders, rear deck, and hood are made of Fiberglas

The Chevrolet Corvette with a 168-hp motor, triple side-draft carburetors, and a dual exhaust system. It is in actual production

This is the Ford Motor Company's Continental Nineteen Fifty X. Its transparent top retracts into leather-covered canopy

The XL-500 developed by Lincoln-Mercury. Less than 57 inches high, it has a scarlet Fiberglas body and an all-glass roof

Rear view of the XL-500. Main bumper protrudes from body while two vertical bumpers are part of tail-light assembly

The Ford Syrtis with Roof-O-Matic top — a hardtop convertible that actually converts

Here the Syrtis is shown with the rear window moved forward to form a tonneau windshield for a four-passenger open car

With the top up. Even when lowered beneath the rear-deck lid, there is ample luggage space below

The Kaiser-Darrin Model KF-161 sports car with Fiberglas body and 100-hp six-cylinder engine

## SPORTS CARS AND EXPERIMENTAL MODELS SHOW THE WAY

The Plymouth XX-500, a custom-built six-passenger sedan

From the very beginning, automobile development has owed a great deal to the luxury market. It was by building fine cars for people who were willing to pay practically any price for distinction and novelty that enabled designers and engineers to try out new and radical ideas which filtered down years later to the mass market.

The cars shown here are a continuation of that trend. Some of them are true experimental models incorporating new engineering features. Others are simply new body designs modeled along sports car lines. But they are all evidence of the rapid progress which the American automobile industry has been making during the postwar years.

The Packard Pan-American sports car with 185-hp Eight-in-line engine which has four-barrel down-draft carburetor

The Nash-Healey 1953 sports car featuring a European custom body styled by Pinin Farina. It has 125-hp engine with two carburetors

A Chrysler sports car styled in Italy by Ghia

The Chrysler D'Elegance with standard Chrysler FirePower V-8 engine has a custom body with black and natural yellow leather interior

Abbé Gavois in his 1891 Panhard photographed in 1911 with a more modern car of same make

# MISCELLANY

## AN 1891 PANHARD THAT WAS DRIVEN
## FOR MORE THAN TWENTY-EIGHT YEARS

*By Abbé Gavois*          *From the October 1911 issue*

My car came into my possession in 1895. Before that time it was in the hands of Mr. Buxtorff, a manufacturer at Jacquart à Troyes, in Champagne, who had been the owner of it since December, 1891. I am quite sure you will wonder how the idea ever sprang up in the brains of a modest chaplain of those days to want a horseless carriage. It was because I was interested in all inventions having to do with mechanical locomotion. I wanted a motor car, whose existence I had predicted at the time of the first appearance of the gas motor.

In 1893, I had visited the first exhibition of motor cars, organized by *Le Petit Journal,* and came away highly enthusiastic. I don't think you will understand fully the scope of my enthusiasm unless I tell you that in those days I was a priest of a hamlet in the Department de la Somme, a place without any means of outside communication.

There was a big gap between my sanguine expectations and their realization. One had to pay three to four thousand francs to get possession of one of the plainest cars on exhibition, and there was no guarantee or proof that they were worth the money. So I had to depend more on circumstances than on the capacity of my purse. In 1894, the firm of Panhard discovered a suitable carriage for me and opened relations with Mr. Buxtorff, who offered me the car for 3000 francs, the price he had paid for it. His offer, however, included all the improvements he had made and also a top or sunshade and an extra seat. I thought this price too high, and even when Mr. Buxtorff came down to 2800 francs, I

believed it was too much for a carriage with only two seats and a double-cylinder, V-shaped motor of 2 hp.

Exactly a year after the break in our negotiations, there came an unexpected letter from Mr. Buxtorff, who offered me his carriage for 1800 francs. At such a moderate price, I decided to accept his proposal.

My first adventure as an automobilist coincided (as often is the case) with my first attempt to operate it. Inexperienced as I was, I had cherished the idea to drive my car 80 miles from Troyes to Amiens. Later on I understood why I should have followed Mr. Buxtorff's advice to make the first part of my trip on a freight car, going by rail to Airaines, a few miles from Belloy, my parish. Nevertheless, I disregarded his advice. I took my place in my carriage amidst a curious and jeering crowd that was inclined to amuse itself at somebody's expense. And then I couldn't make my automobile budge. Finally, my Panhard had to make its entry into the parsonage of Belloy-St. Leonard towed by a horse.

In order to avoid other mishaps with this rather complicated machinery at a time when there was no specialist in sight, I started, with my father's assistance, to take the whole machine apart. Even now I remember the surprise of some of my parishioners at seeing the many different parts scattered around the workshop. At last we overcame our difficulties, and a few days later I undertook the trip to Airaines with one of my colleagues. Everything went smoothly and with the exception of a couple of noisy explosions caused by faulty working of the sparker, we arrived safely at our place of destination.

Alas, I cannot say the same of our return trip! I had omitted to shift the governor of the exhaust valve of one of the cylinders, a necessity with this type of motor, in order to avoid choking. With only one cylinder working, I could not make the carriage go. We decided not to tinker but to spend the night at Airaines. During the night I suddenly thought of my omission. The next morning I got up at daybreak, said my prayers, returned to my motor, put the exhaust mechanism in the proper position, and went on my way.

That is the history of my good old servant, which twice a week makes the trip from Raineville, my new parish, to Amiens; which has no objection to a circuit of fifteen to twenty miles, at a speed of three to four mph and an expense of two cents for each mile (everything included); which has made in twenty years the equivalent of a trip around the world and 10,000 miles more without leaving Picardy.

In all these years I have renewed the Brampton driving chain only five times and the steel tires but twice. The rest of the car's organs remain intact, and though old, their vigorous strength holds a promise of another twenty years of activity—perhaps, please God, for a golden jubilee.

* * *

The Abbé Gavois survived the German invasion of France during the First World War and was still driving his original Panhard in 1919.

## THE BLIND MOTORIST OF ENGLAND

In its March 1904 issue, *Motor* pointed out an absurdity in the new English license law which imposed many severe and unnecessary requirements upon the prospective driver while other things much more important—such as being able to see—were not provided for. To show how illogical the new Motor-Car Act was, the British publication *Motoring Illustrated* succeeded in securing a license for a blind man, Mr. Samuel Sharp of Waterford, who was then legally permitted to drive an automobile on English roads at 20 mph.

## THE AMERICAN AUTOMOBILE IN 1913

*From various issues of* Motor *that year*

In 1903, about 150 American factories were engaged in turning out motor cars. In 1909, there were 743 manufacturers of cars, and today the number cannot be much less than one thousand.

In constructional progress, the ten years we are considering are scarcely less remarkable than they are for industrial advancement. Instead of the four-cylinder, 40-hp car that is typical of today, the 1903 car had a power plant of two cylinders, which developed about 15 hp. The wheelbase of the 1903 car was a scant 83 inches, in place of the 120 inches of today. Planetary gears were still standard ten years ago and drive was by chains. The wheels of the 1903 car were 28 inches, as compared with the 36-inch wheel of the present. Ignition was by jump spark with dry cells. And yet the average price of the 1903 product was $2048 as compared with $2383 of the 1913 car, which has electric lights, dual ignition, an electric starter and a hundred refinements undreamt of by manufacturers ten years ago.

There are in this country more than a million motor cars. To establish the exact number of horse-drawn carriages and

## STORING A CAR FOR THE WINTER IN 1915

*From the November 1915 issue*

In laying up the car, remove the tires and jack up all four wheels. The inner tubes should be removed from the tires and placed in a box. The casings should be cleaned well, wrapped with cloth or heavy paper and kept in a moderately cool, dark room. Grease all parts which are liable to rust and do not overlook the motor parts such as the spark-plug ends, the flywheel teeth if a flywheel starter is used, all chains and open gearing, etc. Grease all polished parts and remove as many as possible and store them in the house. Grease the rims so they will not rust. Drain the gasoline and water systems and leave all oil in the motor, gearset, rear axle, etc. Remove the battery and let the service station take care of it for you, or leave it in the car and charge it once every seven or eight weeks. The car top should be raised, the curtains fitted, and the whole covered with a sheet so as to protect it from dust and dirt.

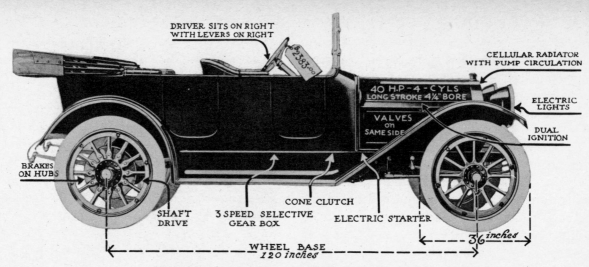

DRIVER SITS ON RIGHT
WITH LEVERS ON RIGHT

CELLULAR RADIATOR
WITH PUMP CIRCULATION

40 H.P - 4 - CYLS
LONG STROKE 4¼" BORE

ELECTRIC
LIGHTS

VALVES
on
SAME SIDE

DUAL
IGNITION

BRAKES
ON HUBS

CONE CLUTCH

SHAFT
DRIVE

3 SPEED SELECTIVE
GEAR BOX

ELECTRIC STARTER

36 inches

WHEEL BASE
120 inches

### THE TYPICAL AMERICAN GASOLINE CAR OF 1913

From a total of 272 cars selling for a total of $648,175, *Motor* computed the various typical features shown in the picture reproduced above. Engines ran from 15 to more than 50 hp; most of them had L-heads and dual ignition. All figures on the 1913 car are based on the number of individual makes. The Model T Ford would therefore count as only one make; otherwise it would heavily overweigh the figures given

wagons is somewhat more difficult, as no official record of these vehicles is kept. We have, however, the estimate of an organization thoroughly competent to form an authoritative opinion, the Carriage Builders' National Association of Mount Vernon, New York. "There were," says the secretary of this association, "manufactured in 1910 somewhat more than one million carriages and small wagons and approximately six hundred thousand business and farm wagons. An equal number of these vehicles has been turned out each year for the last ten years, and as the average life of these wagons is about seven years, it is conservative to say that there are now ten million horse-drawn vehicles."

The million motor cars of 1913 were distributed as follows:

|  | Cars | Per 1000 population |
|---|---|---|
| Middle Western states | 382,410 | 14 |
| Middle Atlantic states | 220,180 | 11 |
| Pacific Coast states | 105,000 | 20 |
| New England states | 97,742 | 15 |
| Southeastern states | 78,866 | 4 |
| Northwestern states | 52,480 | 16 |
| Southwestern states | 44,250 | 7 |
| Rocky Mountain states | 19,325 | 10 |
| Total for United States | 1,000,253 | Average 11 |
| Great Britain | 175,300 | 4 |
| France | 88,300 | 3 |
| Germany | 70,000 | 2 |

Of the American cars being manufactured in 1913, the demand for the various body types was as follows:

Of cars selling for less than $1500, runabouts were 31.3 per cent of the total, touring cars 68 per cent, and closed cars .7 per cent.

In the $1501 to $2000 group, runabouts were 10.4 per cent, touring cars 87.3 per cent, and closed cars 2.3 per cent.

In the $2001 to $2500 group, runabouts were 13.2 per cent, touring cars 85.2 per cent, and closed cars 1.6 per cent.

In the $2501 to $3500 group, runabouts were 23.3 per cent, touring cars 72.3 per cent, and closed cars 4.4 per cent. The mechanical features of fifty early 1913 cars were:

| Electric lighting (in some form) | 89 per cent |
|---|---|
| Starters: | |
| Electric | 26 per cent |
| Explosive | 50 per cent |
| Compressed air | 11 per cent |
| Mechanical | 2 per cent |
| None | 11 per cent |
| Four cylinders | 58 per cent |
| Six cylinders | 14 per cent |
| Both fours and sixes | 28 per cent |
| Long stroke | 76 per cent |
| Left-side driving | 32 per cent |
| Center control | 34 per cent |

In 1913 an automobile was driven for the first time at 100 mph for a full hour. Cars had made such speed before, but only for short distances. *Motor* reporting the event in its April 1913 issue said: "This performance, which will go down in history and be long remembered, was done by a Talbot car on the famous [British] Brooklands track February 15, 1913. The actual distance covered was 103¾ miles. The rated horsepower of twenty-five was attained from four cylinders of 4½-inch by 5-inch bore and stroke, or a piston displacement of 318 cubic inches."

### THE BIRTH OF THE SELF-STARTER

*From the October 1911 issue*

Motoring appears about to be relieved of the most humiliating requirement that still remains for the driver. With the advent of the engine-in-front type of car a decade ago, the ridiculous spectacle of the driver lying on his back in the road under the machine tinkering with its vitals died an early and unmourned death. Soon afterward, the side-entrance body relieved the passengers of the need for stepping into muddy or dusty streets to enter the tonneau. More recently, the always curious spectators who assemble from nowhere when a motorist is in trouble, were robbed of much of their delectation by the introduction of detachable rims, which reduced roadside tire trouble about seventy-five per cent. This year sees the almost general adoption of removable rims that will eliminate practically all tire work and tire inflation in public.

Motorists, however, are still under the painful necessity of providing an awkward exhibition of helplessness when the motor stalls in congested traffic. The driver must de-clutch, retard his ignition, throw back the robe that covers his knees in cool weather, open the side door, worm his way none too gracefully between the steering wheel and levers, walk around to the front of the machine, and then give a good imitation of a Greek hand-organ musician while street cars crowded with impatient riders are held up—with other traffic—until the motor can be started by a crank.

Probably there is no driver of a car who will not welcome the coming retirement of the starting crank. The movement is already in swing, and it is evident that 1912 promises to mark the beginning of the end of that long-tolerated but needless producer of perspiration, profanity, and contusions.

Investigation shows that there are a dozen different so-called self-starters in the market made by as many different companies. The several types may be divided into five classes, as follows: Pneumatic, electric, explosive gas, spring, and lever or mechanical movement. Not all these are, strictly speaking, self-starters in the sense of being automatic to the extent that they require practically no physical effort, although the spring-starter may be so managed as to necessitate rewinding by hand only occasionally.

## A REPORT ON TOLL ROADS IN 1918

*From the June 1918 issue*

The history of the toll road in America dates back to 1792, when the historic Lancaster Pike, between Philadelphia and Lancaster, was handed over to private operation.

In the condition of the country at that time, there was considerable excuse for the toll road. To begin with, the country was comparatively sparsely settled; the distances were great, and taxes to permit road building would have borne heavily on the individual citizen. The alternative of permitting those who used the roads to pay for them as they used them probably appealed to the average stay-at-home American of that day. Little did he realize what he was letting his descendants in for.

After the first plunge had been made with the Lancaster Pike, the toll-road disease spread rapidly. In 1828 there were 3110 miles of toll roads in Pennsylvania, the construction of which had cost the turnpike companies about $10,-000,000. In 1811, the records show that 317 turnpike companies were operating in New York and New England, with a total of 4500 miles and a combined capital of nearly $5,000,000.

The real death blow of the pay-as-you-drive road was the arrival of the motor vehicle. From the very dawn of the motor era, the question of roads became a definite issue. Slowly at first, but later with gathering momentum, public opinion got behind the campaign for more and better roads. Inevitably this growth of good roads sentiment developed the demand for free roads. The toll road was little hindrance to the slow progress of horse-drawn vehicles, but it was a serious obstacle to the course of the motor vehicle.

But the pay-as-you-drive road is vanishing from the highway system of America. In all the New England states there is only one privately owned road left to obstruct free traffic. New York has eliminated practically all of them. New Jersey is almost free from them. One toll road remains in Delaware. Maryland has entered on a carefully planned campaign for ridding its territory of corporate highway enterprise. Pennsylvania, which has always been a stronghold of the toll-road idea, is struggling desperately to get rid of them. The recent announcement that four more stretches of the historic Lancaster Pike will be taken over, aggregating almost 100 miles of this vitally important through route, calls renewed attention to the splendid work that Pennsylvania is doing in the elimination of toll roads and throws into relief the pleasing fact that the toll road is destined soon to become an unwholesome memory of a primitive transportation age.

## WISHFUL THINKING IN 1911

*From the February 1911 issue*

At a meeting of the Carriage Builders' National Association in Cincinnati, one of the speakers said: "While we must frankly admit that there were certain styles of carriages (known among carriage builders as heavy work) that were greatly affected by the automobile, it is not perhaps generally known that these so-called heavy vehicles never exceeded 10 to 15 per cent of horse-drawn vehicles built for pleasure, leaving 85 per cent of the horse-drawn vehicle industry of the country untouched by the automobile.

"In 1906-1907, and coincident with the enormous demand for automobiles, the demand for buggies reached the highest tide in its history. The demand in 1910 would have been even greater than in the wondrous year of 1907 had it not been for the continued unseasonable weather of May and June.

"It seems that the supply of motors has caught up with the demand, temporarily at least, and it would also seem that the tremendous demand for automobiles has simply been a repetition of the enormous demand for buggies from 1785 to 1893, after which time the demand for buggies was in exact proportion to the growth and expansion of the country, its wealth and prosperity. It may be that the car will have the same experience in the future that the buggy had in the past."

# FACTS AND FIGURES

## MOTOR-VEHICLE REGISTRATIONS IN UNITED STATES
### Privately Owned Vehicles

| Year Dec. 31 | Passenger Cars | Buses | Trucks | Total |
|---|---|---|---|---|
| 1895 | 4 | .... | .... | 4 |
| 1896 | 16 | .... | .... | 16 |
| 1897 | 90 | .... | .... | 90 |
| 1898 | 800 | .... | .... | 800 |
| 1899 | 3,200 | .... | .... | 3,200 |
| 1900 | 8,000 | .... | .... | 8,000 |
| 1901 | 14,800 | .... | .... | 14,800 |
| 1902 | 23,000 | .... | .... | 23,000 |
| 1903 | 32,920 | .... | .... | 32,920 |
| 1904 | 54,590 | .... | 700 | 55,290 |
| 1905 | 77,400 | .... | 1,400 | 78,800 |
| 1906 | 105,900 | .... | 2,200 | 108,100 |
| 1907 | 140,300 | .... | 2,900 | 143,200 |
| 1908 | 194,400 | .... | 4,000 | 198,400 |
| 1909 | 305,950 | .... | 6,050 | 312,000 |
| 1910 | 458,377 | .... | 10,123 | 468,500 |
| 1911 | 618,727 | .... | 20,773 | 639,500 |
| 1912 | 901,596 | .... | 42,404 | 944,000 |
| 1913 | 1,190,393 | .... | 67,667 | 1,258,060 |
| 1914 | 1,664,003 | .... | 99,015 | 1,763,018 |
| 1915 | 2,332,426 | .... | 158,506 | 2,490,932 |
| 1916 | 3,367,889 | .... | 250,048 | 3,617,937 |
| 1917 | 4,727,468 | .... | 391,057 | 5,118,525 |
| 1918 | 5,554,952 | .... | 605,496 | 6,160,448 |
| 1919 | 6,679,133 | .... | 897,755 | 7,576,888 |
| 1920 | 8,131,522 | .... | 1,107,639 | 9,239,161 |
| 1921 | 9,212,158 | .... | 1,281,508 | 10,493,666 |
| 1922 | 10,704,076 | .... | 1,569,523 | 12,273,599 |
| 1923 | 13,253,019 | .... | 1,849,086 | 15,102,105 |
| 1924 | 15,436,102 | .... | 2,176,838 | 17,612,940 |
| 1925 | 17,439,701 | 17,808 | 2,483,215 | 19,940,724 |
| 1926 | 19,220,885 | 24,320 | 2,807,354 | 22,052,559 |
| 1927 | 20,142,120 | 27,659 | 2,969,780 | 23,139,559 |
| 1928 | 21,308,159 | 31,982 | 3,171,542 | 24,511,683 |
| 1929 | 23,060,421 | 33,999 | 3,408,088 | 26,502,508 |
| 1930 | 22,972,745 | 40,507 | 3,518,747 | 26,531,999 |
| 1931 | 22,330,402 | 41,880 | 3,489,756 | 25,862,038 |
| 1932 | 20,832,357 | 43,476 | 3,256,776 | 24,132,609 |
| 1933 | 20,586,284 | 44,918 | 3,245,505 | 23,876,707 |
| 1934 | 21,472,078 | 51,530 | 3,430,396 | 24,954,004 |
| 1935 | 22,494,884 | 58,994 | 3,675,865 | 26,229,743 |
| 1936 | 24,108,236 | 62,618 | 4,001,464 | 28,172,318 |
| 1937 | 25,390,773 | 66,166 | 4,249,219 | 29,706,158 |
| 1938 | 25,167,030 | 65,198 | 4,210,477 | 29,442,705 |
| 1939 | 26,139,526 | 68,859 | 4,406,702 | 30,615,087 |
| 1940 | 27,372,397 | 72,641 | 4,590,386 | 32,035,424 |
| 1941 | 29,524,101 | 88,800 | 4,859,244 | 34,472,145 |
| 1942 | 27,868,746 | 102,093 | 4,608,086 | 32,578,925 |
| 1943 | 25,912,730 | 106,702 | 4,480,176 | 30,499,608 |
| 1944 | 25,466,331 | 106,518 | 4,513,340 | 30,086,189 |
| 1945 | 25,691,434 | 112,253 | 4,834,742 | 30,638,429 |
| 1946 | 28,100,188 | 119,937 | 5,725,692 | 33,945,817 |
| 1947 | 30,718,852 | 128,983 | 6,512,628 | 37,360,463 |
| 1948 | 33,213,905 | 132,603 | 7,209,961 | 40,556,469 |
| 1949 | 36,312,380 | 135,002 | 7,692,569 | 44,139,951 |
| 1950 | 40,185,146 | 143,206 | 8,272,153 | 48,600,505 |
| 1951 | 42,525,217 | 143,290 | 8,657,931 | 51.326,438 |

### Privately and Publicly Owned Vehicles

| Year | Passenger Cars | Buses | Trucks | Total |
|---|---|---|---|---|
| 1942 | 27,976,259 | 139,274 | 4,887,067 | 33,002,600 |
| 1943 | 26,009,073 | 152,324 | 4,726,737 | 30,888,134 |
| 1944 | 25,566,464 | 152,592 | 4,760,250 | 30,479,306 |
| 1945 | 25,793,493 | 162,125 | 5,079,802 | 31,035,420 |
| 1946 | 28,213,336 | 173,585 | 5,986,081 | 34,373,002 |
| 1947 | 30,845,350 | 187,457 | 6,808,691 | 37,841,498 |
| 1948 | 33,350,894 | 196,726 | 7,537,911 | 41,085,531 |
| 1949 | 36,453,351 | 208,929 | 8,028,016 | 44,690,296 |
| 1950 | 40,333,591 | 223,652 | 8,637,969 | 49,195,212 |
| 1951 | 42,682,591 | 230,461 | 9,035,754 | 51,948,806 |
| 1952 | 43,810,531 | 240,142 | 9,207,897 | 53,258,570 |

Source: U. S. Bureau of Public Roads 1900 to date. Prior to 1900 estimated by Automobile Manufacturers Association.

## PASSENGER CAR PRODUCTION IN THE UNITED STATES

| Year | Production |
|---|---|
| 1900 | 4,192 |
| 1901 | 7,000 |
| 1902 | 9,000 |
| 1903 | 11,235 |
| 1904 | 22,130 |
| 1905 | 24,250 |
| 1906 | 33,200 |
| 1907 | 43,000 |
| 1908 | 63,500 |
| 1909 | 123,990 |
| 1910 | 181,000 |
| 1911 | 199,319 |
| 1912 | 356,000 |
| 1913 | 461,500 |
| 1914 | 548,139 |
| 1915 | 895,930 |
| 1916 | 1,525,578 |
| 1917 | 1,745,792 |
| 1918 | 943,436 |
| 1919 | 1,651,625 |
| 1920 | 1,905,560 |
| 1921 | 1,468,067 |
| 1922 | 2,274,185 |
| 1923 | 3,624,717 |
| 1924 | 3,185,881 |
| 1925 | 3,735,171 |
| 1926 | 3,783,987 |
| 1927 | 2,936,533 |
| 1928 | 3,815,417 |
| 1929 | 4,587,400 |
| 1930 | 2,784,745 |
| 1931 | 1,973,090 |
| 1932 | 1,135,491 |
| 1933 | 1,573,512 |
| 1934 | 2,177,919 |
| 1935 | 3,252,244 |
| 1936 | 3,669,528 |
| 1937 | 3,915,889 |
| 1938 | 2,000,985 |
| 1939 | 2,866,796 |
| 1940 | 3,717,385 |
| 1941 | 3,779,682 |
| 1942 | 222,862 |
| 1943 | 139 |
| 1944 | 610 |
| 1945 | 69,532 |
| 1946 | 2,148,699 |
| 1947 | 3,558,178 |
| 1948 | 3,909,270 |
| 1949 | 5,119,466 |
| 1950 | 6,665,863 |
| 1951 | 5,338,435 |
| 1952 | 4,320,793 |

## STATE MOTOR-VEHICLE REGISTRATION—1952

|  |  |
|---|---|
| Alabama | 777,285 |
| Arizona | 330,054 |
| Arkansas | 505,281 |
| California | 5,154,326 |
| Colorado | 621,627 |
| Connecticut | 789,483 |
| Delaware | 122,232 |
| Florida | 1,178,682 |
| Georgia | 1,021,722 |
| Idaho | 290,529 |
| Illinois | 2,841,125 |
| Indiana | 1,529,876 |
| Iowa | 1,090,358 |
| Kansas | 921,476 |
| Kentucky | 855,929 |
| Louisiana | 755,590 |
| Maine | 287,525 |
| Maryland | 779,545 |
| Massachusetts | 1,376,058 |
| Michigan | 2,566,628 |
| Minnesota | 1,217,201 |
| Mississippi | 524,062 |
| Missouri | 1,332,747 |
| Montana | 282,578 |
| Nebraska | 619,693 |
| Nevada | 94,178 |
| New Hampshire | 181,497 |
| New Jersey | 1,746,068 |
| New Mexico | 271,848 |
| New York | 3,980,527 |
| North Carolina | 1,171,015 |
| North Dakota | 285,128 |
| Ohio | 3,021,633 |
| Oklahoma | 891,473 |
| Oregon | 711,982 |
| Pennsylvania | 3,266,830 |
| Rhode Island | 270,983 |
| South Carolina | 686,270 |
| South Dakota | 299,909 |
| Tennessee | 933,900 |
| Texas | 3,155,337 |
| Utah | 273,313 |
| Vermont | 125,875 |
| Virginia | 1,034,011 |
| Washington | 988,849 |
| West Virginia | 497,313 |
| Wisconsin | 1,249,265 |
| Wyoming | 156,097 |
| Dist. of Col. | 193,657 |
| Total | 53,258,570 |

## FORD SPECIFICATIONS: 1903-1942

| Year | Model | † Price | Weig't | No. of cylinders | Bore & Stroke | Piston Displacement | Maximum H.P. | Tire Size | Wheelbase |
|---|---|---|---|---|---|---|---|---|---|
| 03 | A | 850 | 1250 | 2 | 4x4 | 100.5 | 8@1000 | 28x3 | 72 |
| 04 | B | 2000 | 1600 | 4 | 4x5 | 251.3 | 24@1200 | 32x3½ | 92 |
| 04 | C | 900 | 1300 | 2 | 4x4 | 100.5 | 10@1000 | 28x3 | 76 |
| 05 | B | 2000 | 1750 | 4 | 4¼x5 | 283.6 | 24@1200 | 32x3½ | 93 |
| 05 | C | 950 | 1250 | 2 | 4¼x4 | 113.4 | 10@900 | 28x3 | 78 |
| 05 | F | 1000 | 1300 | 2 | 4½x4 | 127.2 | 12@900 | 30x3½ | 84 |
| 06 | N | 500 | 700 | 4 | 3⅝x3¼ | 134.2 | 15@900 | 28x2½ | 78 |
| 06 | F | 1000 | 1300 | 2 | 4½x4 | 127.2 | 12@1400 | 30x3½ | 84 |
| 06 | K | 2500 | 2000 | 6 | 4½x4¼ | 405.4 | 40@1600 | 34x4 | 120 |
| 07 | N | 600 | 1000 | 4 | 3¾x3⅜ | 149.0 | 15@1400 | 28x3 | 84 |
| 07 | K | 2800 | 2500 | 6 | 4½x4¼ | 405.4 | 40@1600 | 34x4 | 120 |
| 07 | R | 750 | 1100 | 4 | 3¾x3⅜ | 149.0 | 15@1400 | 28x3 | 84 |
| 08 | N | 600 | 1050 | 4 | 3¾x3⅜ | 149.0 | 15@1400 | 28x3 | 84 |
| 08 | K | 2800 | 2500 | 6 | 4½x5 | 405.4 | 40@1600 | 34x4 | 120 |
| 08 | S | 700 | 1100 | 4 | 3¾x3⅜ | 149.0 | 15@1400 | 30x3 | 84 |
| 09 | T | 850 | 1200 | 4 | 3¾x4 | 176.7 | 20@1400 | ‡30x3½ | 100 |
| 10 | T | 950 | 1250 | 4 | 3¾x4 | 176.7 | 20@1400 | ‡30x3½ | 100 |
| 11 | T | 780 | 1250 | 4 | 3¾x4 | 176.7 | 20@1400 | ‡30x3½ | 100 |
| 12 | T | 690 | 1300 | 4 | 3¾x4 | 176.7 | 20@1400 | ‡30x3½ | 100 |
| 13 | T | 600 | 1300 | 4 | 3¾x4 | 176.7 | 20@1400 | 30x3½ | 100 |
| 14 | T | 550 | 1350 | 4 | 3¾x4 | 176.7 | 20@1400 | 30x3½ | 100 |
| 15 | T | 490 | 1350 | 4 | 3¾x4 | 176.7 | 20@1400 | 30x3½ | 100 |
| 16 | T | 440 | 1400 | 4 | 3¾x4 | 176.7 | 20@1400 | 30x3½ | 100 |
| 17 | T | 360 | 1400 | 4 | 3¾x4 | 176.7 | 20@1400 | 30x3½ | 100 |
| 18 | T | 450 | 1500 | 4 | 3¾x4 | 176.7 | 20@1400 | 30x3½ | 100 |
| 19 | T | 525 | 1500 | 4 | 3¾x4 | 176.7 | 20@1400 | 30x3½ | 100 |
| 20 | T | 525 | 1500 | 4 | 3¾x4 | 176.7 | 20@1400 | 30x3½ | 100 |
| 21 | T | 440 | 1560 | 4 | 3¾x4 | 176.7 | 20@1600 | 30x3½ | 100 |
| 22 | T | 355 | 1500 | 4 | 3¾x4 | 176.7 | 20@1400 | 30x3½ | 100 |
| 23 | T | 393 | 1650 | 4 | 3¾x4 | 176.7 | 20@1600 | 30x3½ | 100 |
| 24 | T | 380 | 1650 | 4 | 3¾x4 | 176.7 | 20@1600 | 30x3½ | 100 |
| 25 | T | 290 | 1662 | 4 | 3¾x4 | 176.7 | 20@1600 | 30x3½ | 100 |
| 26 | T | 290 | 1728 | 4 | 3¾x4 | 176.7 | 20@1600 | 30x3½ | 100 |
| 27 | T | 495 | 1950 | 4 | 3¾x4 | 176.7 | 20@1600 | 29x4.40 | 100 |
| 28 | A | 495 | 2400 | 4 | 3⅞x4¼ | 200.4 | 40@2200 | 30x4.50 | 103½ |
| 29 | A | 625 | 2414 | 4 | 3⅞x4¼ | 200.4 | 40@2200 | 30x4.50 | 103½ |
| 30 | A | 600 | 2467 | 4 | 3⅞x4¼ | 200.4 | 40@2200 | 4.75x19 | 103½ |
| 31 | A | 600 | 2462 | 4 | 3⅞x4¼ | 200.4 | 40@2200 | 4.75x19 | 103½ |
| 32 | B | 590 | 2462 | 4 | 3⅞x4¼ | 200.4 | 40@2200 | 4.75x19 | 103½ |
| 32 | V-8 | 590 | 2495 | 8 | 3 1/16x3¾ | 221.0 | 65@3400 | 5.25x18 | 106 |
| 33 | B | 540 | 2465 | 4 | 3⅞x4¼ | 200.4 | 50@2800 | 5.50x17 | 106 |
| 33 | V-8 | 590 | 2590 | 8 | 3 1/16x3¾ | 221.0 | 65@3400 | 5.50x17 | 106 |
| 34 | V-8 | 575 | 2675 | 8 | 3 1/16x3¾ | 221.0 | 92@3900 | 5.50x17 | 112 |
| 35 | V-8 | 575 | 2767 | 8 | 3 1/16x3¾ | 221.0 | 90@3800 | 6.00x16 | 112 |
| 36 | V-8 | 580 | 2860 | 8 | 3 1/16x3¾ | 221.0 | 90@3800 | 6.00x16 | 112 |
| 37 | V-8, 60 | 625 | 2543 | 8 | 2.6x3.2 | 135.9 | 60@3500 | 5.50x16 | 112 |
| 37 | V-8, 85 | 668 | 2761 | 8 | 3 1/16x3¾ | 221.0 | 90@3800 | 6.00x16 | 112 |
| 38 | V-8, 60 | 707 | 2481 | 8 | 2.6x3.2 | 135.9 | 60@3500 | 5.50x16 | 112 |
| 38 | V-8, 85 | 733 | 2697 | 8 | 3 1/16x3¾ | 221.0 | 85@3800 | 6.00x16 | 112 |
| 39 | V-8, 60 | 687 | 2623 | 8 | 2.6x3.2 | 135.9 | 60@3500 | 5.50x16 | 112 |
| 39 | V-8, 85 | 728 | 2850 | 8 | 3 1/16x3¾ | 221.0 | 85@3800 | 6.00x16 | 112 |
| 40 | V-8, 60 | 707 | 2591 | 8 | 2.6x3.2 | 135.9 | 60@3500 | 5.50x16 | 112 |
| 40 | V-8, 85 | 748 | 2826 | 8 | 3 1/16x3¾ | 221.0 | 85@3800 | 6.00x16 | 112 |
| 40 | 6 | 906 | 2922 | 6 | 3.3x4.4 | 226.0 | 90@3300 | 6.00x16 | 114 |
| 41 | V-8 | 802 | 3121 | 8 | 3 1/16x3¾ | 221.0 | 85@3800 | 6.00x16 | 114 |
| 42 | 6 | 906 | 2922 | 6 | 3.3x4.4 | 226.0 | 90@3300 | 6.00x16 | 114 |
| 42 | V-8 | 943 | 3050 | 8 | 3 1/16x3¾ | 221.0 | 90@3800 | 6.00x16 | 114 |

† NOTE—Open car prices from 1903 to 1926: Closed car prices begin with 1927:
‡ Rear Tires are 30 x 3½. Front are 30 x 3.

# SPECIFICATIONS FOR THREE REPRESENTATIVE AMERICAN CARS

Model T Ford
1908

Model A Ford
1928

The first Ford V8
1932

The modern Ford
1949

Production was suspended during the Second World War, during which no passenger cars were built.

## FORD SPECIFICATIONS — 1946 to 1953

| Year | Model | Price | Weight | No. of Cyl. | Bore & Stroke | Piston Displacement | Max. hp | Tire Size | Wheelbase |
|---|---|---|---|---|---|---|---|---|---|
| 46 | 6 | 1198 | 3050 | 6 | 3.3x4.4 | 226.0 | 90@33 | 6.00x16 | 114 |
| | V8 | 1248 | 3082 | 8 | 3 3/16x3¾ | 239.4 | 100@38 | 6.00x16 | 114 |
| 47 | 7GA | 1195 | 3233 | 6 | 3.30x4.40 | 226.0 | 90@33 | 6.00x16 | 114 |
| | 79GA | 1279 | 3220 | 8 | 3 3/16x3¾ | 239.4 | 100@38 | 6.00x16 | 114 |
| 48 | 87HA | 1334 | 3233 | 6 | 3.30x4.40 | 226.0 | 90@33 | 6.00x16 | 114 |
| | 899A | 1412 | 3246 | 8 | 3 3/16x3¾ | 239.4 | 100@38 | 6.00x16 | 114 |
| 49 | HA | 1472 | 2992 | 6 | 3 3/10x4 4/10 | 225.9 | 95@33 | 6.00x16 | 114 |
| | BA | 1546 | 3032 | 8 | 3 3/16x3¾ | 239.4 | 100@36 | 6.00x16 | 114 |

| Year | Model | Price | Weight | No. of Cyl. | Bore & Stroke | Piston Displacement | Max. hp | Tire Size | Wheelbase |
|---|---|---|---|---|---|---|---|---|---|
| 50 | OHA | 1472 | 3048 | 6 | 3 3/10x4 4/10 | 225.9 | 95@33 | 6.00x16 | 114 |
| | OBA | 1545 | 3083 | 8 | 3 3/16x3¾ | 239.4 | 100@36 | 6.00x16 | 114 |
| 51 | 1HA | 1495 | 3075 | 6 | 3 3/10x4 2/5 | 225.9 | 95@36 | 6.00x16 | 114 |
| | 1BA | 1571 | 3115 | 8 | 3 3/16x3¾ | 239.4 | 100@36 | 6.00x16 | 114 |
| 52 | 1HA | 1757 | 3173 | 6 | 3 9/16x3 3/5 | 215.3 | 101@35 | 6.00x16 | 115 |
| | 1BA | 1848 | 3207 | 8 | 3 3/16x3¾ | 239.4 | 110@38 | 6.00x16 | 115 |
| 53 | 6 | 1766 | 3105 | 6 | 3 9/16x3 3/5 | 215.3 | 101@35 | 6.70x15 | 115 |
| | 8 | 1858 | 3171 | 8 | 3 3/16x3¾ | 239.4 | 110@38 | 6.70x15 | 115 |

## CADILLAC SPECIFICATIONS: 1902-1942

| Year | Model | † Price | Weig't | No. of cylinders | Bore & Stroke | Piston Displacement | Maximum H.P. | Tire Size | Wheelbase |
|---|---|---|---|---|---|---|---|---|---|
| 02 | A | 850 | 1400 | 1 | 5x5 | 98.1 | 7 | 28x3 | 72 |
| 03 | | | 1100 | 1 | 5x5 | 98.1 | 7.3@1000 | 30x3 | |
| 04 | B | 750 | 1350 | 1 | 5x5 | 98.1 | 8 | 30x3 | 84 |
| 05 | E | 750 | 1200 | 1 | 5x5 | 98.1 | 8½ | 28x3 | 74 |
| 05 | B | 750 | 1500 | 1 | 5x5 | 98.1 | 8½ | 30x3 | 76 |
| 05 | F | 950 | 1500 | 1 | 5x5 | 98.1 | 8½ | 30x3½ | 96 |
| 05 | D | 2800 | 2600 | 4 | 4⅜x5 | 300.7 | 30 | 34x4½ | 100 |
| 06 | K | 750 | 1100 | 1 | 5x5 | 98.1 | 10 | 28x3 | 74 |
| 06 | M | 950 | 1350 | 1 | 5x5 | 98.1 | 10 | 30x3½ | 76 |
| 06 | H | 2500 | 2400 | 4 | 4⅜x5 | 300.7 | 30 | 32x4 | 98 |
| 06 | L | 3750 | 2850 | 4 | 5x5 | 392.7 | 40 | ‡36x4½ | 110 |
| 07 | K | 800 | 1100 | 1 | 5x5 | 98.1 | 10 | 30x3 | 74 |
| 07 | M | 950 | 1350 | 1 | 5x5 | 98.1 | 10 | 30x3½ | 76 |
| 07 | G | 2000 | | 4 | 4x4½ | 226.2 | 20 | 32x3½ | 100 |
| 07 | H | 2500 | 2400 | 4 | 4⅜x5 | 300.7 | 30 | 32x4 | 102 |
| 08 | S | 850 | | 1 | 5x5 | 98.1 | 10 | 30x3 | 82 |
| 08 | T | 1000 | | 1 | 5x5 | 98.1 | 10 | 30x3½ | 82 |
| 08 | G | 2000 | | 4 | 4x4½ | 226.2 | 25 | 32x3½ | 100 |
| 08 | H | 2500 | 2400 | 4 | 4⅜x5 | 300.7 | 30 | 32x4 | 102 |
| 09 | S, T | 950 | | 1 | 5x5 | 98.1 | 10 | 30x3½ | 82 |
| 09 | 30 | 1400 | | 4 | 4x4½ | 226.2 | 30 | 32x3½ | 106 |
| 10 | 30 | 1600 | | 4 | 4¼x4½ | 255.3 | 30 | 34x4 | 110 |
| 11 | 30 | 1700 | | 4 | 4½x4½ | 286.3 | 40 | 34x4 | 116 |
| 12 | 30 | 1800 | | 4 | 4½x4½ | 286.3 | 40 | 36x4 | 116 |
| 13 | | 1975 | | 4 | 4½x5¾ | 365.8 | 40-50 | 36x4½ | 120 |
| 14 | 1914 | 1975 | 4095 | 4 | 4½x5¾ | 365.8 | 40-50 | 36x4½ | 120 |
| 15 | 51 | 1975 | 3795 | 8 | 3⅛x5⅛ | 314.4 | 60 | 36x4½ | 122 |
| 16 | 53 | 2080 | 3900 | 8 | 3⅛x5⅛ | 314.4 | 60 | 36x4½ | 122 |
| 17 | 55 | 2240 | 4035 | 8 | 3⅛x5⅛ | 314.4 | 60 | 36x4½ | 125 |
| 18 | 57 | 2805 | 4035 | 8 | 3⅛x5⅛ | 314.4 | 60 | 35x5 | 125 |
| 18 | 57 | 2805 | 4035 | 8 | 3⅛x5⅛ | 314.4 | 60 | 35x5 | 132 |
| 19 | 57 | 3250 | 4035 | 8 | 3⅛x5⅛ | 314.4 | 60 | 35x5 | 125 |
| 20 | 59 | 3490 | 4050 | 8 | 3⅛x5⅛ | 314.4 | 60 | 35x5 | 125, 32 |
| 21 | 59 | 3940 | 4050 | 8 | 3⅛x5⅛ | 314.4 | 60@2700 | 34x4½ | 125, 32 |
| 22 | 61 | 3150 | 4025 | 8 | 3⅛x5⅛ | 314.4 | 60@2700 | 33x5 | 132 |
| 23 | 61 | 2885 | 4025 | 8 | 3⅛x5⅛ | 314.4 | @2760 | 33x5 | 132 |
| 24 | V-63 | 2985 | 4270 | 8 | 3⅛x5⅛ | 314.4 | 72@3000 | 33x5 | 132 |
| 25 | V-63 | 3185 | 4280 | 8 | 3⅛x5⅛ | 314.4 | 72@3000 | 33x5 | 132, 38 |
| 26 | 314 | 3250 | 4300 | 8 | 3⅛x5⅛ | 314.4 | 87@3000 | 33x6.75 | 132, 38 |
| 27 | 314 | 2995 | 4110 | 8 | 3⅛x5⅛ | 314.4 | 87@3000 | 33x6.75 | 132, 38 |
| 28 | V-8, 341 A | 3395 | 4840 | 8 | 3 5/16x4 15/16 | 341.0 | 90@3000 | 32x6.75 | 140 |
| 28 | LaS 303 | 2650 | 4000 | 8 | 3⅛x4 15/16 | 303.0 | 80@3000 | 32x6.00 | 125, 34 |
| 29 | V-8, 341 B | 3495 | 5028 | 8 | 3 5/16x4 15/16 | 341.0 | 90@3000 | 7.00x20 | 140 |
| 29 | LaS 328 | 2450 | 4512 | 8 | 3¼x4 15/16 | 327.7 | 85@3000 | 6.50x19 | 125 |
| 30 | V-8, 353 | 3695 | 5025 | 8 | 3⅜x4 15/16 | 353.0 | 95@3000 | 7.00x19 | 140 |
| 30 | V-16, 452A | 5950 | 5725 | 16 | 3x4 | 452.8 | 185@3400 | 7.00x19 | 148 |
| 30 | LaS 340 | 2565 | 4645 | 8 | 3 5/16x4 15/16 | 341.0 | 90@3000 | 6.50x19 | 134 |
| 31 | V-8, 355A | 2795 | 4660 | 8 | 3⅜x4 15/16 | 353.0 | 95@3000 | 6.50x19 | 134 |

| Year | Model | † Price | Weig't | No. of cylinders | Bore & Stroke | Piston Displacement | Maximum H.P. | Tire Size | Wheelbase |
|---|---|---|---|---|---|---|---|---|---|
| 31 | V-12, 370A | 3895 | 5230 | 12 | 3⅛x4 | 368.0 | 135@3400 | 7.00x19 | 140, 4 |
| 31 | V-16, 452A | 5950 | 5740 | 16 | 3x4 | 452.8 | 165@3400 | 7.00x19 | 148 |
| 31 | LaS 345A | 2205 | 4650 | 8 | 3⅜x4 15/16 | 353.0 | 95@3000 | 6.50x19 | 134 |
| 32 | V-8, 355B | 2895 | 4900 | 8 | 3⅜x4 15/16 | 353.0 | 115@3000 | 7.00x17 | 134, 4 |
| 32 | V-12, 370B | 3595 | 5190 | 12 | 3⅛x4 | 368.0 | 135@3400 | 7.50x17 | 134, 4 |
| 32 | V-16, 452B | 4595 | 5640 | 16 | 3x4 | 452.5 | 165@3500 | 7.50x18 | 143, 4 |
| 32 | LaS 345B | 2495 | 4855 | 8 | 3⅜x4 15/16 | 353.0 | 115@3000 | 7.00x17 | 130, 3 |
| 33 | V-8, 355C | 2895 | 5000 | 8 | 3⅜x4 15/16 | 353.0 | 115@3000 | 7.00x17 | 134, 4 |
| 33 | V-12, 370C | 3595 | 5335 | 12 | 3⅛x4 | 368.0 | 135@3400 | 7.50x17 | 134, 4 |
| 33 | V-16, 452C | 6250 | 6070 | 16 | 3x4 | 452.8 | 165@3400 | 7.50x17 | 143, 4 |
| 33 | LaS 345C | 2245 | 2245 | 8 | 3⅜x4 15/16 | 353.0 | 115@3000 | 7.00x17 | 130, 3 |
| 34 | V-8, 355D | 2495 | 4735 | 8 | 3⅜x4 15/16 | 353.0 | 130@3400 | 7.00x17 | 128, 3 |
| 34 | V-12, 370D | 4445 | 5700 | 12 | 3⅛x4 | 368.0 | 150@3800 | 7.50x17 | 146 |
| 34 | V-16, 452D | 6650 | 6085 | 16 | 3x4 | 452.8 | 185@3800 | 7.50x17 | 154 |
| 34 | LaS 50 | 1595 | 3995 | 8 | 3x4¼ | 240.3 | 90@3700 | 7.00x16 | 119 |
| 35 | V-8, 355E | 2445 | 4715 | 8 | 3⅜x4 15/16 | 353.0 | 130@3400 | 7.00x17 | 128,3 |
| 35 | V-12, 370E | 3995 | 5735 | 12 | 3⅛x4 | 368.0 | 150@3600 | 7.50x17 | 146 |
| 35 | V-16, 452E | 7000 | 6085 | 16 | 3x4 | 452.0 | 185@3800 | 7.50x17 | 154 |
| 35 | LaS 350 | 1695 | 3960 | 8 | 3x4¼ | 240.3 | 95@3600 | 7.00x16 | 119 |
| 35 | LaS 35-50 | 1295 | 3650 | 8 | 3x4⅜ | 248.0 | 105@3600 | 7.00x16 | 120 |
| 36 | V-8, 60 | 1695 | 4010 | 8 | 3⅜x4½ | 322.2 | 125@3200 | 7.00x16 | 121 |
| 36 | V-8, 70, 75 | 2445 | 4670 | 8 | 3½x4½ | 346.0 | 135@3400 | 7.50x16 | 131, 3 |
| 36 | V-12, 80, 85 | 2645 | 4945 | 12 | 3⅛x4 | 368.0 | 150@3600 | 7.50x16 | 131, 3 |
| 36 | V-16, 90 | 7450 | 6085 | 16 | 3x4 | 452.2 | 185@3800 | 7.50x17 | 154 |
| 36 | LaS 50 | 1225 | 3635 | 8 | 3x4⅜ | 248.0 | 104@3600 | 7.00x16 | 120 |
| 37 | V-8, 60 | 1660 | 3845 | 8 | 3½x4½ | 346.0 | 135@3400 | 7.00x16 | 124 |
| 37 | V-8, 65, 70 | 2090 | 4385 | 8 | 3½x4½ | 346.0 | 135@3400 | 7.50x16 | 131 |
| 37 | V-8, 75 | 2815 | 4745 | 8 | 3½x4½ | 346.0 | 135@3400 | 7.50x16 | 138 |
| 37 | V-12, 85 | 3535 | 5050 | 12 | 3⅛x4 | 368.0 | 150@3600 | 7.50x16 | 138 |
| 37 | V-16, 90 | 7595 | 6190 | 16 | 3x4 | 452.0 | 185@3800 | 7.50x17 | 154 |
| 37 | LaS 50 | 1260 | 3810 | 8 | 3⅜x4½ | 322.0 | 123@3400 | 7.00x16 | 124 |
| 38 | V-8, 60S, 60 | 1785 | 3940 | 8 | 3½x4½ | 346.0 | 135@3400 | 7.00x16 | 124, 2 |
| 38 | V-8, 65 | 2290 | 4540 | 8 | 3½x4½ | 346.0 | 135@3400 | 7.50x16 | 132 |
| 38 | V-8, 75 | 3080 | 4865 | 8 | 3½x4½ | 346.0 | 140@3400 | 7.50x16 | 141 |
| 38 | V-16, 90 | 5140 | 5105 | 16 | 3¼x3¼ | 431.0 | 175@3600 | 7.50x16 | 141 |
| 38 | LaS 50 | 1385 | 3830 | 8 | 3⅜x4½ | 322.0 | 125@3400 | 7.00x16 | 124 |
| 39 | V-8, 61 | 1680 | 3770 | 8 | 3½x4½ | 346.0 | 135@3400 | 7.00x16 | 126 |
| 39 | V-8, 60S | 2090 | 4110 | 8 | 3½x4½ | 346.0 | 135@3400 | 7.00x16 | 127 |
| 39 | V-8, 75 | 2995 | 4785 | 8 | 3½x4½ | 346.0 | 140@3400 | 7.50x16 | 141 |
| 39 | V-16, 90 | 5140 | 5105 | 16 | 3¼x3¼ | 431.0 | 185@3600 | 7.50x16 | 141 |
| 39 | LaS 50 | 1320 | 3740 | 8 | 3⅜x4½ | 322.0 | 125@3400 | 7.00x16 | 120 |
| 40 | V-8, 62, 60S | 1745 | 4032 | 8 | 3½x4½ | 346.0 | 135@3400 | 7.00x16 | 127 |
| 40 | V-8, 72, 75 | 2670 | 4679 | 8 | 3½x4½ | 346.0 | 140@3400 | 7.50x16 | 139 |
| 40 | V-16, 90 | 5140 | 5152 | 16 | 3¼x3¼ | 431.0 | 185@3600 | 7.50x16 | 141 |
| 40 | LaS 50, 52 | 1320 | 3790 | 8 | 3⅜x4½ | 322.0 | 130@3400 | 7.00x16 | 123 |
| 41 | 60S, 61, 62, 63 | 1445 | 4032 | 8 | 3½x4½ | 346.0 | 150@3400 | 7.00x15 | 126 |
| 41 | 67, 75 | 2595 | 4679 | 8 | 3½x4½ | 346.0 | 150@3400 | 7.50x16 | 136, 3 |
| 42 | 60S, 61, 62, 63 | 1647 | 4115 | 8 | 3½x4½ | 346.0 | 150@3400 | 7.00x15 | 126 |
| 42 | 67, 75 | 2896 | 4525 | 8 | 3½x4½ | 346.0 | 150@3400 | 7.50x16 | 136, 3 |

‡ Rear tires are 36x4½. Fronts are 36x4.

† Note—open car prices from 1902 to 1926, closed car prices begin with 192

## CADILLAC SPECIFICATIONS — 1946 to 1953

| Year | Model | Price | Weight | No. of Cyl. | Bore & Stroke | Piston Displacement | Max. hp | Tire Size | Wheelbase |
|---|---|---|---|---|---|---|---|---|---|
| 46 | 61 | 2176 | 4115 | 8 | 3½x4½ | 346.3 | 150@34 | 7.00x15 | 126 |
| | 62 | 2359 | 4080 | 8 | 3½x4½ | 346.3 | 150@34 | 7.00x15 | 129 |
| | 60S | 3099 | 4250 | 8 | 3½x4½ | 346.3 | 150@34 | 7.00x15 | 133 |
| | 75 | 4298 | 4705 | 8 | 3½x4½ | 346.3 | 150@34 | 7.50x16 | 136 |
| 47 | 61 | 2175 | 4165 | 8 | 3½x4½ | 346.0 | 150@34 | 7.00x15 | 126 |
| | 62 | 2360 | 5232 | 8 | 3½x4½ | 346.0 | 150@34 | 7.00x15 | 129 |
| | 60S | 2990 | 4370 | 8 | 3½x4½ | 346.0 | 150@34 | 7.00x15 | 133 |
| | 75 | 4190 | 4848 | 8 | 3½x4½ | 346.0 | 150@34 | 7.50x16 | 136 |
| 48 | 61 | 2833 | 4165 | 8 | 3½x4½ | 346.0 | 150@36 | 7.00x15 | 126 |
| | 62 | 2996 | 5232 | 8 | 3½x4½ | 346.0 | 150@36 | 7.00x15 | 129 |
| | 60S | 3820 | 4370 | 8 | 3½x4½ | 346.0 | 150@36 | 7.00x15 | 133 |
| | 75 | 4990 | 4848 | 8 | 3½x4½ | 346.0 | 150@36 | 7.50x16 | 136 |
| 49 | 61 | 2893 | 3991 | 8 | 3 13/16x3⅝ | 331.0 | 160@38 | 8.20x15 | 126 |
| | 62 | 3050 | 3852 | 8 | 3 13/16x3⅝ | 331.0 | 160@38 | 8.20x15 | 126 |
| | 60 | 3828 | 4125 | 8 | 3 13/16x3⅝ | 331.0 | 160@38 | 8.20x15 | 133 |
| | 75 | 4750 | 4581 | 8 | 3 13/16x3⅝ | 331.0 | 160@38 | 7.50x16 | 136¼ |

| Year | Model | Price | Weight | No. of Cyl. | Bore & Stroke | Piston Displacement | Max. hp | Tire Size | Wheelbase |
|---|---|---|---|---|---|---|---|---|---|
| 50 | 61 | 2866 | 3870 | 8 | 3 13/16x3⅝ | 331.0 | 160@36 | 8.00x15 | 122 |
| | 60 | 3233 | 4010 | 8 | 3 13/16x3⅝ | 331.0 | 160@36 | 8.00x15 | 126 |
| | 62 | 3797 | 4150 | 8 | 3 13/16x3⅝ | 331.0 | 160@36 | 8.00x15 | 130 |
| | 75 | 4770 | 4556 | 8 | 3 13/16x3⅝ | 331.0 | 160@36 | 8.20x15 | 146¾ |
| 51 | 61 | 2917 | 3839 | 8 | 3 13/16x3⅝ | 331.0 | 160@38 | 8.00x15 | 122 |
| | 62 | 3468 | 3983 | 8 | 3 13/16x3⅝ | 331.0 | 160@38 | 8.00x15 | 126 |
| | 60 | 4167 | 4155 | 8 | 3 13/16x3⅝ | 331.0 | 160@38 | 8.00x15 | 130 |
| | 75 | 4982 | 4622 | 8 | 3 13/16x3⅝ | 331.0 | 160@38 | 8.20x15 | 146¾ |
| 52 | 62 | 3638 | 4151 | 8 | 3 13/16x3⅝ | 331.0 | 190@40 | 8.00x15 | 126 |
| | 60 | 4270 | 4258 | 8 | 3 13/16x3⅝ | 331.0 | 190@40 | 8.00x15 | 130 |
| | 75 | 5361 | 4699 | 8 | 3 13/16x3⅝ | 331.0 | 190@40 | 8.20x15 | 146¾ |
| 53 | 62 | 3666 | 4142 | 8 | 3 13/16x3⅝ | 331.0 | 210@41 | 8.00x15 | 126 |
| | 60 | 4305 | 4351 | 8 | 3 13/16x3⅝ | 331.0 | 210@41 | 8.00x15 | 130 |
| | 75 | 5408 | 4803 | 8 | 3 13/16x3⅝ | 331.0 | 210@41 | 8.20x15 | 146¾ |

Production was suspended during the Second World War, during which no passenger cars were built.

## STUDEBAKER SPECIFICATIONS: 1904-1942

| Year | * Model | † Price | Weig't | No. of cylinders | Bore & Stroke | Piston Displacement | Maximum H.P. | Tire Size | Wheel base |
|---|---|---|---|---|---|---|---|---|---|
| 04 | 202 | 1100 | 1550 | 2 | 5x5½ | 215.9 | 16 | 30x3½ | 88 |
| 05 | 9503 | 3000 | 2100 | 4 | 3⅞x4½ | 212.3 | 20-24 | x4 | 96 |
| 05 | 9502 | 1350 | 2080 | 2 | 5x5½ | 215.9 | 14-16 | 30x3½ | 80 |
| 06 | E | 2600 | 2400 | 4 | 3⅞x4½ | 212.3 | 20 | 32x4 | 98 |
| 06 | F | 3000 | 2700 | 4 | 4⅜x4¾ | 285.6 | 28 | 34x4 | 104 |
| 06 | G | 3700 | 2700 | 4 | 4⅛x5¼ | 280.6 | 30-35 | 34x4½ | 104 |
| 07 | L | 3000 | 2500 | 4 | 4⅜x4¾ | 285.6 | 28-32 | 34x4 | 104 |
| 07 | G, H | 3700 | 2400 | 4 | 4⅛x5¼ | 280.6 | 30-35 | 34x4 | 104 |
| 08 | A, H | 3500 | | 4 | 4⅛x5¼ | 280.6 | 30 | 34x4 | 104 |
| 08 | B | 4250 | 3050 | 4 | 4¾x5¼ | 372.1 | 40 | 34x4½ | 114 |
| 09 | Stu-EMF | 1250 | | 4 | 4x4½ | 226.2 | 30 | 32x3½ | 106 |
| 09 | EMF 30 | 1250 | 2100 | 4 | 4x4½ | 226.2 | 30 | 32x3½ | 106 |
| 09 | A,C | 3500 | 2850 | 4 | 4⅛x5¼ | 280.6 | 30 | 34x4 | 104 |
| 09 | B, D | 4000 | 3150 | 4 | 4¾x5¼ | 372.1 | 40 | 34x4½ | 114, 17 |
| 10 | Flandrs 20 | 750 | 1300 | 4 | 3⅝x3¾ | 154.8 | 20 | 32x3 | 100 |
| 10 | EMF, A, 30 | 1250 | 2100 | 4 | 4x4½ | 226.2 | 30 | 32x3½ | 108 |
| 10 | Garford H | 3750 | | 6 | 4¼x4 | 340.5 | 42 | ‡37x5 | 127 |
| 10 | Garfrd G7 | 4000 | 3400 | 4 | 4¾x5¼ | 372.1 | 40 | 36x4½ | 117½ |
| 10 | EMF 30 | 1250 | 2040 | 4 | 4x4½ | 226.2 | 30 | 34x3½ | 107 |
| 10 | Flandrs 20 | 790 | | 4 | 3⅝x3¾ | 154.8 | 20 | 32x3 | 100 |
| 11 | G840 | 3500 | 3600 | 4 | 4¾x5¼ | 372.1 | 40 | ‡36x4½ | 117½ |
| 11 | Finds S, 20 | 700 | 1200 | 4 | 3⅝x3¾ | 154.8 | 20 | 32x3 | 100 |
| 11 | EMF, A, 30 | 1000 | 2150 | 4 | 4x4½ | 226.2 | 30 | 32x3½ | 110 |
| 11 | Garfd G10 | 3500 | 3150 | 4 | 4¼x5¼ | 297.8 | | 36x4 | 116 |
| 12 | Findrs 20S | 800 | | 4 | 3⅝x3¾ | 154.8 | 20 | ‡30x3½ | 102 |
| 12 | EMF, 30, A | 1100 | | 4 | 4x4½ | 226.2 | 30 | 32x3½ | 112 |
| 13 | SA, 25 | 885 | | 4 | 3½x5 | 192.4 | 25 | 30x3½ | 102 |
| 13 | AA, 35 | 1290 | | 4 | 4⅛x5 | 267.3 | 35 | 34x4 | 115½ |
| 13 | E, Six | 1550 | | 6 | 3½x5 | 288.6 | 40 | 34x4 | 121 |
| 13 | 20 | 800 | | 4 | 3⅝x3¾ | 154.8 | 20 | ‡30x3½ | 102 |
| 13 | 30 | 1100 | | 4 | 4x4½ | 226.2 | 30 | 32x3½ | 112 |
| 13 | Finds 50 | 2250 | | 6 | 4x4¾ | 358.1 | | 36x4½ | 130 |
| 14 | Four | 1050 | | 4 | 3½x5 | 192.4 | | 32x3½ | 108 |
| 14 | Six | 1575 | | 6 | 3½x5 | 288.6 | | 34x4 | 121 |
| 15 | Four, SD | 985 | 2350 | 4 | 3½x5 | 192.4 | 20 | 33x4 | 108 |
| 15 | Six, EC | 1385 | 2860 | 6 | 3½x5 | 288.6 | 30 | 34x4 | 121 |
| 16 | 4-40, SF | 885 | 2675 | 4 | 3⅞x5 | 235.8 | 40 | 34x4 | 112 |
| 16 | 6-50, ED | 1050 | 2930 | 6 | 3⅞x5 | 353.8 | 50 | 34x4 | 122 |
| 17 | 6-50 | 1180 | 2990 | 6 | 3⅞x5 | 353.8 | 50 | 34x4 | 122 |
| 17 | 4-40 | 940 | 2790 | 4 | 3⅞x5 | 235.8 | 40 | 34x4 | 112 |
| 18 | Lgt. 4, SH | 1050 | 2500 | 4 | 3½x5 | 192.4 | 40 | 32x3½ | 112 |
| 18 | Big Six, EG | 1385 | 2990 | 6 | 3⅞x5 | 353.8 | 50 | 33x4½ | 126 |
| 18 | Lgt Six EH | 1395 | 2695 | 6 | 3½x5 | 288.6 | 51 | 32x4 | 119 |
| 19 | EH | 1585 | 2750 | 6 | 3½x5 | 288.6 | 51 | 32x4 | 119 |
| 19 | EG | 1985 | 3050 | 6 | 3⅞x5 | 353.8 | 62 | 33x4½ | 126 |
| 19 | SH | 1135 | 2500 | 4 | 3½x5 | 192.4 | 40 | | |
| 20 | Spec 6, EU | 1685 | 2995 | 6 | 3½x5 | 288.6 | 51@2000 | 32x4 | 119 |
| 20 | Big 6, EG | 2135 | 3175 | 6 | 3⅞x5 | 353.8 | 65@2000 | 33x4½ | 126 |
| 20 | Light Six | 1435 | 2400 | 6 | 3⅛x4½ | 207.1 | | 32x4 | 112 |
| 21 | Light Six | 1485 | 2400 | 6 | 3⅛x4½ | 207.1 | 45@2000 | 32x4 | 112 |
| 21 | Special Six | 1750 | 2995 | 6 | 3½x5 | 288.6 | 55@2000 | 32x4 | 119 |
| 21 | Big Six | 2150 | 3125 | 6 | 3⅞x5 | 353.8 | 60@2000 | 33x4½ | 126 |
| 22 | Light Six | 1150 | 2550 | 6 | 3⅛x4½ | 207.1 | 45@2000 | 32x4 | 112 |
| 22 | Special Six | 1635 | 3035 | 6 | 3½x5 | 288.6 | 55@2000 | 32x4 | 119 |
| 22 | Big Six | 1985 | 3230 | 6 | 3⅞x5 | 353.8 | 65@2000 | 33x4½ | 126 |
| 23 | Light Six | 975 | 2645 | 6 | 3⅛x4½ | 207.1 | 40@2000 | 31x4 | 112 |
| 23 | Special Six | 1275 | 3300 | 6 | 3½x5 | 288.6 | 50@2000 | 32x4 | 119 |
| 23 | Big Six | 1750 | 3310 | 6 | 3⅞x5 | 353.8 | 60@2000 | 33x4½ | 126 |
| 24 | Light Six | 995 | 2800 | 6 | 3⅛x4½ | 207.1 | 40@2400 | 31x4 | 112 |
| 24 | Special Six | 1350 | 3445 | 6 | 3½x5 | 288.6 | 50@2000 | 32x4 | 119 |
| 24 | Big Six | 1750 | 3770 | 6 | 3⅞x5 | 353.8 | 60@2000 | 33x4½ | 126 |
| 25 | Standrd 6 | 1145 | 2870 | 6 | 3⅜x4½ | 241.6 | 50@2200 | 31x5.25 | 113 |
| 25 | Special 6 | 1450 | 3660 | 6 | 3½x5 | 288.6 | 65@2400 | 32x6.20 | 120 |
| 25 | Big 6 | 1875 | 3785 | 6 | 3⅞x5 | 353.8 | 75@2400 | 34x7.30 | 127 |
| 26 | Standrd 6 | 1145 | 2870 | 6 | 3⅜x4½ | 241.6 | 50@2200 | 31x5.25 | 113 |
| 26 | Special 6 | 1445 | 3475 | 6 | 3½x5 | 288.6 | 65@2400 | 32x6.20 | 120 |
| 26 | Big 6 | 1575 | 3785 | 6 | 3⅞x5 | 353.8 | 75@2400 | 34x7.30 | 127 |
| 27 | Standrd 6 | 1230 | 2945 | 6 | 3⅜x4½ | 241.6 | 50@2200 | 31x5.25 | 113 |
| 27 | Special 6 | 1480 | 3470 | 6 | 3½x5 | 288.6 | 65@2400 | 32x6.00 | 120 |
| 27 | Big 6, ES | 1785 | 3835 | 6 | 3⅞x5 | 353.8 | 75@2400 | 32x6.75 | 120, 27 |
| 27 | Erskine 6 | 975 | 2425 | 6 | 2⅝x4½ | 146.1 | 40@3200 | 28x4.40 | 107 |
| 28 | Erskine, 51 | 965 | 2425 | 6 | 2¾x4½ | 160.4 | 40@3200 | 29x4.75 | 107 |
| 28 | Dicta6, GE | 1195 | 3302 | 6 | 3⅜x4½ | 241.6 | 50@2200 | 30x5.50 | 113 |
| 28 | Com. 6, GB, GH | 1495 | 3594 | 6 | 3⅞x5 | 353.8 | 75@2400 | 30x5.50 | 120 |
| 28 | President 8, FA, FB | 1985 | 4000 | 8 | 3⅜x4⅜ | 313.1 | 100@2600 | 31x6.20 | 131 |
| 29 | Erskine 52 | 945 | 2600 | 6 | 2¾x4½ | 160.4 | 43@3000 | 4.75x20 | 109 |
| 29 | Dicta, GE | 1265 | 3280 | 6 | 3⅜x4½ | 241.6 | 67@2800 | 5.50x20 | 113 |
| 29 | Com 6, GJ | 1375 | 3235 | 6 | 3⅜x4⅝ | 248.3 | 74@3000 | 5.50x19 | 119½ |
| 29 | Com 8, FD | 1525 | 3255 | 8 | 3 1/16x4¼ | 250.4 | 80@3600 | 5.50x19 | 119½ |
| 29 | President 8, FE, FH | 2350 | 4235 | 8 | 3½x4⅜ | 336.7 | 114@3200 | 6.50x19 | 125, 35 |
| 30 | 6, 53 | 965 | 2950 | 6 | 3¼x4⅛ | 205.3 | 70@3200 | 5.25x19 | 114 |
| 30 | Dicta6, GL | 1165 | 3080 | 6 | 3⅜x4⅛ | 221.4 | 68@3200 | 5.00x19 | 115 |
| 30 | Dicta8, FC | 1285 | 3095 | 8 | 3 1/16x3¾ | 221.0 | 70@3200 | 5.50x19 | 115 |
| 30 | Com. 6, GJ | 1425 | 3235 | 6 | 3⅜x4⅝ | 248.3 | 75@3000 | 5.50x19 | 120 |
| 30 | Com 8, FD | 1515 | 3310 | 8 | 3 1/16x4¼ | 250.4 | 80@3600 | 5.50x19 | 120 |
| 30 | President 8, FE, FH | 1995 | 4305 | 8 | 3½x4⅜ | 336.7 | 115@3200 | 6.50x19 | 125, 35 |
| 31 | 6, 54 | 895 | 2900 | 6 | 3¼x4⅛ | 205.3 | 70@3200 | 5.25x19 | 114 |
| 31 | Dicta 8, 61 | 1150 | 3095 | 8 | 3 1/16x3¾ | 221.0 | 81@3200 | 5.25x19 | 114 |
| 31 | Com 8, 70 | 1585 | 3520 | 8 | 3 1/16x4¼ | 250.4 | 101@3200 | 6.00x19 | 124 |
| 31 | President 8 80, 90 | 1850 | 4250 | 8 | 3½x4⅜ | 336.7 | 122@3200 | 6.50x19 | 130, 36 |
| 32 | Rock 6, 65 | 585 | 2595 | 6 | 3⅛x4⅛ | 189.8 | 65@3200 | 5.25x18 | 100 |
| 32 | Rock 6, 75 | 685 | 3000 | 6 | 3¼x4⅛ | 205.3 | 72@3200 | 5.50x18 | 114 |
| 32 | 6, 55 | 895 | 3150 | 6 | 3¼x4⅝ | 230.2 | 80@3200 | 5.50x18 | 117 |
| 32 | Dicta 8, 62 | 1150 | 3240 | 8 | 3 1/16x3¾ | 221.0 | 85@3200 | 5.50x18 | 117 |
| 32 | Com. 8, 71 | 1585 | 3545 | 8 | 3 1/16x4¼ | 250.4 | 101@3200 | 6.00x18 | 125 |
| 32 | Presi. 8, 91 | 1850 | 4260 | 8 | 3½x4⅜ | 336.7 | 122@3200 | 6.50x18 | 135 |
| 33 | Rock Six 10 | 635 | 2675 | 6 | 3⅛x4⅛ | 189.8 | 70@3200 | 5.25x17 | 110 |
| 33 | 6, 56 | 915 | 3310 | 6 | 3¼x4⅝ | 230.0 | 85@3200 | 5.50x17 | 117 |
| 33 | Com. 8, 73 | 1075 | 3385 | 8 | 3 1/16x4 | 235.7 | 100@3800 | 6.00x17 | 117 |
| 33 | Pres. 8, 82 | 1385 | 3725 | 8 | 3 1/16x4¼ | 250.4 | 110@3600 | 6.50x17 | 125 |
| 33 | Sp. President 8, 92 | 1685 | 4465 | 8 | 3½x4⅜ | 336.7 | 132@3400 | 7.00x17 | 135 |
| 34 | Dicta 6, A | 695 | 2900 | 6 | 3¼x4⅛ | 205.3 | 88@3600 | 5.50x17 | 114 |
| 34 | Com. 8, B | 895 | 3300 | 8 | 3 1/16x3¾ | 221.0 | 103@4000 | 6.00x17 | 119 |
| 34 | Pres. 8, C | 1095 | 3480 | 8 | 3 1/16x4¼ | 250.4 | 110@3600 | 6.50x17 | 123 |
| 35 | Dr 6, 1A, 2A | 750 | 3030 | 6 | 3¼x4⅛ | 205.3 | 88@3600 | 6.00x16 | 114 |
| 35 | Com. 8, 1B | 985 | 3600 | 8 | 3 1/16x4¼ | 250.4 | 107@3800 | 6.50x16 | 119 |
| 35 | Pres. 8, 1C | 1330 | 3900 | 8 | 3 1/16x4¼ | 250.4 | 110@3600 | 7.00x16 | 123 |
| 36 | Dr 6, 3A, 4A | 745 | 3120 | 6 | 3¼x4⅜ | 217.8 | 90@3400 | 6.00x16 | 116 |
| 36 | Pres. 8, 2C | 1045 | 3605 | 8 | 3 1/16x4¼ | 250.4 | 115@3600 | 6.50x16 | 125 |
| 37 | Dr 6, 5A, 6A | 880 | 3130 | 6 | 3¼x4⅜ | 217.8 | 90@3400 | 6.00x16 | 116 |
| 37 | Pres. 8, 3C | 1165 | 3620 | 8 | 3 1/16x4¼ | 250.4 | 115@3600 | 6.50x16 | 125 |
| 38 | 6, 7A | 965 | 3190 | 6 | 3 5/16x4⅜ | 226.2 | 90@3400 | 6.00x16 | 116½ |
| 38 | Com. 6, 8A | 1040 | 3215 | 6 | 3 5/16x4⅜ | 226.2 | 90@3400 | 6.00x16 | 116½ |
| 38 | Pres. 8, 4C | 1205 | 3455 | 8 | 3 1/16x4¼ | 250.4 | 110@3600 | 6.50x16 | 122 |
| 39 | Cha. 6, G | 700 | 2330 | 6 | 3x3⅞ | 164.3 | 78@4000 | 5.50x16 | 110 |
| 39 | Com. 6, 9A | 965 | 3200 | 6 | 3 5/16x4⅜ | 226.2 | 90@3400 | 6.00x16 | 116½ |
| 39 | Pres. 8, 5C | 1110 | 3440 | 8 | 3 1/16x4¼ | 250.4 | 110@3600 | 6.50x16 | 122 |
| 40 | Cha. 6, 2G | 740 | 2365 | 6 | 3x3⅞ | 164.3 | 78@4000 | 5.50x16 | 110 |
| 40 | Com 6, 10A | 965 | 3200 | 6 | 3 5/16x4⅜ | 226.2 | 90@3400 | 6.25x16 | 116½ |
| 40 | Pres. 8, 6C | 1095 | 3440 | 8 | 3 1/16x4¼ | 250.4 | 110@3600 | 6.50x16 | 122 |
| 41 | Cha. 6, 3G | 770 | 2435 | 6 | 3x4 | 169.6 | 80@4000 | 5.50x16 | 110 |
| 41 | Com 6, 11A | 985 | 3150 | 6 | 3 5/16x4⅜ | 226.2 | 94@3600 | 6.25x16 | 119 |
| 41 | Pres. 8, 7C | 1115 | 3500 | 8 | 3 1/16x4¼ | 250.4 | 117@4000 | 7.00x16 | 125 |
| 42 | Cha. 6, 4G | 870 | 2520 | 6 | 3x4 | 169.6 | 80@4000 | 5.50x16 | 110 |
| 42 | Com 6, 12A | 1128 | 3265 | 6 | 3 5/16x4⅜ | 226.2 | 94@3600 | 6.25x16 | 119 |
| 42 | Pres. 8, 8C | 1262 | 3485 | 8 | 3 1/16x4¼ | 250.4 | 117@4000 | 7.00x15 | 124 |

* Cars listed bear the Studebaker name except as otherwise stated. Name abbreviations are: Flandrs, Flands—Flanders, Garfrd, Garfd—Garford, Rock—Rockne.
† NOTE—Open car prices from 1904 to 1926, closed car prices begin with 1927. ‡ Rear tire size is shown. Front tires have ½-inch smaller section.

## STUDEBAKER SPECIFICATIONS — 1946 to 1953

| Year | Model | Price | Weight | No. of Cyl. | Bore & Stroke | Piston Displacement | Max. hp | Tire Size | Wheelbase |
|---|---|---|---|---|---|---|---|---|---|
| 46 | Champ. Six G | 1097 | 2525 | 6 | 3x4 | 169.6 | 80@40 | 5.50x16 | 110 |
| 47 | 6G | 1292 | 2735 | 6 | 3x4 | 169.6 | 80@40 | 5.50x16 | 112 |
| | 14A | 1544 | 3265 | 6 | 3 5/16x4⅜ | 226.2 | 94@36 | 6.50x15 | 119 |
| 48 | 7G | 1636 | 2735 | 6 | 3x4 | 169.6 | 80@40 | 5.50x15 | 112 |
| | 15A | 1956 | 3265 | 6 | 3 5/16x4⅜ | 226.2 | 94@36 | 6.50x15 | 119 |
| 49 | 8G | 1688 | 2745 | 6 | 3x4 | 169.6 | 80@40 | 6.40x15 | 112 |
| | 16A | 2019 | 3215 | 6 | 3 5/16x4¾ | 245.6 | 100@34 | 6.50x15 | 119 |
| 50 | 9G | 1519 | 2750 | 6 | 3x4 | 169.6 | 85@40 | 6.40x15 | 113 |
| | 17A | 1903 | 3255 | 6 | 3 5/16x4¾ | 245.6 | 102@32 | 7.60x15 | 120 |
| 51 | 10G | 1494 | 2720 | 6 | 3x4 | 169.6 | 85@40 | 6.40x15 | 115 |
| | H | 1747 | 3120 | 8 | 3⅜x3¼ | 232.6 | 120@40 | 7.10x15 | 115 |
| 52 | 12G | 1752 | 2720 | 6 | 3x4 | 169.6 | 85@40 | 6.40x15 | 115 |
| | 3H | 2107 | 3085 | 8 | 3⅜x3¼ | 232.6 | 120@40 | 7.10x15 | 115 |
| 53 | 14G | 1767 | 2710 | 6 | 3x4 | 169.6 | 85@40 | 6.40x15 | 116½ and 120½ |
| | 4H | 2121 | 3075 | 8 | 3⅜x3¼ | 232.6 | 120@40 | 7.10x15 | 116½ and 120½ |

# SOME OF THE MORE THAN TWO THOUSAND AMERICAN CARS

More than 2000 different makes of cars have been manufactured in the United States. Some of them never got out of the experimental stage; others made a hesitant start and died young; still others, like the Locomobile, the Pierce-Arrow, the Mercer, the Stutz, and the Franklin, were among the best of their day but were unable to survive competition.

The list given here is a comparatively short one. It covers only the more important, better known, or more interesting cars. It does not attempt to list some of the strange names like Brownie Kar, Peter Pan, Dodo, Dragon, Frontmobile, or the Mighty Michigan.

Much basic research still remains to be done on automobile makes and makers, particularly on the years in which the companies started in business and were liquidated. Until such research is completed, many blanks and occasional inaccuracies will occur in every list.

| NAME OF CAR | BEGUN | ENDED | MANUFACTURER | LOCATION |
|---|---|---|---|---|
| Abbott-Detroit | 1909 | 1917 | Abbott Motor Co. | Detroit |
| Ajax (Nash) | 1925 | 1926 | Ajax Motor Co. | Racine, Wis. |
| Alco | 1909 | 1914 | American Locomotive Co. | Providence, R.I. |
| Allen | 1913 | 1922 | Allen Motor Co. | Fostoria, O. |
| American Bantam | 1937 | 1941 | American Bantam Car Co. | Butler, Pa. |
| American (Underslung) | 1903 | 1914 | American Motors Co. | Indianapolis |
| Amplex | 1908 | 1912 | Simplex Motor Car Co. | Mishawaka, Ind. |
| Anderson | 1919 | 1925 | Anderson Motor Co. | Rock Hill, So. Car. |
| Apperson | 1905 | 1926 | Apperson Bros. Auto Co. | Kokomo, Ind. |
| Auburn | 1903 | 1936 | Auburn Automobile Co. | Auburn, Ind. |
| Austin | 1906 | 1919 | Austin Automobile Co. | Grand Rapids, Mich. |
| Autocar | 1897 | Going | Autocar Co. (Makes Trucks) | Ardmore, Pa. |
| Baker | 1899 | 1924 | Baker Motor Vehicle Co. | Cleveland, O. |
| Bergdoll | 1909 | 1913 | Louis J. Bergdoll | Philadelphia |
| Biddle | 1915 | 1923 | Biddle Motor Car Co. | Phila.-New York |
| Black Crow | 1907 | 1915 | Crow Elkhart Co. | Elkhart, Ind. |
| Bour-Davis | 1915 | 1922 | Bour-Davis Motor Co. | Detroit |
| Brewster | 1916 | 1926 | Brewster & Co. | Long Island City |
| Briscoe (Earl) | 1914 | 1921 | Briscoe Motor Corp. | Jackson, Mich. |
| Brush | 1907 | 1912 | Brush Runabout Co. | Detroit |
| Buick | 1904 | Going | Buick Motor Co. | Flint, Mich. |
| Bush | 1916 | 1924 | Bush Motor Co. | Chicago, Ill. |
| Cadillac | 1902 | Going | Cadillac Motor Car Co. | Detroit |
| Cameron | 1903 | 1917 | Cameron Car Co. | Norwalk, Conn. |
| Cartercar | 1907 | 1915 | Motorcar Co. | Pontiac, Mich. |
| Case | 1910 | 1927 | J. I. Case Threshing Mach. Co. | Racine, Wis. |
| Chadwick | 1905 | 1916 | Chadwick Engineering Works | Pottstown, Pa. |
| Chalmers | 1908 | 1924 | Chalmers Motor Co. | Detroit |
| Chandler | 1912 | 1929 | Chandler Motor Car Co. | Cleveland |
| Chevrolet (see Little) | 1911 | Going | Chevrolet Motor Co. | Flint, Mich. |
| Chrysler | 1923 | Going | Chrysler Motor Car Co. | Detroit |
| Cleveland | 1919 | 1926 | Cleveland Auto Co. | Cleveland |
| Cole | 1909 | 1925 | Cole Motor Car Co. | Indianapolis |
| Columbia | 1897 | 1913 | Columbia Motor Car Co. | Hartford, Conn. |
| Columbia | 1916 | 1925 | Columbia Motors Co. | Detroit |
| Cord | 1929 | 1937 | Auburn Automobile Co. | Auburn, Ind. |
| Correja | 1908 | | Vandewater & Co. | Iselin, N. Y. |
| Crane | 1912 | | Crane Motor Co. | Bayonne, N. J. |
| Crawford (Dagmar) | 1905 | 1924 | Crawford Automobile Co. | Hagerstown, Md. |
| Crosley | 1939 | 1952 | Crosley Motors | Cincinnati |
| Crow-Elkhart | 1911 | 1923 | Crow-Elkhart Motor Co. | Elkhart, Ind. |
| Cunningham | 1911 | | Cunningham Sons Co. | Rochester, N. Y. |
| Dagmar | 1924 | 1926 | Crawford Auto Co. | Hagerstown, Md. |
| Daniels | 1915 | 1926 | Daniels Motor Car Co. | Reading, Pa. |
| Davis | 1910 | 1929 | Geo. W. Davis Motor Car Co. | Richmond, Ind. |

| NAME OF CAR | BEGUN | ENDED | MANUFACTURER | LOCATION |
|---|---|---|---|---|
| DeSoto (Chrysler) | 1928 | Going | DeSoto Motor Corp. | Detroit |
| Detroit | 1900 | 1922 | (Became Thomas-Detroit) | Detroit |
| DeVaux | 1931 | 1932 | Continental DeVaux Co. | Grand Rapids, Mich. |
| Diamond T | 1907 | Going | Diamond T Motor Car Co. (Makes-Trucks) | Chicago |
| Diana | 1925 | 1929 | Diana Motor Car Co. | St. Louis |
| Dixie Flyer (National Four) | 1916 | 1923 | Dixie Motor Car Co. | Louisville, Ky. |
| Doble (steam) | 1916 | | Detroit Steam Motors Co. | Detroit |
| Dodge Brothers (Chrysler) | 1914 | Going | Dodge Bros. | Detroit |
| Dorris | 1906 | 1926 | Dorris Motor Car Co. | St. Louis |
| Dort | 1915 | 1925 | Dort Motor Car Co. | Flint, Mich. |
| Duesenberg | 1920 | 1937 | Duesenberg Motors Co. | Indianapolis |
| Dupont | 1920 | 1929 | Dupont Motors Mfg. Co. | Wilmington, Del. |
| Durant | 1921 | 1932 | Durant Motors, Inc. | Elizabeth, N. J. |
| Duryea | 1893 | | Charles Edgar Duryea | Springfield, Mass. |
| Duryea | 1895 | | Duryea Motor Wagon Co. | Springfield, Mass. |
| Duryea | 1905 | | Duryea Power Co. | Reading, Pa. |
| Earl | 1921 | 1924 | Earl Motors, Inc. | Jackson, Mich. |
| Edwards-Knight | 1912 | | Edwards-Knight Motor Car Co. | L. I. City, N. Y. |
| Elcar | 1909 | 1930 | Elkhart Carriage & Motor Car Co. | Elkhart, Ind. |
| Elgin | 1916 | 1924 | Elgin Motor Car Co. | Chicago |
| Elmore | 1901 | 1912 | Elmore Mfg. Co. | Clyde, O. |
| E-M-F (Studebaker) | 1908 | 1909 | Everett-Metzger-Flanders Co. | Detroit |
| Empire | 1910 | 1918 | Empire Automobile Co. | Indianapolis |
| Enger | 1914 | 1917 | Enger Motor Car Co. | Cincinnati |
| Erskine (Studebaker) | 1927 | 1930 | Studebaker Corp. | South Bend, Ind. |
| Essex | 1919 | 1933 | Hudson Motor Car Co. | Detroit |
| Everitt | 1910 | 1912 | Metzger Motor Car Co. | Detroit |
| Fageol | 1917 | | Fageol Motor Co. | Oakland, Cal. |
| Falcon-Knight | 1927 | 1929 | Falcon Motors Corp. | Detroit |
| Flanders | 1910 | | Flanders Motor Co. | Detroit |
| Flint | 1924 | 1928 | Flint Motor Co. | Flint, Mich. |
| Ford | 1903 | Going | Ford Motor Co. | Detroit |
| Fox | 1922 | 1925 | Fox Motor Co. | Philadelphia |
| Franklin | 1902 | 1934 | Franklin Automobile Co. | Syracuse, N. Y. |
| Gardner | 1919 | 1931 | Gardner Motor Car Co. | St. Louis |
| Gearless | 1907 | 1921 | Gearless Transmission Co. | Rochester, N. Y. |
| Glide | 1901 | 1920 | Bartholomew Co. and Avery Co. | Peoria, Ill. |
| Graham (Paige) | 1930 | 1941 | Graham Motor Co. | Detroit |
| Grant | 1915 | 1923 | Grant Motor Car Co. | Cleveland |
| Gray | 1922 | 1926 | Gray Motor Corp. | Detroit |
| Great Western | 1909 | 1916 | Great Western Auto Co. | Peru, Ind. |
| Grout | 1914 | 1915 | Grout Bros. Auto Co. | Orange, Mass. |
| H-A-L | 1916 | 1918 | H-A-L Motor Car Co. | Cleveland |
| Halladay | 1907 | 1922 | Halladay Motor Car Co. | Attica, Ind. |
| Handley-Knight | 1921 | 1923 | Handley-Knight Co. | Kalamazoo, Mich. |
| Harroun | 1916 | 1922 | Harroun Motor Corp. | Wayne, Mich. |
| Hatfield | 1907 | | Cortland Cart & Carriage Co. | Sidney, N. Y. |
| Havers | 1911 | 1914 | Havers Motor Car Co. | Port Huron, Mich. |
| Haynes-Apperson (Haynes) | 1895 | 1905 | Haynes-Apperson Automobile Co. | Kokomo, Ind. |
| Haynes | 1905 | 1925 | Haynes Automobile Co. | Kokomo, Ind. |
| H-C-S | 1920 | 1925 | H-C-S Automobile Co. | Indianapolis |
| Henry J | 1951 | Going | Kaiser-Frazer Corp. | Willow Run, Mich. |
| Herff-Brooks | 1914 | 1916 | Herff-Brooks Corp. | Indianapolis |
| Herreshoff | 1909 | 1915 | Herreshoff Motor Co. | Detroit |
| Hollier | 1915 | 1920 | Lewis Spring & Axle Co. | Chelsea, Mich. |
| Holmes | 1918 | 1923 | Holmes Automobile Co. | Canton, O. |
| Holsman | 1902 | | Holsman Automobile Co. | Chicago |
| Howard (Lexington-Howard) | 1903 | 1914 | Lexington-Howard Co. | Connersville, Ind. |
| Hudson | 1909 | Going | Hudson Motor Car Co. | Detroit |

| NAME OF CAR | BEGUN | ENDED | MANUFACTURER | LOCATION |
|---|---|---|---|---|
| Hupmobile | 1908 | 1941 | Hupp Motor Car Co. | Detroit |
| Imperial | 1907 | 1916 | Imperial Automobile Co. | Jackson, Mich. |
| Jackson | 1904 | 1923 | Jackson Motors Corp. | Jackson, Mich. |
| Jeffery | 1914 | 1917 | Thos. B. Jeffery Co. | Kenosha, Wis. |
| Jewett (Paige-Detroit) | 1922 | 1926 | Paige-Detroit Motor Car Co. | Detroit |
| Jordan | 1916 | 1932 | Jordan Motor Car Co. | Cleveland |
| Kaiser | 1947 | Going | Kaiser-Frazer Sales Corp. | Willow Run, Mich. |
| Keeton | 1908 | 1914 | Keeton Motor Car Co. | Detroit |
| King | 1910 | 1924 | King Motor Car Co. | Detroit |
| Kissel | 1903 | 1931 | Kissel Motor Car Co. | Hartford, Wis. |
| Kline | 1909 | 1924 | Kline Motor Car Corp. | Richmond, Va. |
| Knox | 1900 | 1915 | Knox Automobile Co. | Springfield, Mass. |
| K-R-I-T | 1902 | 1915 | Krit Motor Car Co. | Detroit |
| Lafayette | 1920 | 1924 | Lafayette Motor Car Co. | Indianapolis |
| Lambert | 1904 | 1917 | Buckeye Mfg. Co. | Anderson, Ind. |
| LaSalle | 1927 | 1940 | Cadillac Motor·Car Co. | Detroit |
| Lexington (Lexington-Howard) | 1913 | 1926 | Lexington Motor Co. | Connersville, Ind. |
| Liberty | 1916 | 1924 | Liberty Motor Car Co. | Detroit |
| Lincoln | 1917 | Going | Ford Motor Co. | Detroit |
| Little (Chevrolet) | 1911 | 1913 | Little Motor Car Co. | Flint, Mich. |
| Locomobile | 1899 | 1929 | Locomobile Co. of America | Bridgeport, Conn. |
| Lozier | 1902 | 1914 | Lozier Motor Co. | N. Y.—Detroit |
| Marion (Marion-Handley) | 1905 | 1915 | Marion Motor Car Co. | Indianapolis |
| Marion-Handley | 1916 | 1918 | Mutual Motors Co. | Jackson, Mich. |
| Marmon | 1903 | 1933 | Nordyke & Marmon Co. | Indianapolis |
| Marquette | 1909 | 1912 | Marquette Motor Co. | Saginaw—Detroit |
| Matheson | 1903 | 1913 | Matheson Motor Car Co. | Wilkes-Barre, Pa. |
| Maxwell (Plymouth) | 1904 | 1925 | Maxwell Motor Co. | Detroit |
| McFarlan | 1910 | 1928 | McFarlan Motor Car Co. | Connersville, Ind. |
| McIntyre | 1908 | 1916 | W. H. McIntyre Co. | Auburn, Ind. |
| Mercury | 1938 | Going | Ford Motor Company | Dearborn, Mich. |
| Mercer | 1906 | 1925 | Mercer Automobile Co. | Trenton, N. J. |
| Meteor | 1919 | 1922 | Meteor Motors, Inc. | Philadelphia |
| Metz (Waltham) | 1909 | 1921 | The Metz Co. | Waltham, Mass. |
| Mitchell | 1903 | 1923 | Mitchell Motor Car Co. | Racine, Wis. |
| Moline | 1904 | 1918 | Moline Automobile Co. | Moline, Ill. |
| Moline-Knight | 1917 | 1921 | Root & Van Dervoort Eng. Co. | E. Moline, Ill. |
| Monroe | 1914 | 1924 | Monroe Motor Co. | Indianapolis |
| Moon (Windsor) | 1906 | 1929 | Moon Motor Car Co. | St. Louis |
| Mora | 1906 | 1910 | Mora Motor Car Co. | Rochester, N. Y. |
| Nash (See Rambler & Jeffrey) | 1917 | Going | Nash Motors Co. | Detroit, Mich. |
| National | 1900 | 1924 | National Motor Vehicle Co. | Indianapolis |
| Nelson | 1917 | 1920 | E. A. Nelson Motor Car Co. | Detroit |
| Northern | 1902 | 1908 | Northern Mfg. Co. | Detroit |
| Oakland (Pontiac) | 1907 | 1931 | Oakland Motor Car Co. | Pontiac, Mich. |
| Ogren | 1912 | 1917 | Ogren Motor Works | Chicago |
| Ohio | 1909 | 1914 | Ohio Motor Car Co. | Cincinnati |
| Oldsmobile | 1897 | Going | Olds Motor Works | Lansing, Mich. |
| Orient | 1900 | 1910 | Waltham Mfg. Co. | Waltham, Mass. |
| Otto | 1909 | 1912 | Otto Gas Engine Works | Philadelphia |
| Overland (Willys) | 1938 | Going | Willys-Overland Motors, Inc. | Toledo |
| Overland (Whippet) | 1903 | 1926 | Willys-Overland Co. | Toledo |
| Owen-Magnetic | 1916 | 1920 | Owen-Magnetic Motor Car Co. | Wilkes-Barre, Pa. |
| Packard | 1899 | Going | Packard Motor Car Co. | Detroit |
| Palmer-Singer | 1908 | 1914 | Palmer-Singer Mfg. Co. | L. I. City, N. Y. |
| Partin-Palmer | 1913 | 1917 | Partin-Palmer Mfg. Co. | Chicago |
| Paterson | 1908 | 1923 | W. A. Paterson Co. | Flint, Mich. |
| Pathfinder | 1911 | 1918 | Motor Car Mfg. Co. | Indianapolis |
| Peerless | 1900 | 1932 | Peerless Motor Car Co. | Cleveland |

| NAME OF CAR | BEGUN | ENDED | MANUFACTURER | LOCATION |
|---|---|---|---|---|
| Pierce-Arrow | 1901 | 1938 | Pierce-Arrow Motor Car Co. | Buffalo |
| Pilgrim | 1914 | 1918 | Pilgrim Motor Car Co. | Detroit |
| Pilot | 1911 | 1924 | Pilot Motor Car Co. | Richmond, Ind. |
| Plymouth | 1929 | Going | Chrysler Motor Corp. | Detroit |
| Pontiac (See Oakland) | 1926 | Going | (Pontiac Motor Division) | Pontiac, Mich. |
| Pope-Hartford | 1897 | 1912 | Pope Mfg. Co. | Hartford, Conn. |
| Pope-Toledo | 1901 | 1910 | Pope Mfg. Co. | Toledo |
| Pope-Tribune | 1904 | | Pope Mfg. Co. | Hartford, Conn. |
| Pratt-Elkhart | 1910 | 1917 | Elkhart Carriage & Harness Co. | Elkhart, Ind. |
| Premier | 1903 | 1925 | Premier Motor Mfg. Co. | Indianapolis |
| Pullman | 1905 | 1917 | York Motor Car Co. | York, Pa. |
| Queen | 1905 | | Blomstrom Motor Co. | Detroit |
| Rambler (Jeffery) | 1900 | 1913 | Thomas B. Jeffery Co. | Kenosha, Wis. |
| Rainier | 1909 | 1911 | Rainier Motor Co. | New York |
| R-C-H | 1911 | 1915 | R. C. H. Corp. | Detroit |
| Regal | 1908 | 1918 | Regal Motor Car Co. | Detroit |
| Reo | 1904 | Going | Reo Motor Car Co. (Makes Trucks) | Lansing, Mich. |
| Rickenbacker | 1922 | 1927 | Rickenbacker Motor Co. | Detroit |
| Roamer | 1916 | 1928 | Roamer Motor Car Co. | Kalamazoo, Mich. |
| Rockne (Studebaker) | 1932 | 1933 | Studebaker Corp. | South Bend, Ind. |
| Roosevelt (Marmon Six) | 1929 | 1930 | Nordyke & Marmon Co. | Indianapolis |
| Royal Tourist | 1904 | 1908 | Royal Motor Car Co. | Cleveland |
| R & V Knight | 1914 | 1924 | Root & Van Dervoort Eng. Co. | E. Moline, Ill. |
| Saxon | 1911 | 1923 | Saxon Motor Car Co. | Detroit |
| Scripps-Booth | 1911 | 1922 | Scripps-Booth Corp. | Detroit |
| Selden | 1906 | 1914 | Selden Motor Vehicle Co. | Rochester, N. Y. |
| S-G-V | 1908 | 1916 | S. G. V. Co. | Reading, Pa. |
| Simplex | 1907 | 1918 | Simplex Automobile Co. | New Brunswick, N. J. |
| Singer | 1915 | 1921 | Singer Motor Co. | Mt. Vernon, N. Y. |
| Speedwell | 1908 | 1915 | Speedwell Motor Car Co. | Dayton |
| St. Louis | 1899 | 1909 | St. Louis Motor Carriage Co. | St. Louis |
| Standard-8 | 1913 | 1923 | Standard Steel Car Co. | Pittsburgh |
| Stanley Steamer | 1896 | 1926 | Stanley Motor Carriage Co. | Newton, Mass. |
| Star (Durant) | 1922 | 1928 | Durant Motor Co. | Flint, Mich. |
| Staver | 1908 | 1913 | Staver Carriage Co. | Chicago |
| Stearns-Knight | 1898 | 1929 | F. B. Stearns Co. | Cleveland |
| Stephens | 1917 | 1925 | Moline Plow Co. | Freeport, Ill. |
| Stevens-Duryea | 1902 | 1926 | Stevens-Duryea Co. | Chicopee Falls, Mass. |
| Stoddard-Dayton | 1905 | 1913 | Dayton Motor Car Co. | Dayton |
| Stoddard-Knight | 1911 | | Dayton Motor Car Co. | Dayton |
| Studebaker | 1904 | Going | Studebaker Corp. of America | South Bend, Ind. |
| Stutz | 1912 | 1936 | Stutz Motor Car Co. | Indianapolis |
| Templar | 1916 | 1924 | Templar Motor Corp. | Cleveland |
| Terraplane (Hudson) | 1934 | 1938 | Hudson Motor Car Co. | Detroit |
| Thomas-Detroit (Chalmers) | 1904 | 1908 | E. R. Thomas Motor Co. | Buffalo |
| Thomas Flyer | 1902 | 1913 | E. R. Thomas-Detroit Co. | Buffalo |
| Velie | 1909 | 1929 | Velie Motors Corp. | Moline, Ill. |
| Viking (Oldsmobile) | 1929 | 1930 | Olds Motor Works | Lansing, Mich. |
| Walter | 1903 | 1909 | Walter Automobile Co. | New York |
| Waltham | 1900 | 1922 | Waltham Mfg. Co. | Waltham, Mass. |
| Welch | 1901 | 1911 | Welch Motor Car Co. | Pontiac, Mich. |
| Welch-Detroit | 1910 | 1911 | Welch-Detroiter Motor Car | Detroit, Mich. |
| Westcott | 1897 | 1925 | Westcott Motor Car Co. | Springfield, O. |
| White Steam | 1902 | 1912 | White Sewing Mach. Co. | Cleveland |
| Wills-Sainte Claire | 1921 | 1926 | C. H. Wills & Co. | Marysville, Mich. |
| Willys | 1903 | Going | Willys-Overland Co. | Toledo |
| Willys-Knight | 1903 | 1933 | Willys-Overland Co. | Toledo |
| Winton | 1897 | 1924 | Winton Motor Carriage Co. | Cleveland |
| Yale | 1903 | 1906 | Kirk Mfg. Co. | Toledo |

# A SHORT CHRONOLOGY OF THE AMERICAN AUTOMOBILE

1876 • Two-cycle, liquid petroleum engine invented by G. B. Brayton exhibited at Philadelphia Centennial Exposition

1879 • George B. Selden applied for U.S. patent on an automobile

1892 • Hiram Percy Maxim built a one-cylinder engine for a tricycle

1893 • Charles E. and J. Frank Duryea built a one-cylinder automobile
• Ransom E. Olds produced a steam-driven automobile

1894 • Elmer and Edgar Apperson constructed a one-cylinder, 1-hp automobile designed by Elwood Haynes

1895 • Charles E. and J. Frank Duryea formed the Duryea Motor Wagon Co., first American company organized to make gasoline cars
• George Selden granted U.S. patent on automobile
• J. Frank Duryea won first American automobile race, averaging 5.05 mph over 52.4 mi. course in Chicago, Ill.

1896 • Duryea Motor Wagon Co. made the first sale of an American gasoline car
• Henry Ford successfully operated a motor vehicle with a two-cylinder, 4-hp engine
• A Riker Electric Stanhope won the first American track race for motor vehicles, averaging 26.8 mph for the first of five one-mile heats
• Experimental automobiles were built by Ransom Olds, Charles B. King, and Alexander Winton

1897 • A Winton was driven a mile in 1 min. 48 sec. and from Cleveland to New York in 10 days
• Olds Motor Vehicle Co. organized
• Studebaker Bros. began experimenting with motor cars
• Stanley Steam Car appeared

1898 • William E. Metzger opened first independent car dealership

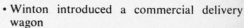

• Winton introduced a commercial delivery wagon
• John Wilkinson built a four-cylinder, valve-in-head, air-cooled engine (from which Franklin engines later evolved)
First American exhibition of motor cars held in Boston, Mass.

1899 • James W. and Warren D. Packard and George L. Weiss organized the Ohio Automobile Co.

1900 • First National Automobile Show was held in Madison Square Garden, New York City
• The Ohio, built by Packard, introduced a steering wheel instead of conventional tiller
• First automobile license, called an "Engineer's Certificate," was issued in New York City

1901 • R. E. Olds built 1,500 Oldsmobiles, becoming first mass producer of gasoline cars
• New York State licensed motor vehicles
• Electric Vehicle Co., holder of the Selden Patent, threatened to sue infringers
• George N. Pierce Co. announced the Pierce Motorette

1902 • The Rapid Motor Vehicle Co. was organized to build trucks
• Thomas B. Jeffery Co. introduced and built 1,500 Ramblers
• Detroit Automobile Co. became the Cadillac Automobile Co.
• The National Assn. of Automobile Manufacturers adopted a 60-day guarantee on new cars
• American Automobile Assn. was founded
• J. Stevens Arms & Tool Co. began manufacture of the Stevens-Duryea
• Ohio Automobile Co. became the Packard Motor Car Co.
• Locomobile became the first American car with a four-cylinder, water-cooled, front-mounted, gasoline engine

1903 • *Motor* first issued in October
• Ford Motor Co. organized by Henry Ford
• Olds racing car covered 5-mile straightaway at Daytona Beach in 6½ min.
• First transcontinental trip made in a gasoline automobile, taking two months, three days
• The Assn. of Licensed Automobile Manufacturers, composed of firms paying royalties under the Selden patent, was organized
• Buick Motor Co. was formed and began producing valve-in-head engines
• Ford sued as an infringer of the Selden patent
• T-head engine, sliding transmissions, mechanically operated intake valves, and shock absorbers appeared
• Cadillac, Ford, and Overland cars were produced for the first time

1904 • First Vanderbilt Cup Race was run
• R. E. Olds sold his interest in Olds Motor Works and organized Reo Motor Co.
• Studebaker sold its first gasoline motor vehicle
• Henry Ford, driving "999," set world's mile speed record at 91.37 mph
• William K. Vanderbilt broke Ford's record by driving a 90-hp Mercedes 92.307 mph

1905 • A Pierce Arrow won the first Glidden Tour, organized by the AAA as a reliability run
• Society of Automobile Engineers was formed
• Cars first sold on installment plan
• American Motor Car Manufacturers Assn. was organized

1906 • Ford introduced a six-cylinder model
• A Stanley Steamer did a mile in 28⅕ sec., averaging 127.66 mph
• Front bumpers appeared as optional equipment

1907 • Oakland Motor Car Co. was formed
• Assn. of Licensed Automobile Manufacturers devised a formula for figuring horsepower which was adopted by a number of states as a means of taxation

1908 • General Motors Co. incorporated in New Jersey on September 16
• Model T Ford introduced
• Buick, Oldsmobile, and Oakland became General Motors units
• Fisher Body Co. organized
• First successful four-wheel drive developed
• A Thomas Flyer won the New York-to-Paris Race
• Fourth Vanderbilt Cup Race was won by a Locomobile, first American victory in the event

1909 • Louis Chevrolet began working on a six-cylinder passenger car
• The Selden patent was sustained in a suit to compel Ford to pay royalties
• Hupmobile featured a multiple-disc clutch in unit with engine
• Indianapolis Speedway completed
• Hudson Motor Car Co. formed
• Cadillac became part of General Motors

1910 • Four-Wheel Drive Auto Co. began manufacturing four-wheel-drive vehicles
• Buick produced a six-cylinder model
• Cars offered "completely equipped" for the first time

1911 • Chevrolet Motor Co. organized and began production
• In reversal, U.S. Court of Appeals declared the Selden patent valid but not infringed by Ford and other manufacturers
• Cadillac began using electric starter developed by Charles F. Kettering

Not only <u>one</u> good performance distinguishes the HAYNES-APPERSON Automobiles, but a consistent winning with stock machines of every contest ever entered—17 in all. The car you buy is the kind that made this record.

HAYNES-APPERSON CO., · Kokomo, Ind., U.S.A.

• Diamond-T Motor Car Co. discontinued production of passenger cars to make trucks
• First 500-mile Indianapolis Speedway Race was won by Ray Harroun
• Studebaker Bros., changing name to Studebaker Corp., halted manufacture of electric vehicles to concentrate on gasoline cars
• Automobile stocks first listed on N. Y. Stock Exchange

1912 • Cadillac adopted generator-battery lighting, ignition system, and starter
• Oakland and Hupmobile offered all-steel bodies

1913 • Willys-Knight with sleeve-valve engine introduced
• National Automobile Chamber of Commerce was formed

1914 • Cadillac designed first American V8 engine for its 1915 models
• Pierce-Arrow put headlights in fenders
• Horace and John Dodge began production of the Dodge car

1915 • Packard offered first American twelve-cylinder model
• Oldsmobile offered top and windshield as standard equipment

1916 • Charles W. Nash took over the Thomas B. Jeffery Co. and formed Nash Motors Co.
• Hand-operated windshield wipers, stoplights, and rearview mirrors appeared as standard equipment

1917 • Henry M. Leland formed Lincoln Motor Co.
• First Nash featured a six-cylinder, valve-in-head engine
• Automotive companies, cooperating in the war effort, participated in the development and production of Liberty aircraft engines

1918 • Chevrolet became part of General Motors
• The industry turned to producing shells, helmets, aircraft engines, tanks, guns and gun carriages, as well as military vehicles

1919 • Ralph De Palma set new speed record of 149.8 mph in a Packard
• A two-range transmission perfected

1920 • Duesenberg Eight with four-wheel brakes appeared
• Pierre S. du Pont became president of General Motors, succeeding W. C. Durant

1921 • W. C. Durant left General Motors to organize Durant Motors
• Hudson offered an adjustable front seat
• Hydraulic brakes first offered

1922 • Balloon tires and air cleaners introduced
• Ford bought Lincoln Motor Co.
• The Essex coach, first inexpensive closed car, appeared

1923 • Dodge offered all-steel closed bodies
• Four-wheel brakes and power-operated windshield wipers became standard equipment on several makes

1924 • *Motor* became a business publication after 21 years as a consumer magazine
• Maxwell-Chalmers Corp. introduced the Chrysler Light Six, featuring high compression engine, seven-bearing crankshaft, four-wheel hydraulic brakes, and replaceable cartridge oil filter
• Balloon tires appeared as standard equipment
• Nash Motors bought Lafayette Motors Corp.

1925 • Maxwell-Chalmers becomes Chrysler Corp.
• Bumpers became standard equipment

1926 • Packard offered hypoid gears
• Ford announced plans to discontinue the Model T

- Pontiac introduced as companion to Oakland
- General Motors bought Fisher Body Corp.
- Hot-water car heaters introduced
1927 • Cadillac introduced the LaSalle V8
- Ford introduced the Model A
- An electric drive with no gearshift developed
- Lockheed introduced an internal hydraulic brake system
1928 • Cadillac introduced synchromesh
- Chrysler Corp. acquired Dodge Bros.
- Studebaker took control of Pierce-Arrow
- Ford offered shatterproof glass as standard equipment
- Four-speed transmissions returned
- Chrysler entered low-priced field with Plymouth and also offered De Soto as a new line
1929 • Automobile radios, foot-controlled dimmer switches, and dual tail lights made their first appearance
- Oldsmobile introduced V8 Viking
- Cord used front wheel drive in its initial offering
- Chrysler adopted downdraft carburetor
1930 • Cadillac offered V16 and V12 models
- Studebaker introduced free-wheeling
- Chrysler offered an Eight for first time
1931 • The Oakland line was discontinued and Pontiac offered Sixes and Eights
- Oldsmobile adopted a downdraft carburetor and synchromesh transmission
1932 • Ford V8 supplanted the Model A
- Pierce-Arrow introduced hydraulic valve lifters in its new models
- Buick, LaSalle, and Cadillac offered vacuum-operated clutches
- Fred Duesenberg killed in crash
1933 • Use of the accelerator pedal for starting became general
- Independent wheel suspension introduced
- Lincoln Continental made first appearance
1934 • Chrysler and De Soto introduced Airflow design, along with automatic-transmission overdrive
- Graham offered a model equipped with a supercharger
- Knee-action introduced in America
1935 • Ford introduced Lincoln-Zephyr
- Fisher introduced the all-steel "turret top"
1936 • Reo discontinued passenger car production to concentrate on trucks
- Diamond-T built a Diesel-powered truck
- Nash Motors merged with Kelvinator Corp. to become Nash-Kelvinator Corp.
1937 • Ford offered a choice of 60- or 85-hp engines
- Steering-column gearshifts were revived
- Oldsmobile and Buick offered automatic transmissions

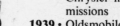

1938 • Ford began production of Mercury
- Chrysler introduced fluid coupling for transmissions
1939 • Oldsmobile offered hydramatic drive
- "Automatic" overdrive became available
1940 • Automotive Committee for Air Defense was established to facilitate air production
- Cadillac discontinued LaSalle
- Sealed-beam headlights were introduced on most makes
1941 • Willys began to deliver the Jeep
- Automotive Council for War Production was formed
1942 • All manufacturers halted production of civilian passenger cars and trucks, and car rationing began
1943 • Nonessential driving banned in 17 states
1944 • Basic gas ration reduced to 2 gal. per week
- The War Production Board authorized manufacture of light civilian trucks for the first time since early 1942
1945 • The WPB authorized reconversion to motor-vehicle production
- Restrictions on manufacture of replacement parts were lifted
- Kaiser-Frazer Corp. organized
- Gasoline rationing ended
1946 • Kaisers and Frazers made first appearance
- Bendix introduced power steering for trucks
1947 • Henry Ford and Wm. C. Durant died
1948 • Willys-Overland introduced six-cylinder Jeep station wagon and convertible Jeepster
- Goodrich introduced tubeless tires
- General Motors developed a new high-compression engine, using high-octane fuel
- Buick introduced Dynaflow (hydraulic torque converter) transmission
- 100,000,000th American motorcar was made
1949 • Nash Rambler was introduced
- GM introduced hardtops in Cadillac, Oldsmobile, and Buick lines
- Chrysler introduced disc brakes
1950 • Kaiser offered Henry J
- Buick introduced tinted window glass
1951 • Chrysler introduced power steering for passenger cars
- Chrysler introduced 180-hp, hemispherical combustion chamber V8
1952 • Willys offered a passenger car line
- Lincoln introduced ball-joint front suspension
- Cadillac, Buick, and Oldsmobile introduced four-barrel carburetors
1953 • *Motor* marked its 50th year
- 12-volt ignition systems were reintroduced on some cars
- Cadillac boosted horsepower to 210
- Kaiser-Frazer bought Willys-Overland Motors

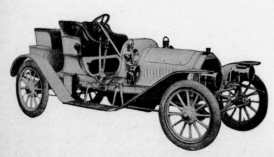

# INDEX